The Essentials of Conditioning and Learning

Second Edition

MICHAEL DOMJAN
University of Texas at Austin

 **Wadsworth**
Thomson Learning™

Australia • Canada • Denmark • Japan • Mexico • New Zealand • Philippines
Puerto Rico • Singapore • South Africa • Spain • United Kingdom • United States

Senior Psychology Editor: *Marianne Taflinger*
Assistant Editor: *Jennifer Wilkinson*
Editorial Assistants: *Rachael Bruckman/Suzanne Wood*
Marketing Manager: *Jenna Opp*
Project Editor: *Matt Stevens*
Print Buyer: *April Reynolds*

Permissions Editor: *Joohee Lee*
Copy Editor: *Michele Kornegay*
Compositor: *Pre-Press Company, Inc.*
Cover Designer: *Bill Stanton*
Cover Image: © *International Stock*
Printer/Binder: *Webcom Ltd.*

Printed in Canada

1 2 3 4 5 6 7 03 02 01 00 99

For permission to use material from this text, contact us:
   Web: www.thomsonrights.com
   Fax: 1-800-730-2215
   Phone: 1-800-730-2214

**Library of Congress
Cataloging-in-Publication Data**
The essentials of conditioning and learning /
   Michael Domjan. — 2nd ed.
      p.   cm.
   Includes bibliographical references and index.
   ISBN 0-534-35642-7 (ppk. : alk. paper)
   1. Conditioned response. 2. Reinforcement (Psychology) 3. Learning, Psychology of. I. Title.
BF319.D653   2000
153.1'526—dc21   99-27558
                                  CIP

For more information, contact

Wadsworth/Thomson Learning
10 Davis Drive
Belmont, CA 94002-3098
USA
www.wadsworth.com

International Headquarters
Thomson Learning
290 Harbor Drive, 2nd Floor
Stamford, CT 06902-7477
USA

UK/Europe/Middle East
Thomson Learning
Berkshire House
168-173 High Holborn
London WC1V 7AA
United Kingdom

Asia
Thomson Learning
60 Albert Street #15-01
Albert Complex
Singapore 189969

Canada
Nelson/Thomson Learning
1120 Birchmount Road
Scarborough, Ontario M1K 5G4
Canada

This book is printed on acid-free recycled paper.

To Karen

BRIEF CONTENTS

ONE *Basic Concepts and Definitions* 1

TWO *The Structure of Unconditioned Behavior* 13

THREE *Habituation and Sensitization* 25

FOUR *Pavlovian Conditioning and Extinction* 41

FIVE *Stimulus Relations in Pavlovian Conditioning* 63

SIX *Instrumental or Operant Conditioning* 81

SEVEN *Schedules of Reinforcement* 99

EIGHT *Theories of Reinforcement* 120

NINE *Punishment* 135

TEN *Avoidance Learning* 149

ELEVEN *Stimulus Control of Behavior* 167

TWELVE *Memory Mechanisms* 185

CONTENTS

Preface   xiii

CHAPTER ONE
Basic Concepts and Definitions   *1*

Fundamental Features of Learning   2
Learning and Other Forms of Behavior Change   *2*
Learning, Performance, and Levels of Analysis   *4*
A Definition of Learning   *6*
Naturalistic versus Experimental Observations   6
The Fundamental Learning Experiment   8
The Control Problem in Studies of Learning   *9*
Summary   11
Technical Terms   12

CHAPTER TWO
The Structure of Unconditioned Behavior   *13*

Shaping and Homogeneous versus
    Heterogeneous Substrates of Behavior   14
The Concept of the Reflex   15
Complex Forms of Elicited Behavior   17
Fixed-Action Patterns   *17*
Sign Stimuli   *19*

The Organization of Elicited Behavior   20
Motivational Factors   21
Appetitive and Consummatory Behavior   21
Behavior Systems   22
Summary   24
Suggested Readings   24
Technical Terms   24

CHAPTER THREE

Habituation and Sensitization   25

General Principles of Regulation   27
Effects of the Repeated Presentation
of an Eliciting Stimulus   28
Characteristics of Habituation Effects   31
Characteristics of Sensitization Effects   35
The Dual-Process Theory of
Habituation and Sensitization   36
The S-R System and the State System   36
Implications of the Dual-Process Theory   37
Summary   39
Suggested Readings   40
Technical Terms   40

CHAPTER FOUR

Pavlovian Conditioning and Extinction   41

Pavlov's Proverbial Bell   42
Some Common Misconceptions   42
Contemporary Pavlovian Conditioning Preparations   44
Appetitive Conditioning   44
Aversive Conditioning   45
The Nature of the Conditioned Response   46
Skeletal versus Glandular Conditioned Responses   47
Similarity of Conditioned and Unconditioned Responses   47
The Behavior System Approach   48

The Contents of Pavlovian Associations   49
   Effects of US Devaluation   49
   Effects of US Inflation   51
The Selectivity of Associations   52
The Control Problem in
   Pavlovian Conditioning   54
Extinction of Pavlovain Conditioned Behavior   57
   Extinction and Habituation   57
   Extinction as Unlearning   58
   Extinction as a Form of Inhibition   59
   Clinical Implications   60
Summary   60
Suggested Readings   61
Technical Terms   62

CHAPTER FIVE
Stimulus Relations in Pavlovian Conditioning 63

Temporal Relation between CS and US   64
   Simultaneous Conditioning   64
   Delayed Conditioning   65
   Trace Conditioning   65
   Effects of the CS-US Interval   65
   Temporal Encoding of US Occurrence   67
Signal Relation between CS and US   67
   The Blocking Effect   67
   CS/US Contingency   69
Higher-Order Relations in Pavlovian Conditioning:
   Conditioned Inhibition   70
   Inhibitory Conditioning Procedures   71
   Behavioral Manifestations of Conditioned Inhibition   73
   Stimulus Relations in Conditioned Inhibition   75
Higher-Order Relations in Pavlovian Conditioning:
   Conditioned Facilitation   76
   Stimulus Relations in Conditioned Facilitation   77
   Distinguishing between B-US and B(A-US) Relations   78
Summary   79

Suggested Readings   80
Technical Terms   80

CHAPTER SIX

Instrumental or Operant Conditioning   81

The Traditions of Thorndike and Skinner   83
Methodological Considerations   84
The Establishment of an Instrumental
or Operant Response   87
Learning Where and What to Run For   87
Constructing New Responses from Familiar Components   88
Shaping New Responses   88
The Importance of Immediate Reinforcement   91
Event Relations in Instrumental Conditioning   92
The S-R Association: Thorndike's Law of Effect   93
S-S* and S(R-S*) Relations   93
Implications for Neural Mechanisms   95
Implications for Constraints on Instrumental Conditioning   95
Summary   97
Suggested Readings   97
Technical Terms   98

CHAPTER SEVEN

Schedules of Reinforcement   99

The Cumulative Record   100
Simple Schedules of Reinforcement   101
Ratio Schedules   102
Interval Schedules   103
Mechanisms of Schedule Performance   106
Feedback Functions for Ratio Schedules   106
Feedback Functions for Interval Schedules   107
Feedback Functions and Schedule Performance   108
Chained Schedules of Reinforcement   108
Heterogeneous Chains   109
Homogeneous Chains   109
Training Response Chains   110
Concurrent Schedules   111

Extinction of Instrumental Behavior   113
  The Partial Reinforcement Extinction Effect   114
  Explanations of the PREE   115
Summary   118
Suggested Readings   118
Technical Terms   119

CHAPTER EIGHT

Theories of Reinforcement   120

Thorndike and the Law of Effect   121
Hull and Drive Reduction Theory   122
  Primary Reinforcers   123
  Secondary Reinforcers and Acquired Drives   124
  Sensory Reinforcement   124
Reinforcers as Responses   125
  The Premack Principle   125
  The Premack Revolution   126
  Applications of the Premack Principle   126
  Theoretical Problems   127
The Response Deprivation Hypothesis   128
  Response Deprivation and the Law of Effect   128
  Response Deprivation and Response Probability   129
  Response Deprivation and the Locus of Reinforcement Effects   129
The Behavioral Regulation Approach   130
  The Behavioral Bliss Point   130
  Imposing an Instrumental Contingency   130
  Responding to Schedule Constraints   132
  Contributions of Behavioral Regulation   133
Summary   133
Suggested Readings   134
Technical Terms   134

CHAPTER NINE

Punishment   135

Effective and Ineffective Punishment   136
  When Punishment Fails   137
  When Punishment Succeeds   138

Research Evidence on Punishment   138
  Response-Reinforcer Contingency   139
  Response-Reinforcer Contiguity   140
  Intensity of the Aversive Stimulus   140
  Signaled Punishment   141
  Punishment and Mechanisms Maintaining the Punished Response   142
  Punishment and Reinforcement of Alternative Behavior   143
  Paradoxical Effects of Punishment   143
Can and Should We Create a Society Free of Punishment?   144
Alternatives to Punishment   146
  Time-Out   146
  Differential Reinforcement of Other Behavior   147
Summary   148
Suggested Readings   148
Technical Terms   148

CHAPTER TEN

Avoidance Learning   *149*

Dominant Questions in the Analysis of Avoidance Learning   150
Origins of the Study of Avoidance Learning   151
Contemporary Avoidance Conditioning Procedures   152
  Discriminated Avoidance   152
  Nondiscriminated or Free-Operant Avoidance   154
Theoretical Approaches to Avoidance Learning   156
  Test of the Role of the Instrumental Contingency   156
  Two-Factor Theory of Avoidance   157
  Conditioned Temporal Cues   159
  Safety Signals in Avoidance Learning   160
  Avoidance Learning and Unconditioned Defensive Behavior   162
Summary   165
Suggested Readings   166
Technical Terms   166

CHAPTER ELEVEN

Stimulus Control of Behavior   *167*

Measurement of Stimulus Control   168
  Identifying Relevant Stimuli   169
  Identifying Relevant Stimulus Features   170
  Measurement of the Degree of Stimulus Control   171

Determinants of Stimulus Control:
Stimulus and Organismic Factors 173
Sensory Capacity   174
Sensory Orientation   174
Stimulus Intensity or Salience   174
Motivational Factors   175
Determinants of Stimulus Control: Learning Factors   176
Pavlovian and Instrumental Conditioning   176
Stimulus Discrimination Training   177
Multiple Schedules of Reinforcement   179
Differential Reinforcement and Stimulus Control   180
Interdimensional versus Intradimensional Discriminations   181
Shaping of Discrimination and Perceptual Concept Learning   183
Summary   184
Suggested Readings   184
Technical Terms   184

CHAPTER TWELVE

Memory Mechanisms   185

Stages of Information Processing   186
The Matching-to-Sample Procedure   187
Simultaneous and Delayed Matching-to-Sample   189
Procedural Controls for Memory   189
Types of Memory   190
Reference Memory and Working Memory   190
Active and Passive Memory   191
Retrospective and Prospective Memory   192
Sources of Memory Failure   195
Interference   195
Retrieval Failure   197
Summary   199
Suggested Readings   200
Technical Terms   200

Glossary   201
References   215
Name Index   231
Subject Index   233

Michael Domjan is Professor and Chair of the Psychology Department at the University of Texas at Austin, where he has been teaching undergraduate and graduate courses in learning since 1973. He has served as Editor of the *Journal of Experimental Psychology: Animal Behavior Processes* and Associate Editor of *Learning and Motivation*. He is noted for his research on food-aversion learning and learning mechanisms in sexual behavior. He is recipient of the G. Stanley Hall Award from the American Psychological Association, and his research on sexual conditioning was selected for a MERIT Award by the National Institutes of Mental Health. His textbook, *The Principles of Learning and Behavior*, is now in its fourth edition.

PREFACE

The principles of conditioning and learning are used in many areas of psychology and allied disciplines. The purpose of this book is to provide a concise, current, and sophisticated summary of the essentials of conditioning and learning for students and professionals in those areas.

Concepts from conditioning and learning have been used in the design of behavior therapy procedures and in various educational settings, including special education, rehabilitation training, and elementary education. The principles of conditioning and learning are also important in behavioral neuroscience, physiological psychology, developmental psychology, psychopharmacology, and comparative psychology. Researchers in these areas are interested in how nonverbal organisms learn, process, and remember information. Asking animal and nonverbal human subjects how they learn and think invariably requires using conditioning procedures in some way. Therefore, interpretation of the results of such experiments necessitates understanding the underlying processes and mechanisms that are responsible for conditioning and learning effects.

The basic procedures of habituation, classical conditioning, and instrumental conditioning have not changed in the past 50 years and are familiar to many students and professionals. Our understanding of these procedures has changed dramatically, however, with the result that common presumptions about learning are no longer valid. Consider, for example, the following claims:

- Learning can be directly observed in the behavior of organisms, just as aggression, maternal behavior, and other important activities.
- Pavlovian conditioning involves the learning of new conditioned responses to previously ineffective stimuli.
- Extinction is the opposite of conditioning and involves the unlearning of an association.

- Avoidance responses occur because they prevent the delivery of an aversive event.
- Using a larger reinforcer makes instrumental behavior more resistant to extinction.

All of these claims seem reasonable, but none of them is valid in light of contemporary perspectives. The purpose of this book is to summarize contemporary perspectives to enable students and professionals to use concepts from conditioning and learning more effectively in their work.

The book can serve as the primary source for an introductory course on conditioning and learning. It can also serve as a supplemental text for courses in behavior modification, behavioral neuroscience, special education, and related areas. Finally, the book can be used to provide the foundations for an advanced course in which students are required to read a collection of specialized articles.

In preparing this book, I was guided by my students, who over the past quarter century have encouraged me to keep searching for ways to explain concepts more simply and directly. The goals of the first edition were followed in preparing the second edition. The second edition includes more human examples to improve the accessibility of the information, and each chapter now ends with a summary. This edition also includes new references and suggested readings, where appropriate.

I am grateful for the suggestions provided by the reviewers: George Cicala, University of Delaware; Hank Gorman, Austin College; Roger Thompson, Franklin & Marshall College; Richard Walls, West Virginia University; David Washburn, Language Research Center, Decatur, Georgia; and Michael Zeiler, Emory University.

I would like to thank Marianne Taflinger of Wadsworth-Brooks/Cole for encouraging me to prepare the revision, the reviewers, who helped keep me on track, and Matt Stevens, who guided the book through the production process.

Michael Domjan
Austin, Texas

CHAPTER ONE

Basic Concepts and Definitions

DID YOU KNOW THAT:

- Learning can result in either an increase or a decrease in responding.
- Learning is not always evident in the actions of an organism. It can be behaviorally silent.
- Learning may be investigated at the behavioral, neurophysiological, or cellular level.
- Learning is a special type of cause of behavior.
- Learning can be investigated only with experimental methods. Naturalistic observations may provide suggestive evidence but cannot prove that a behavior is caused by learning.
- Learning is inferred based on a difference in behavior between individuals given a particular type of experience and individuals lacking that experience.
- Control procedures are as important in studies of learning as are training or experimental procedures.

Learning is of great interest because it is a pervasive feature of human behavior that is also evident in many other animal species. It has been found in creatures as diverse as fruit flies, sea slugs, honeybees, rodents, birds, and monkeys. **Learning** is one of the basic features of behavior.

Fundamental Features of Learning

People learn to recognize friends as different from strangers. They learn how to hold a telephone and to pick it up when it rings. They also learn to swim, to ride a bicycle, and to avoid stepping in potholes. In all of these cases, *learning is identified by a change in behavior.* An experienced swimmer or cyclist behaves very differently than someone who has not yet learned to swim or ride a bike.

Learning to swim or ride a bicycle involves learning new hand, leg, and body movements and coordinating those movements to achieve balance and forward locomotion. Many, but not all, instances of learning involve the acquisition of new responses. We also learn *not* to do certain things. Children have to learn to keep quiet during a sermon, to hold still when being examined by a doctor, and not to be alarmed when they are picked up by a grandparent rather than by a stranger. Learning to inhibit or suppress behavior is often as important as learning new responses. Riding a bicycle, for example, requires learning to pedal as well as learning not to lean too much to one side or the other. Thus, *the change in behavior that is used to identify learning can be either an increase or a decrease in a particular response.*

LEARNING AND OTHER FORMS OF BEHAVIOR CHANGE

Although all learning is identified by some kind of a change in **behavior**, not all cases in which behavior is altered are instances of learning (see Figure 1.1). Therefore, it is important to distinguish learning from other sources of behavior change.

A major feature of learning that makes it different from other forms of behavior change is that *learning is relatively long-lasting*, which distinguishes it from various short-term or temporary changes in behavior. Physiological factors such as **fatigue** and drowsiness can cause widespread and dramatic changes in behavior (for example, your actions may become slower and less vigorous). However, such changes are temporary and can be reversed easily by a good rest. Major short-term changes in behavior also can be caused by changes in **motivation**. For example, people are much more reactive to stimuli related to food when they are hungry than when they are full. Changes in stimulus conditions can also cause widespread but short-term changes in behavior. A fire alarm can quickly turn a quietly seated audience into an anxiously scrambling mob, but the same people will again sit quietly the next time they go to the movies. Learning, by contrast, involves longer-term changes. The assumption is that once something is learned, it will be

Sources of Behavior Change

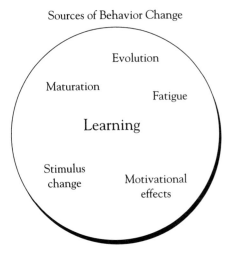

F I G U R E 1.1 **Possible mechanisms that can result in changes in behavior.**
Note that learning is only one of several possible sources of behavior change.

remembered for some time. You are not considered to have learned a new
concept discussed in class if you cannot remember it the next day.

Although learning involves enduring changes in behavior, not all long-
term changes are caused by learning. Long-term changes in behavior also
can be produced by physical growth or **maturation**. Children become more
skillful in lifting heavy objects and reaching a cookie jar on a high shelf as
they get older. However, these changes are not caused by learning. Rather,
they result from physical growth and maturation. Children become taller
and stronger as they get older.

Behavioral changes caused by learning and changes caused by maturation can be interrelated and difficult to distinguish from one another. As a
child becomes stronger and taller with age, those physical changes facilitate
the learning of new skills. However, one important difference between
learning and maturation is that maturation does not require practice with
things specifically related to the skill that is being acquired. A child will become better able to reach high shelves as she gets older whether or not she
ever practices reaching for cookies. **Practice** is not needed for maturation,
but it is required for learning.

Practice is obviously necessary to learn a skill such as swimming or riding a bicycle. One cannot become a good swimmer without spending a lot
of time rehearsing various swim strokes, and one cannot become an expert
bicycle rider without extensive practice with pedaling, steering, and balanc-
ing. In contrast, other things can be learned very quickly. A child will learn
not to touch a burning log in a fireplace after just one painful encounter

with a burning log. Regardless of the amount of practice involved, however, all *learning requires some practice or experience specifically related to the acquired behavior*.

Another difference between maturation and learning is that the same maturational process can produce behavioral changes in a variety of situations. As a child grows taller, she will be able to reach taller shelves, climb taller trees, and catch butterflies that are flying higher off the ground. Physical growth and maturation can result in changes in behavior in many different contexts. In contrast, *behavior changes caused by learning are more limited to the practiced response*. Learning to operate a kitchen stove will help you cook indoors but will not improve your skill in building a fire for cooking outdoors. This is not to say that learning about one thing cannot help you do something else. Some generalization of learning can occur. However, generalization of learning tends to be limited. What you learn about one situation only generalizes to other similar situations. For example, learning to operating a particular gas stove will improve your ability to work other similar gas stoves but may not help if you are trying to cook with a microwave oven.

Another type of long-term change that has to be distinguished from learning is change due to **evolution**. Evolution serves to shape not only physical attributes of organisms but also their behavior. Furthermore, evolutionary changes, like learning, are a result of interactions with the environment. However, evolutionary changes occur across generations. In contrast, learning results in behavioral changes within the lifetime of an individual organism.

Although learning is clearly distinguishable from evolution, the two forms of behavior change are clearly interrelated. Considering how pervasive learning is in the animal kingdom, it is safe to assume that learning has evolved because it provides organisms with an evolutionary advantage. Thus, learning mechanisms are no doubt the products of evolutionary processes. Learning and evolution may interact in the other direction as well. That is, learning may influence the course of evolution by altering the reproductive fitness of particular organisms. A recent study of Pavlovian conditioning in gourami fish illustrates this point (Hollis, Pharr, Dumas, Britton, & Field, 1997). In that study, fish that were exposed to a conditioned stimulus previously associated with a sexual partner produced far more offspring than fish in a control group that did not get the conditioned stimulus.

LEARNING, PERFORMANCE, AND LEVELS OF ANALYSIS

Although the occurrence of learning can only be identified by observing a change in behavior, the change in behavior may be evident only under special circumstances. A physics student, for example, may not be able to provide an adequate definition of a quark, suggesting that he has not learned the concept. However, the same student may be able to pick out the correct definition from a list of alternative possibilities. Children can learn many things about driving a car by watching adults drive. They can learn what the steering wheel is good for and what the functions of the gas and the brake pedals are. However, they may show no evidence of this knowledge until they are old enough to take driving lessons. These examples illustrate that *sometimes learning is behaviorally silent*—it does not produce a visible change in behavior. In such cases, special procedures have to be used to determine what the individual has learned.

Learning may not be evident in the actions of an organism for a variety of reasons. One possibility is that what is learned is a relationship between stimuli or events in the environment rather than a particular response. For example, we may learn to associate the color red with ripe apples. The learning of an association between two stimuli is called S-S learning, or **stimulus-stimulus learning**. A learned association between red and ripeness will not be reflected in what we do unless we are given a special task, such as judging the ripeness of apples. S-S learning is usually not evident in the actions of an organism unless special test procedures are used.

The things an individual does, a person's observable actions, are collectively referred to as **performance**. Performance depends on many factors, including motivation and the stimulus conditions or behavioral opportunities provided by the environment. Learning is just one of the many factors that determine performance. You may be an excellent flute player, but if you do not have the opportunity or inclination to play the flute, no one will be able to tell what an accomplished musician you are.

I will describe a number of behaviorally silent forms of conditioning and learning in the following chapters. Examples of behaviorally silent learning suggest that learning cannot be equated with a change in behavior. Rather, learning involves a change in the kinds of things an organism could do given the right circumstances. Thus, *learning involves a change in the potential for doing something.*

Where does the change in the potential for action reside? Behavior is regulated by the nervous system. Therefore, learning involves long-lasting changes in the neural mechanisms of behavior. In fact, early neuroscientists such as Ivan Pavlov considered behavioral studies of learning to be studies of how the nervous system works. They regarded learning procedures as techniques for the investigation of neural function.

Because learning involves changes in the nervous system, it may be investigated at a variety of different levels of analysis (see Figure 1.2). We may study learning at the level of molecular changes within nerve cells or neurons. We may also study changes in neurotransmitter systems or neural circuits associated with learning. Finally, we may study learning at the level of changes in the behavior of intact organisms.

Studies of learning began at the level of the intact organism, where learning is manifest in changes in observable behavior, and learning has been

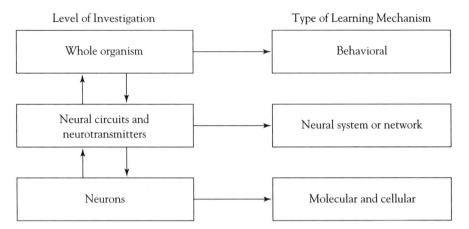

FIGURE   1.2   Levels of analysis of learning.
Learning mechanisms may be investigated at the organismic level, at the level of
neural circuits and transmitter systems, and at the level of nerve cells or neurons.

investigated most extensively at that level. However, with recent advances in
the neurosciences, concepts and terms that have been developed for the behavioral analysis of learning have been applied to investigations at the level
of neural circuits and neurotransmitter systems and at the cellular and
molecular level. One of the challenges facing the study of learning in the
coming years will be to integrate the findings from these diverse levels of
analysis.

A DEFINITION OF LEARNING

The preceding discussion identified a number of characteristics of learning.
Learning involves a change in the potential or neural mechanisms of behavior. The change is relatively long-lasting and is the result of experience with
environmental events specifically related to the behavior in question. These
characteristics are combined in the following definition:

> Learning is a relatively enduring change in the potential to engage in a par-
> ticular behavior resulting from experience with environmental events
> specifically related to that behavior.

Naturalistic versus Experimental Observations

Behavior occurs in many ways and in many situations. However, basically
just two approaches to the study of behavior are available: naturalistic
observations and experimental observations. **Naturalistic observations**

involve observing and measuring behavior as it occurs under natural conditions, in the absence of interventions or manipulations introduced by the investigator. In contrast, **experimental observations** involve measuring behavior under conditions specifically designed by the investigator to test particular factors or variables that might influence the learning or performance of the behavior.

Consider, for example, activities involved in foraging for food by tree squirrels. Foraging can be investigated using naturalistic observations. One could watch squirrels in a park, for example, and count how often they picked up a seed, how often they ate the seed right away, and how often they buried the seed for later retrieval. Making such observations throughout the day would provide detailed information about the foraging behavior of the squirrels in that park. Such observations would not reveal, however, *why* the squirrels did what they did. Observing squirrels undisturbed cannot tell us why they select one type of seed instead of another, why they devote more effort to foraging in one part of the day than another, or why they eat some seeds right away and bury others to eat later. Naturalistic observations cannot provide answers to questions that probe the *causes* of behavior. They may help us formulate questions or hypotheses about why animals do certain things, but naturalistic observations cannot provide the answers.

The causes of behavior can only be discovered using experimental observations. Experimental observations require the investigator to manipulate the environment in special ways that facilitate reaching a causal conclusion. Using naturalistic observations, you may find that squirrels bury more seeds in the fall than in the winter. What might cause this outcome? Naturalistic observations cannot answer this question because environmental conditions in the fall differ from conditions in the winter in many respects. Food is more plentiful in the fall than in the winter, and the climate is warmer. Daylight gets shorter from day to day in the fall and longer from day to day as winter turns to spring. Trees have more leaves in the fall than in the winter, making it easier for squirrels to hide seeds without being seen.

To determine what factors encourage squirrels to bury seeds, the environment has to be manipulated to isolate each possible causal variable. Consider, for example, whether the availability of excess food causes seed burying. We could test this possibility by comparing squirrels under two different conditions. In one condition, the squirrels would be provided with excess food by spreading lots of store-bought peanuts in the observation area. In the second condition, only a subsistence food supply would be available. The squirrels would not be provided with extra peanuts, and some of the food growing in their habitat would be harvested by the experimenter to reduce the food supply. In all other relevant respects, the two test conditions would be the same. Temperature, changes in daylight from day to day, and the extent of foliage in the trees would be identical. Given these identical conditions, if the squirrels buried more seeds when food was plentiful than when food was scarce, we could conclude that excess food encourages or causes the burying of seeds.

Although experimental observations permit drawing conclusions about the causes of behavior, it is important to realize that the causes of behavior cannot be observed directly. Rather, causes are inferred from differences in behavior seen under different experimental conditions. When we conclude that excess food causes seed burying, we are not describing something we have actually observed. What we saw in our hypothetical experiment is that squirrels bury more seeds when food is plentiful than when food is scarce. The conclusion that excess food causes seed burying is an inference arrived at by comparing the two experimental conditions. *Causal conclusions are inferences based on a comparison of two (or more) experimental conditions.* Causes cannot be observed directly.

Uncontrolled naturalistic observations can provide a wealth of descriptive information about behavior. We have learned a great deal from naturalistic observations about foraging for food, courtship and sexual behavior, maternal behavior, parental behavior, and defensive and territorial behavior. Considering that learning is ultimately evident in the behavior of humans and other animals, one might suppose that observational techniques are useful in the study of learning. In fact, some have advocated that detailed investigations of learning should begin with naturalistic observations of learning phenomena (Miller, 1985). However, naturalistic observations are inherently unsuitable for studies of learning because they cannot identify causal variables.

The Fundamental Learning Experiment

According to the definition developed in this chapter, learning is a relatively enduring change in behavioral potential resulting from experience with environmental events specifically related to that behavior. A critical aspect of this definition is that learning is a result of past experiences. As such, learning is a causal variable. It is a causal variable that involves past experience with particular environmental events. To conclude that learning has occurred, we have to be sure that the change in behavior we are seeing is caused by past experience.

As I noted earlier, causes cannot be observed directly. Instead, they must be inferred from experimental observations. This idea has profound implications for the study of learning. Because learning is a causal variable, it cannot be observed directly. Rather, learning can be investigated only with experimental manipulations that serve to isolate a specific past experience as the cause of a change in behavior.

To conclude that a change in behavior has been caused by a specific past experience or learning, one has to compare individuals with and without that experience under otherwise identical circumstances. Consider, for example, the fact that most 8-year-old children can ride a bicycle proficiently, whereas 4-year-olds cannot. A reasonable interpretation is that the older children are expert riders because they have had more time to practice riding a bicycle. That is, the change in behavior from 4 to 8 years of age may be caused by experience with bicycles. To support this conclusion, it is not enough to point to the fact that 8-year-olds are better riders than 4-year-olds. Such an age difference could be due to physical growth and maturation. It is also not compelling to point out that 8-year-olds spend more time riding bicycles than 4-year-olds because that may be an effect rather than a cause of the higher skill of 8-year-olds. Some kind of an experiment must be conducted to prove that proficient riding is a result of past experience or learning.

One way to prove that bicycle riding is a learned skill would be to conduct an experiment with 4-year-old children who have never ridden a bicycle. We could assign the children randomly to one of two treatment groups, an experimental group and a control group. The experimental group would receive three 1-hour lessons in riding a bicycle. The control group would also receive three 1-hour lessons in which they would become familiar with bicycles. However, the control group would not be taught to ride. Rather, they would be told about various parts of a bicycle and how the parts fit together. At the end of the lessons, both groups of children would be tested for their skill in riding. If proficient riding is learned through relevant practice, then the children in the experimental group should be more proficient than the children in the control group.

This example illustrates the **fundamental learning experiment**. To conclude that a behavior change is a result of learning, we must compare the behavior of individuals under two conditions. In the **experimental condition**, participants are provided with the relevant environmental experience or training. In the **control condition**, participants do not receive the relevant training but are treated identically in all other respects. The occurrence of learning is inferred from a comparison between the two conditions. One cannot conclude that learning has occurred by observing only individuals who have acquired the skill of interest. Conclusions about learning require a comparison between the experimental and control conditions.

THE CONTROL PROBLEM IN STUDIES OF LEARNING

Are there any special consequences of the fact that learning can only be inferred through a comparison of individuals with a particular training history and others who lack that history? Yes. One important consequence is that *learning cannot be investigated with naturalistic observations*. Under natural circumstances, individuals with a particular training history often differ in a number of respects from individuals lacking that history. Therefore, the requirements of the fundamental learning experiment are difficult to satisfy under entirely natural circumstances.

A second important consequence of the fact that learning depends on the comparison of an experimental and a control condition is that the control procedure must be designed with as much care as the experimental procedure is. In fact, some landmark contributions to the study of learning have come not from analyses of experimental procedures for producing learning but from analyses of control procedures (Church, 1964; Rescorla, 1967). Different training procedures require different control procedures. I will discuss this issue in greater detail as I discuss various types of learning in the following chapters. For now, suffice it to say that the design of a control procedure is dictated by the particular aspect of past experience one wishes to isolate as being responsible for the behavioral change that is of interest.

In the example of children learning to ride a bicycle, we were interested in whether practice riding is critical for becoming a skillful rider. Children who practice riding also learn a lot about how a bicycle works (how the pedals make the wheels turn, for example). That is why we designed the procedure for the control group so that the children in that group got to learn about the parts of a bicycle and how those parts go together. However, the children in the control group were not provided with practice in sitting on a bicycle and pedaling it. Thus, the design of the control procedure allowed us to isolate practice in riding a bicycle as the critical factor involved in learning to ride.

A third important consequence of the fact that learning can only be inferred from a comparison of experimental and control conditions is that learning is usually investigated with at least two independent groups of participants, an experimental group and a control group. Thus, traditional studies of learning involve the use of **between-subjects** experimental designs.

An important exception to traditional between-subjects experimental designs was developed in the Skinnerian tradition of learning research (Sidman, 1960). Skinner advocated the extensive investigation of individual subjects rather than groups of participants. However, even **single-subject experiments** involve comparisons between experimental and control conditions (see Figure 1.3). Basically, single-subject experiments require that the individual's behavior be understood well enough to permit accurate assumptions about how the individual would have behaved if he did not receive the training procedure of interest.

Consider, for example, a 4-year-old child who is unable to catch a ball tossed to him. If we spend several hours a day teaching the child how to catch a ball, he might become proficient within a few days. From this we may conclude that the child has learned to catch a ball. Notice, however, that this conclusion is based on our assumption that the child would not have acquired the skill as rapidly if he had not received instruction. Only if we have sufficient knowledge to make this assumption can we infer that the child has learned to catch the ball. Thus, the study of learning in individual subjects also involves a comparison between an experimental and a control condition. The only difference is that the control condition is not provided by an explicit control group.

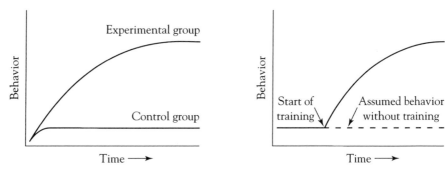

FIGURE 1.3 Two versions of the fundamental learning experiment.
In the left panel, two groups of individuals are compared. The training procedure is provided for participants in the experimental group but not for participants in the control group. In the right panel, a single individual is observed before and during training. The individual's behavior during training is compared to what we assume his behavior would have been without training.

Summary

Although learning is a common human experience, what it is and how it must be investigated are not obvious. Learning is evident in a change in behavior—either the acquisition of a new response or the suppression of an existing response. Not all instances of altered behavior involve learning, however, and not all instances of learning produce immediately observable changes in behavior. The term "learning" is restricted to cases in which an enduring change in the potential to engage in a particular behavior results from prior experience with environmental events specifically related to that behavior.

Learning mechanisms may be examined at the level of intact organisms, at the level of neural circuits or systems, or at the level of nerve cells or neurons. However, because learning is a causal variable, it can be investigated only with experimental methods. Naturalistic observations may provide suggestions about learning but cannot provide definitive evidence. The basic learning experiment involves comparing an experimental and a control condition. The experimental condition includes the training procedure or experience being tested. The control condition is similar but omits the relevant training experience. Learning is inferred from a difference in outcomes between the experimental and control conditions. Because of this, the design of control procedures is as critical for studies of learning as is the design of experimental procedures.

Technical Terms

Behavior
Between-subjects experiment
Control condition
Evolution
Experimental condition
Experimental observation
Fatigue
Fundamental learning experiment

Learning
Maturation
Motivation
Naturalistic observation
Performance
Practice
Single-subject experiment
Stimulus-stimulus learning

CHAPTER TWO

The Structure of Unconditioned Behavior

DID YOU KNOW THAT:

- Learning is constrained by the organism's unconditioned behavior.
- Unconditioned behavior is organized in complex and systematic ways.
- Organized elicited behavior can result in well-coordinated social interactions.
- Species-typical or instinctive behavior is not invariant.
- Some forms of elicited behavior are modulated by the animal's motivational state.
- Behavior in a complex environment can be governed by small isolated stimulus features.

Learning enables organisms to benefit from experience. Through learning, behavior can be altered in ways that make the organism more effective in interacting with its environment. Animals can forage more effectively by learning where and when food is likely to be available (Kamil & Clements,1990), they can defend themselves more successfully by learning when and where they are likely to encounter a predator (Hollis, 1990), and they can be more effective in reproduction by learning when and where they are likely to encounter a potential sexual partner (Domjan, 1994; Hollis, 1990).

Shaping and Homogeneous versus Heterogeneous Substrates of Behavior

In all instances of learning, the behavior of an organism is modified or shaped by its prior experience. B. F. Skinner introduced the term "shaping" in reference to a particular type of conditioning procedure described in greater detail in Chapter 6. For our present purposes, it is sufficient to point out that, through shaping, an organism's behavior can be gradually changed to enable it to perform entirely new responses. A child's uncoordinated arm and leg movements, for example, can be gradually shaped to enable her to swim rapidly across a pool.

Skinner chose the term "shaping" by analogy with how a sculptor gradually changes and molds a lump of clay into a recognizable object (Skinner, 1953). A sculptor interested in making a statue of a swan, for example, starts with an unformed lump of clay. She then cuts away excess clay here and there and molds what remains in special ways. As this process continues, a recognizable swan gradually emerges. In an analogous fashion, learning can change or shape an organism's behavior, with the result that the individual comes to respond in ways that are entirely new.

The analogy of molding a block of clay into a swan captures some of the aspects of how behavior is changed through learning. However, the analogy has a serious shortcoming. Clay is a homogeneous substance that can be molded in any direction with equal ease. Behavior is not like that. Behavior cannot be changed in any direction with equal ease. Changes in behavior occur in the context of genetically programmed predispositions that make certain changes easier to produce than others. For example, it is much easier to train animals to approach and manipulate food-related stimuli (Hearst & Jenkins, 1974) than it is to train them to release or withdraw from such stimuli (Breland & Breland, 1961; Timberlake, Wahl, & King, 1982).

Learning procedures do not shape new behavior in the way that a sculptor shapes clay into a new object. A more apt analogy for the behavioral substrate for learning is wood rather than clay (Rachlin, 1976). Unlike clay, wood has a heterogeneous or uneven consistency. It is grainy and has knots. Cutting with the grain is easier and results in a smoother line than cutting against the grain, and cutting around knots is easier than cutting through them. Because of this heterogeneity, if you are carving a statue out of wood, you have to pay close attention to how the statue is oriented in relation to the grain and the knots in the wood. In an analogous fashion, learning psychologists have to pay close attention to how what they are trying to teach an organism fits with the organism's preexisting behavioral tendencies.

All instances of learning reflect an interaction between the training procedures that are used and the individual's preexisting behavior. Changes brought about by learning are not applied to a homogeneously modifiable substrate. Rather, learning is superimposed on a heterogeneous preexisting behavioral structure. Therefore, understanding how learning occurs requires an appreciation of the heterogeneous behavioral substrate that organisms bring into a learning situation.

The dependence of learning on unlearned aspects of behavior has been emphasized in some areas of learning moreso than in others. The interaction of conditioned and unconditioned aspects of behavior has been the focus of attention in studies of Pavlovian conditioning and avoidance learning (see Chapters 4 and 10). However, we will also see numerous examples of how learning effects depend on unlearned behavioral tendencies in analyses of other aspects of learning.

The Concept of the Reflex

The smallest unit of unconditioned behavior is the **reflex** (see Figure 2.1). The concept of a reflex was formulated by French philosopher René Descartes (1596–1650). Descartes made numerous contributions to Western philosophy, including ideas about behavior that are familiar to most of us today but were innovative in the seventeenth century. Descartes believed, as did other philosophers of his time, that important aspects of human behavior were voluntary. However, he was also impressed with the seemingly automatic and involuntary nature of some actions and proposed the concept of the reflex to characterize involuntary behavior.

Descartes based his concept of the reflex on animated statues that he saw in public parks in France. Sophisticated animated characters such as those created by Disney Studios were not available in Descartes's time, but some of the parks Descartes frequented had statues whose limbs would move when someone walked by. To enable the statues to move, its limbs were attached with joints. Through a series of levers and linkages, the limbs and joints were connected to stepping stones along the walkway near the statue. Whenever someone stepped on one of these stones, the pressure was transferred to the statue, causing the statue's arm or leg to move.

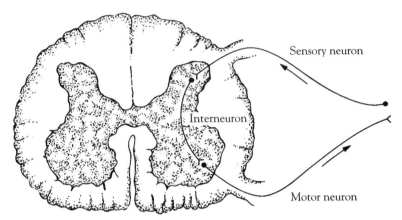

Cross-section of spinal cord

FIGURE 2.1 Neural organization of simple reflexes.
The environmental stimulus for the reflex response activates a sensory neuron, which transmits the sensory message to the spinal cord. Here the neural impulses are relayed to an interneuron, which in turn passes the impulses to the motor neuron. The motor neuron activates muscles involved in the reflex response.

The moving statues appeared lifelike, and it occurred to Descartes that some aspects of human and animal behavior were similar to the behavior of the statues. Descartes pointed out that animals and people also perform certain actions in response to a particular environmental stimulus. For example, we quickly withdraw our finger when we touch a hot stove, we "instinctively" flinch when we hear a sudden noise, and we extend our arm when we lose our footing. Such responses to particular stimuli are examples of **elicited behavior**.

In the statues Descartes saw, the movements were in a sense reflections of the eliciting stimulus, or the force that was applied to the associated stepping stone. Descartes coined the term **reflex** to capture this idea of behavior being a reflection of an eliciting stimulus. The entire unit from stimulus input to response output was called the **reflex arc**.

Reflexes are involved in many aspects of behavior important for sustaining critical life functions. Respiratory reflexes provide us with sufficient air intake. The suckling reflex provides a newborn's first contact with milk, and chewing, swallowing, and digestive reflexes are important in obtaining nutrients throughout life. Postural reflexes enable us to maintain stable body positions, and withdrawal reflexes protect us from focal sources of injury.

For about 250 years after Descartes, investigators of reflexes were primarily concerned with physiological questions. Scientists studied the neural circuitry of the reflex arc, the mechanisms of neural conduction, and the role of reflexes in various physiological systems. These investigations continued at an accelerated pace in the twentieth century. In addition, the idea of elicited behavior came to be extended to more complex forms of overt behavior. Much of this work was done in the newly emerging field of **ethology**, a specialty within biology that is concerned with the evolution and development of functional units of behavior (Baerends, 1988).

Complex Forms of Elicited Behavior

Ethologists discovered that complex social behavior in various species is made up of response components that are elicited by social stimuli. Male stickleback fish, for example, establish a small territory and build a nest tunnel during the mating season. After the territory has been set up, the approach of a male intruder elicits an aggressive defensive response from the resident. In contrast, if a female enters the territory, the resident male engages in courtship zig-zag swimming motions (see Figure 2.2). The courtship zig-zag motions stimulate the female to follow the resident male to the nest tunnel. Once the female is in the tunnel, with her head at one end and her tail at the other, the male prods the base of the female's tail. This causes the female to release her eggs. The female then leaves the nest and the male enters and fertilizes the eggs. After that, he chases the female away and fans the eggs to provide oxygen until the eggs hatch (see Tinbergen, 1952).

In this complex behavioral duet, the male and female each have their special roles. Stimuli provided by the female trigger certain actions on the part of the resident male (zig-zag swimming); the male's behavior in turn provides stimuli that trigger other responses on the part of the female (following the resident male to the nest); the female's behavior then leads to further responses from the male, and so on. The outcome is a sequence of nicely coordinated social responses. The behavior sequence progresses only if the male's behavior provides the necessary stimulation to elicit the next response from the female, and vice versa. If the response of one participant is inadequate to trigger the next response in its partner, the sequence of actions is interrupted and the social interaction may come to an end.

FIXED-ACTION PATTERNS

Careful observations by ethologists have revealed numerous examples of complex social and nonsocial behaviors that are made up of sequences of elicited responses of the sort illustrated by the sexual behavior of sticklebacks. Elicited responses have been shown to be involved in, among other things, nest building, incubation, parental feeding of the young, grooming, foraging, and defensive behavior (Alcock, 1993). Each unit of elicited behavior is made up of a characteristic response and its corresponding eliciting stimulus.

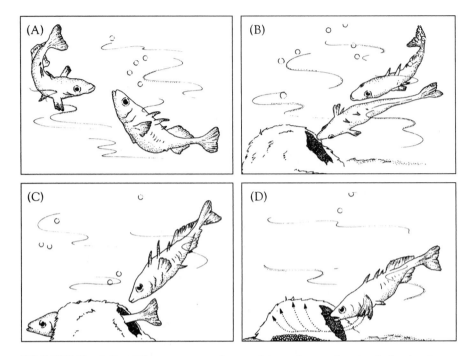

FIGURE 2.2. The sequence of courtship and reproductive behavior in the stickleback.
(A) The male swims towards the female with zig-zag motions. (B) The male guides the female to the nest. (C) The female enters the nest and releases her eggs. (D) After fertilizing the eggs, the male fans them to provide sufficient oxygen for development. (After Tinbergen, 1952.)

These units of elicited behavior are commonly called **fixed-action patterns**, or FAPs. The phrase "action pattern" is used instead of "response" because the activities involved are not restricted to a single muscle movement such as the blink of the eye or the flexion of a leg muscle. Elicited responses involved in grooming, foraging, courtship, and parental behavior require a coordinated set of a number of different muscles. The word "fixed" is used to signify that most members of the species perform the action pattern in question and do so in a highly stereotyped, or "fixed," fashion. An action pattern is a characteristic of the species. For example, infant mammals typically feed by suckling, infant gulls typically feed by gaping and receiving food from a parent, and infant chickens typically feed by pecking small spots on the ground. Because fixed-action patterns are characteristic of a species, they are examples of **species-typical behavior**.

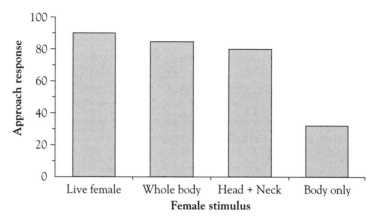

F I G U R E   2.3 Approach response of sexually experienced male quail to a live female and to taxidermic models consisting of the whole body of a female, a female's head and neck only, or a female's body without the head and neck. (After Domjan & Nash, 1988.)

SIGN STIMULI

Fixed-action patterns occur in the context of rich and complex arrays of stimulation. Consider, for example, a male quail or male turkey that becomes sexually attracted to a female who comes into view. The female is a source of many visual cues. Visual cues are provided by her various body parts (head, neck, torso, legs) and by her movements. She may also provide auditory and olfactory stimulation, and if she comes close enough to the male, she provides tactile stimulation. Interestingly, most of these cues are not critical for eliciting male sexual behavior.

To determine which of the various stimuli provided by a female is sufficient to elicit male sexual behavior, experimenters have tested males with live females and with taxidermic models of females. In one study (Domjan & Nash, 1988), for example, some of the models consisted of the head and the entire body of a female. Other models consisted of just the head and neck of the female or just the body without the head. Figure 2.3 shows the tendency of male quail to approach and remain near these various types of female stimuli.

The male quail responded as vigorously to a complete taxidermic model of a female as they responded to a live female. This result shows that movement cues and auditory and olfactory stimuli provided by a live female are not necessary to elicit the approach response. The birds also responded vigorously to just the visual cues of a female's head and neck. In fact, they approached the head-and-neck model almost as much as they responded to a

Figure 2.4.   The sign stimulus for the pecking response of gull chicks is a red spot near the tip of the parent's bill.

complete female model. This is a remarkable outcome. Evidently, male quail can identify a female only by the visual cues of the female's head and neck. The rest of her body, her calls, her smell, and her movements are all unnecessary.

The restricted set of stimuli that are required to elicit a fixed-action pattern is called a **sign stimulus**. As far as male quail and male turkeys are concerned, the female's head and neck are the "signs" that she is a female (Schein & Hale, 1965).

A sign stimulus is often a remarkably small part of the cues that ordinarily precede a fixed-action pattern. The pecking response of gull chicks, for example, is elicited by a prominent red spot on the parent's bill (see Figure 2.4). The pointed shape of the parent's bill, together with this prominent spot, stimulates the chicks to peck the parent's bill, which then causes the parent to feed the chick by regurgitating food. Other aspects of the parent (the shape of her head, her eyes, how she lands on the edge of the nest, and the noises she makes) are not important (Tinbergen & Perdeck, 1950).

The Organization of Elicited Behavior

If each reflex or fixed-action pattern occurred automatically whenever its eliciting stimulus was encountered, behavior would be a bit disorganized. Elicited responses do not occur independently of each other. Rather, they are organized in special ways. As we will see in the following chapters, some of this organization is a result of learning and experience. This section considers aspects of behavioral organization that are not obviously a product of learning.

MOTIVATIONAL FACTORS

One prominent factor that serves to coordinate fixed-action patterns is the internal state of the organism. The occurrence of many action patterns depends on the organism's motivational state. For example, in numerous species courtship and sexual responses occur only during the breeding season. In fact, the situation can be even more restrictive. For a male stickleback to court a female, it not only has to be in the breeding season, but it also has to have established a territory and built a nest. These preconditions serve to prime or create the motivation for courtship behavior.

Motivational factors have been identified for a variety of fixed-action patterns, including aggression, feeding, and various aspects of parental behavior. The motivational state sets the stage for a fixed-action pattern, whose actual occurrence is then triggered by a sign stimulus. In a sense, the sign stimulus releases the fixed action pattern when the animal is in a particular motivational state. Because of this, a sign stimulus is also sometimes referred to as a **releasing stimulus**.

Ethologists considered the motivational state of the organism to be one of the key factors involved in the organization of behavior (Lorenz, 1981). Using motivational concepts, they formulated an influential model for how fixed-action patterns are organized, referred to as the **hydraulic model** of behavior. The hydraulic model assumes that certain factors lead to the buildup of a particular type of motivation or drive. The hunger drive, for example, is created by the expenditure of energy and the utilization of nutrients. This drive in turn induces selective attention to food-related stimuli and lowers the threshold for activating food-related fixed-action patterns. Once food is found and eaten, the motivational state of hunger is discharged. Thus, the motivational state facilitates fixed-action patterns related to eating, and the opportunity to perform those responses in turn reduces the motivational state.

APPETITIVE AND CONSUMMATORY BEHAVIOR

Elicited behavior is also organized in a sequential fashion. Certain responses tend to occur before others. Ethologists characterize the response sequence involved in the discharge of a drive state as consisting of two major components. The first of these is **appetitive behavior**. In the case of the feeding system, appetitive behavior consists of responses involved in searching for a patch of food. Appetitive behavior is fairly variable and occurs in response to general spatial cues. For example, in searching for a patch of food, a squirrel will focus on spatial cues that help identify trees and bushes that contain nuts and fruit. Appetitive behavior tends to occur over a wide area and involves a range of possible activities. During the course of its foraging, the squirrel may run across open grass, climb over rocks, climb trees, jump from one tree limb to another, and so on.

Once the squirrel encounters an edible nut, its behavior becomes much more stereotyped and restricted. Now the squirrel remains in one place, sits back on its hind legs and tail, takes the nut in its front paws, cracks it open, and chews and swallows the food. These more stereotyped species-typical activities are called **consummatory behaviors**. The elicited behavior sequence ends with these fixed-action patterns because these responses discharge the motivation or drive state.

The term "consummatory" refers to the completion, or "consummation," of an instinctive response sequence. In the feeding system, consummatory behavior involves the consumption of food, but the similarity in the labels in this case is just a coincidence. In the sexual behavior system, consummatory behavior consists of the copulatory responses that serve to complete a sexual interaction. In the defensive behavior system, consummatory behavior consists of circa strike responses against the attacker.

Another way to think about appetitive and consummatory behavior is to see appetitive behavior as consisting of activities that enable an organism to come into contact with stimuli that will elicit the fixed-action patterns that serve to end the response sequence. For example, male appetitive sexual behavior involves searching for a female. Once the female is encountered, the stimuli provided by the female elicit a more restricted range of courtship and copulatory responses. Copulatory responses then discharge the motivation to engage in sexual behavior and consummate or end the sexual behavior sequence.

BEHAVIOR SYSTEMS

Recent research on the structure of unconditioned behavior has suggested that elicited behavior sequences should be subdivided into more than just appetitive and consummatory behavior. Timberlake (1994), for example, has characterized the feeding system as consisting of at least three components (see Figure 2.5). According to this more detailed view, the feeding behavior sequence starts with a general search mode. In the **general search mode**, the animal reacts to general features of the environment with responses that enable it to come in contact with a variety of potential sources of food. A honeybee, for example, may fly all around looking for bushes or other plants with flowers.

Once an animal has identified a potential source of food, it switches to a more restricted response mode, the **focal search mode**. In the focal search mode, the bee will concentrate on one bush, going from flower to flower. Upon encountering a specific flower, the behavior of the bee will change to the food handling and consumption mode. This response mode is similar to what ethologists referred to as consummatory behavior and

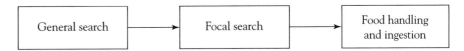

FIGURE 2.5 Components of the feeding behavior system.
The feeding behavior sequence begins with a general search for potential food sites. Once a potential food site has been identified, the animal engages in a focal search of that site. Upon finding the food, the animal engages in food handling and ingestion responses.

consists of responses required to extract nectar from the flower and ingest the nectar.

Behavior systems have been described for a variety of different functions that organisms must accomplish in their lives: caring of young, grooming, defense, and reproduction. Several features of behavior systems are noteworthy:

1. Behavior systems often consist of a sequence of three or more modes of behavior, rather than just appetitive and consummatory behavior. The organism moves from one mode of responding to another (general search to focal search) depending on the environmental events that it encounters.

2. The sequence of response modes is linear. The organism typically moves from one response to the next without skipping a step in the sequence. A squirrel cannot handle food, for example, without first having encountered the food in a focal search mode.

3. Although the response sequence is linear, it is not one-directional. An animal may go forward or backward in the sequence depending on the circumstances. If through its focal search behavior a squirrel does not find nuts that are worth the trouble to break open and eat, it will move back to a more general search mode.

4. Finally, each response mode involves not only characteristic responses but also increased sensitivity or attention to particular kinds of stimuli. In the general search mode, a foraging bee is likely to be looking for flowering bushes as opposed to ones that don't have flowers. In a focal search mode, it is apt to focus on where the flowers are in the bush it has chosen to search. Finally, in the food-handling mode, it will focus on the part of the flower that contains the nectar. Thus, various modes of behavior differ not only in terms of the types of responses that are involved but also in terms of the types of stimuli that guide the behavior.

Summary

All instances of learning reflect an interaction between the training procedures used and the individual's preexisting behavior. Therefore, understanding how learning occurs requires an appreciation of unconditioned behavioral mechanisms. Unconditioned behavior is not homogeneous and modifiable in any direction; it has its own set structure. The simplest unit of unconditioned behavior is the reflex, which consists of a specific eliciting stimulus and a corresponding elicited response. More complex forms of elicited behavior, studied by ethologists, involve fixed-action patterns that are elicited by sign stimuli. Ethologists have identified motivational factors involved in the control of fixed-action patterns and have pointed out that elicited behavior consists of a predictable sequence of activities that begins with appetitive responses and ends with consummatory behavior. These ideas have been extended in contemporary conceptualizations of behavior systems. A behavior system consists of a sequentially organized set of response modes, each of which is characterized by particular responses and increased sensitivity to particular types of stimuli.

Suggested Readings

BAERENDS, G. P. (1988). Ethology. In R. C. Atkinson, R. J. Herrnstein, G. Lindzey, & R. D. Luce (Eds.), *Stevens' handbook of experimental psychology* (Vol. 1, pp. 765–830). New York: Wiley.

RACHLIN, H. (1976). *Behavior and learning.* San Francisco: W. H. Freeman. See especially Chapter 3 (pp. 102–154).

TIMBERLAKE, W. (1994). Behavior systems, associationism, and Pavlovian conditioning. *Psychonomic Bulletin & Review, 1,* 405–420.

TINBERGEN, N. (1951). *The study of instinct.* Oxford: Clarendon Press.

Technical Terms

Appetitive behavior
Behavior system
Consummatory behavior
Elicited behavior
Ethology
Fixed-action pattern
Focal search mode

General search mode
Hydraulic model
Reflex
Reflex arc
Releasing stimulus
Sign stimulus
Species-typical behavior

CHAPTER THREE

Habituation and Sensitization

DID YOU KNOW THAT:

- Reflexive behavior is not automatic and invariant but can increase or decrease as a result of experience.
- The vigor of elicited behavior is regulated by opposing habituation and sensitization processes.
- Elicited behavior is determined not only by the eliciting stimulus but also by other recently encountered events.
- Habituation effects are evident in decreased responding; sensitization effects are evident in increased responding.
- Habituation and sensitization effects are both determined by the intensity and frequency of the eliciting stimulus.
- Habituation is more specific to the eliciting stimulus than sensitization.
- Habituation is an inherent property of all elicited behavior.
- Sensitization reflects a modulatory influence on the mechanisms of elicited behavior.

Having considered the structure of unconditioned behavior in Chapter 2, we are now ready examine some of the ways in which behavior can be changed or modified by experience. We begin with the phenomena of habituation and sensitization. These are good to start with because habituation and sensitization are two of the simplest and most common forms of behavior change. In addition, habituation and sensitization can occur in all of the more complex learning phenomena that are the subject of discussion in subsequent chapters.

Habituation and sensitization have been investigated most extensively in reflex systems. A reflex is a fairly simple response that occurs in reaction to a specific eliciting stimulus. Suckling, for example, can be elicited in a newborn infant by placing a soft object in the infant's mouth. As I noted in Chapter 2, the concept of the reflex was originally formulated by Descartes, who assumed that reflexes have two major features. According to Descartes, the vigor of the elicited response is directly related to the intensity of the eliciting stimulus. In fact, Descartes claimed that the energy required for the reflex response was provided by the eliciting stimulus. Second, Descartes assumed that a reflex response would always occur when its eliciting stimulus was presented. Reflexes were assumed to be "automatic" or inevitable reactions to eliciting stimuli.

Descartes was correct in pointing out that certain actions are triggered by eliciting stimuli. But he was wrong in characterizing reflexes as invariant and energized by their eliciting stimuli. Nevertheless, his views continue to dominate how laypersons think about reflexes. People commonly consider reflexes to be automatic and fixed. In fact, the term "reflexive" is sometimes used as a synonym for "automatic." However, scientists have shown that reflexes do not occur in the same way each time an eliciting stimulus is presented. In fact, as we will see in this chapter, elicited behavior can be remarkably flexible. Responses to an eliciting stimulus can increase (showing sensitization) or decrease (showing habituation), depending on the circumstances. In addition, the energy for reflex action is not provided by the eliciting stimulus.

Why should reflexive behavior be modifiable? Why do we need habituation and sensitization? Basically, habituation and sensitization keep us from wasting effort on things that are irrelevant and allow us to focus our actions on things that are important. Habituation and sensitization regulate our reflex responses and increase the efficiency of our interactions with the environment. Animals (both human and nonhuman) live in complex environments that provide many forms of stimulation all the time. Even during an activity as seemingly uneventful as sitting quietly in a chair, a person is bombarded by all sorts of visual, auditory, olfactory, tactile, and internal physiological stimuli. All of these stimuli can elicit responses, but if we responded to all of the stimuli, we would be reacting to all sorts of things that are unimportant. Without habituation and sensitization, behavior would be totally enslaved to the vicissitudes of the environment.

Consider, for example, the **orienting response**. We orient and turn toward novel visual and auditory stimuli (someone entering the room, for example). However, if all of the stimuli in our environment elicited an orienting response, we would be wasting much of our effort. Many stimuli are not important enough to warrant our attention. While talking to someone in the living room, we need not orient to the sounds of a refrigerator humming in the background or a car going by on the street. Habituation and sensitization serve to regulate and organize our responsivity to environmental events. They ensure that we respond vigorously to some stimuli while ignoring others.

Organizational concepts for elicited behavior that were introduced in Chapter 2 noted that the intensity of elicited behavior is determined by motivational factors and that the sequence of elicited responses is determined by an inherent structure set by the behavior system being activated. I also noted in passing that response systems are sometimes organized by learning and experience. Habituation and sensitization are the first principles of behavioral organization based on experience that we will consider.

General Principles of Regulation

Before turning to specific mechanisms of habituation and sensitization, let us consider in more general terms what it means to "regulate" something. Something is regulated if its functions are maintained within acceptable limits or within a defined target range. The temperature in a house, for example, is regulated by a thermostat so that the house remains comfortable. In the winter, the thermostat may be set to turn on the heater whenever the temperature falls below 70 °F and to turn off the heater if the temperature hits 74 °F. In this case the target range is 70–74 °F. A driver regulates the speed of a car so that the car does not go too much above or below the posted speed limit. A cook regulates the taste of pasta to make sure it is salty enough but not too salty. In all these instances, regulation serves to keep something within acceptable limits, within a target range.

Physiology is replete with examples of regulation, and in physiological systems the target range is typically referred to as the **homeostatic level**. Perhaps the most obvious example of a homeostatic system is temperature regulation in warm-blooded animals, or endotherms. The body temperature of endotherms is regulated so precisely by physiological and behavioral mechanisms that a deviation from the homeostatic level of just one or two degrees is interpreted as a sign of illness. Other familiar homeostatic systems include respiration and blood sugar level. Our respiratory system is designed to limit the accumulation of carbon dioxide in the blood. An increase in serum carbon dioxide above the acceptable level causes drowsiness, coma, and eventual death. Blood sugar levels are also maintained within a target range. A drastic drop in serum glucose level can also result in coma. In contrast, too much serum glucose can cause convulsions.

How is regulation generally achieved? To maintain a system within a desired range, forces that push the system in one direction have to be opposed by mechanisms that serve to return the system to the desired or homeostatic level. Exposure to cold and a consequent drop in body temperature elicits shivering, which produces body heat and counteracts the drop in body temperature. A buildup of carbon dioxide in the blood stimulates breathing, which reduces carbon dioxide and increases oxygen intake. A drop in blood sugar triggers the release of stored glucose from the liver and also induces hunger and eating, all of which increase blood sugar level.

In general, regulation is achieved by the activation of **opponent processes**, processes that counteract or oppose each other. Opponent process concepts have been used in a variety of areas of conditioning and learning. Our first encounter with such processes is in this chapter. Habituation and sensitization are opposing influences that regulate the vigor of elicited behavior. Habituation causes decrements in reactivity; sensitization causes increments in responding.

Effects of the Repeated Presentation of an Eliciting Stimulus

The general characteristics described here for habituation and sensitization may be observed with just about any form of elicited behavior. A common experimental preparation for the study of habituation and sensitization in human infants is illustrated in Figure 3.1. The infant is seated comfortably in front of a screen that is used to present visual stimuli. When a stimulus appears on the screen, the infant looks at the display. The infant's visual attention is measured by noting how long its eyes remain fixed on the stimulus before the infant shifts its gaze elsewhere. How long the infant looks at the stimulus depends on what the stimulus is and how often it has been presented.

Figure 3.2 shows the results of an experiment conducted with two groups of 4-month-old babies (Bashinski, Werner, & Rudy, 1985). For each group, a 10-sec visual stimulus was presented eight times, with a 10-sec interval between trials. The complexity of the visual stimulus differed for the two groups. For one group the visual stimulus was a 4 × 4 checkerboard pattern. For the other group it was a more complex 12 × 12 checkerboard pattern. Notice that the duration of the visual fixation that was elicited by each stimulus was not invariant or "automatic." Rather, fixation time changed in different ways depending on the stimulus. With the complex 12 × 12 pattern, fixation increased from Trial 1 to Trial 2, and then declined thereafter. With the simpler 4 × 4 pattern, visual fixation declined from each trial to the next.

FIGURE   3.1   Experimental set-up for the study of visual attention in infants.
The infant is seated in front of a screen that is used to present various visual stimuli. How long the infant looks at the display before diverting its gaze elsewhere is measured on each trial.

A decrease in the vigor of elicited behavior is called a **habituation effect**. In contrast, an increase in responsivity is called a **sensitization effect**. Habituation was evident throughout the experiment with the 4 × 4 checkerboard pattern. Habituation was also evident with the 12 × 12 pattern from Trial 2 to Trial 8, but sensitization occurred from Trial 1 to Trial 2.

Another common experimental preparation for the study of habituation and sensitization involves the **startle response**. The startle response is a sudden movement or flinch caused by a novel stimulus. If someone broke a balloon behind you (making a loud popping sound), you would suddenly hunch your shoulders and pull in your neck. Startle is a common human reaction in a variety of cultures (Simons, 1996). The sudden movement that characterizes the startle reflex can be easily measured, and this has encouraged numerous studies of habituation and sensitization of the startle reflex in laboratory rats (e.g., Davis, 1974; Davis, Hitchcock, & Rosen, 1987).

A sudden but soft sound may cause you to startle the first few times it occurs, but you will quickly stop responding to the sound. Similar results are obtained with mild tactile stimuli. When you first put on a comfortable pair of shoes, you feel the gentle pressure of the shoes against your feet. However, this reaction quickly habituates. Soon you will be entirely oblivious to wearing the shoes.

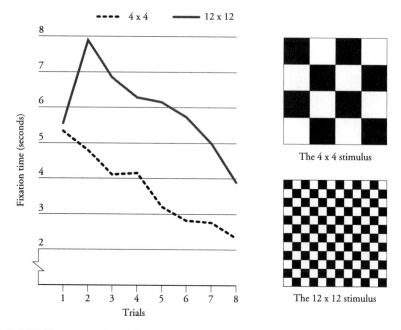

FIGURE   3.2   Visual fixation time for two groups of infants presented with a visual stimulus on eight successive trials.
The stimulus was a 12 × 12 checkerboard pattern for one group and a 4 × 4 checkerboard pattern for the other group. Adapted from Bashinski et al. (1985).

If the tactile stimulus is more intense, it is more difficult to get used to it, and the pattern of responding may be similar to what we saw in the infants' visual attention to a 12 × 12 checkerboard pattern in Figure 3.2. In this case, responding increases somewhat at first but then declines. Such results are also obtained with the startle reflex if the eliciting stimulus is an intense tone.

If the eliciting stimulus is very intense, repetition of it may result in a sustained increase in responding. If your shoes provide intense pressure, your irritation will increase with continued exposure to the pressure, and you may never come to ignore the shoe. Similarly, a sustained increase in the startle response may occur if the eliciting stimulus is an intense noise. Soldiers and civilians in a war zone may never get used to the noise of gun shots. The stress and arousal of combat experience can cause long-term sensitization to the sound of gun shots.

As these examples illustrate, under some circumstances elicited behavior shows a monotonic habituation pattern. In other cases, a sensitization effect occurs at first, followed by a decline in responding. Elicited behavior can also show evidence of sustained sensitization.

CHARACTERISTICS OF HABITUATION EFFECTS

Numerous factors have been found to influence the course of habituation and sensitization effects. Here I consider some of the major variables.

Effects of stimulus change.   Perhaps the most important feature of habituation is that it is specific to the particular stimulus that has been repeatedly presented. If the stimulus is altered, the habituated response recovers, with the degree of recovery determined by how similar the new stimulus is to the one that had been previously presented. Stimulus specificity is a defining feature of habituation (Thompson & Spencer, 1966) and has been used profitably to study information processing in infants (e.g., Cohen, 1988; Kaplan, Werner, & Rudy, 1990).

Before they are able to talk, infants cannot tell us in words which stimuli they consider to be similar and which they consider to be different. However, they can provide answers to such questions in their response to test stimuli following habituation. Consider the following hypothetical experiment involving the visual attention or fixation response of infants: A small green spot of light is presented repeatedly on the stimulus screen until the infant stops fixating at the light. Then, the light is presented again, but in different places on the screen. Let us assume that all of the test stimuli fall on an imaginary horizontal line, with the original habituated stimulus in the middle. How will the baby respond to the various test stimuli? Which test stimuli will the infant consider to be different from the habituation training stimulus, and which will he consider to be similar?

The likely outcome is illustrated in Figure 3.3. In this figure, the response to each test stimulus is plotted as a function of how close that test stimulus was to the spot where the light had been presented during habituation training. Notice that the lowest level of responding (most evidence of habituation) is obtained with the stimulus presented exactly where it had occurred during habituation training. The baby also does not respond much to stimuli presented close to the original training position. Thus, the effects of habituation training transfer to other nearby locations. This is called **stimulus generalization of habituation**. Test stimuli that are presented greater distances from the original training position elicit progressively more responding. This illustrates the stimulus specificity of habituation. The habituated response recovers when the eliciting stimulus is sufficiently different from the training stimulus.

The stimulus specificity of habituation helps to rule out an important potential explanation of habituation effects. One might assume that responding declines with repeated stimulations in a habituation procedure

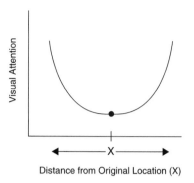

FIGURE 3.3 **Stimulus specificity of habituation.**
The visual fixation response of infants is initially habituated to a spot of green light presented at a particular location. The location of the light is then varied during a series of test trials. Notice that responding increases as the green light is moved away from its original location. (Note: Data are hypothetical.)

___

because of fatigue. The participant may simply get tired of performing the elicited response. Recovery of responding with a change in the eliciting stimulus rules out fatigue. If habituation were caused by fatigue, the participant would not respond to the altered stimulus.

Tests with novel stimuli are routinely carried out in studies of habituation with infants. Infants can stop looking at a visual stimulus for a variety of reasons. They may become tired or fussy or may fall asleep. To be sure that they are still paying attention and are actively participating in the experiment, novel stimuli are introduced after habituation. The results of the experiment are considered valid only if there is recovery in responding to a novel stimulus.

Effects of time-out from stimulation.   Habituation effects are often temporary. They dissipate or are lost as time passes without presentation of the eliciting stimulus. A loss of the habituation effect is evident in a recovery of responding. This is illustrated in Figure 3.4. Because the response recovery is produced by a period without stimulation (a period of rest), the phenomenon is called **spontaneous recovery**.

Spontaneous recovery is a common feature of habituation (Thompson & Spencer, 1966). If your roommate turns on the radio while you are studying, you may notice this at first but will come to ignore the sound if it is not too loud. However, if the radio is turned off for a while and then comes back on, you will again notice that the radio is playing. In fact, if your roommate repeatedly turns the radio on and off, you may become very annoyed.

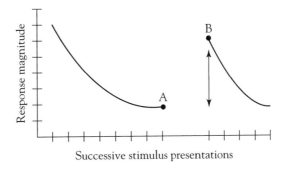

Successive stimulus presentations

FIGURE 3.4 Spontaneous recovery of a habituated response.
A period of rest without stimulus presentations occurred between points A and B, which caused a recovery of the habituated response. (Note: Data are hypothetical.)

The degree of spontaneous recovery is related to the duration of the period of rest. Longer periods without presentation of the eliciting stimulus result in greater recovery of the response. In some cases, however, responding does not recover even with rest periods of several weeks. For example, no spontaneous recovery is evident in habituation of the novelty response to taste.

Animals, including people, are cautious about ingesting a food or drink that has an unfamiliar flavor. This phenomenon is known as **flavor neophobia**. Flavor neophobia probably evolved because things that taste new or unfamiliar could well be poisonous. With repeated exposure to the new taste, the neophobic response becomes attenuated. Coffee, for example, often elicits an aversion response in a child who tastes it for the first time. However, after drinking coffee without ill effect, the child's neophobic response will become diminished or habituated. Furthermore, the habituation is likely to be long-lasting. Having become accustomed to the flavor of coffee, a person is not likely to show a neophobic response even if he goes a couple of weeks without having any coffee. Studies with laboratory rats have shown no spontaneous recovery of flavor neophobia over periods as long as 17 and 24 days (Domjan, 1976; Siegel, 1974).

Habituation effects have been classified by whether or not they exhibit spontaneous recovery. Cases in which substantial spontaneous recovery occurs are called **short-term habituation**, and cases in which significant spontaneous recovery does not occur are called **long-term habituation**. Short-term and long-term habituation are not mutually exclusive phenomena. Sometimes both effects are observed. This is the case if a period of rest produces some recovery in the habituated response, but the recovery is not complete (e.g., Leaton, 1976). Factors that promote long-term as opposed to short-term habituation are not entirely understood (Whitlow & Wagner, 1984; but see Marlin & Miller, 1981).

Effects of stimulus frequency.   The frequency of a stimulus refers to how often the stimulus is repeated in a block of time—how often the stimulus occurs per minute, for example. The higher the stimulus frequency, the shorter the period of rest between repetitions of the stimulus. As we saw in the phenomenon of spontaneous recovery, the duration of rest between stimulations can significantly influence responding. Because higher stimulus frequencies permit less spontaneous recovery between trials, in general, responding declines more rapidly with more frequent stimulation (Davis, 1970). In contrast, responding does not decline as rapidly if the frequency of stimulation is low.

Effects of stimulus intensity.   Habituation is also determined by the intensity of the stimulus. In general, responding declines more slowly if the eliciting stimulus is more intense (Groves, Lee, & Thompson, 1969). For example, laboratory rats are slower to lose their neophobic response to strong flavors than to weak ones (Domjan & Gillan, 1976).

Effects of exposure to a second stimulus.   One of the remarkable features of habituation is that it is not determined solely by the eliciting stimulus. The degree of habituation is also influenced by other stimuli the organism experiences. In particular, exposure to a second stimulus can result in recovery of a previously habituated response. This phenomenon is called **dishabituation** (Thompson & Spencer, 1966).

The results of one experiment on dishabituation are summarized in Figure 3.5. The visual fixation time of human infants was measured in response to a 4 × 4 checkerboard pattern (Kaplan et al., 1990). As expected, repetition of the visual stimulus eight times resulted in a decline or habituation of the looking response of the infants. After Trial 8, a tone (1000 Hz, 75 dB) was presented as a dishabituating stimulus with the checkerboard pattern. As Figure 3.5 shows, presentation of the tone caused significant recovery of visual fixation to the 4 × 4 pattern. The response to the original habituated stimulus (the checkerboard pattern) was enhanced by presentation of the dishabituating stimulus (the tone).

Unfortunately, the term dishabituation is used inconsistently in the research literature. In studies with human infants, dishabituation is sometimes used to refer to the recovery of responding that occurs when the original habituated stimulus is replaced by a novel stimulus. In contrast, in research with other species and responses, dishabituation is reserved for cases in which the introduction of a new stimulus produces recovery in responding

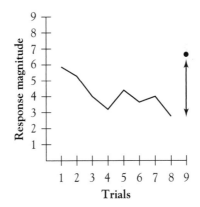

FIGURE 3.5   Dishabituation of a habituated response.
Visual fixation in infants became habituated to a checkerboard stimulus presented
in Trials 1–8. Presentation of a tone with the visual stimulus caused dishabituation
of the attentional response in Trial 9. Adapted from Kaplan et al. (1990).

---

to the original habituated stimulus. I follow the second convention because
it is historically more accurate (Thompson & Spencer, 1966).

Effects of time after a dishabituating stimulus.   The effects of a dishabituating stimulus are short-lasting. If a period of rest follows presentation of
the dishabituating stimulus, the dishabituation effect will dissipate and the
recovery of the habituated response will be lost (Thompson & Spencer,
1966). In the example described earlier and summarized in Figure 3.5, the
dishabituating stimulus was the tone. If a period of rest had been provided
after presentation of the tone, less recovery would have occurred in orientation to the habituated visual stimulus.

CHARACTERISTICS OF SENSITIZATION EFFECTS

Sensitization effects are influenced by the same stimulus intensity and time
factors that govern habituation phenomena. In general, greater sensitization
effects (greater increases in responding) occur with more intense eliciting
stimuli (Groves et al., 1969).

Like habituation, sensitization effects can be short-term or long-term
(e.g., Davis, 1974; Heiligenberg, 1974). **Short-term sensitization** decays as
a result of time without stimulation. Unlike the decay of short-term habituation, which is called "spontaneous recovery," the decay of short-term sensitization has no special name. It is not called "spontaneous recovery" because
responding declines (rather than recovers) as sensitization dissipates. In

contrast to short-term sensitization, **long-term sensitization** is evident even after appreciable periods without stimulation.

One important respect in which sensitization is different from habituation is that sensitization effects are not as specific to a particular stimulus as habituation effects. As I noted earlier, habituation produced by repeated exposure to one stimulus will not be evident if the stimulus is altered substantially (see Figure 3.3). In contrast, sensitization is not as stimulus-specific. For example, the reactivity of laboratory rats to auditory cues can be increased or sensitized by exposing the animals to cutaneous pain (Davis et al., 1987). Once sensitized by pain, the rats show increased reactivity to a wide range of auditory cues. Likewise, the experience of illness increases or sensitizes the reactivity of laboratory rats to taste stimuli, and once taste reactivity has been sensitized, the animals show heightened finickiness to a variety of different taste stimuli (Domjan, 1977).

The Dual-Process Theory of Habituation and Sensitization

So far, I have described the behavioral phenomena of habituation and sensitization. I have not discussed what underlying processes or machinery might produce these behavioral effects. Here we consider a prominent theory of habituation and sensitization, the **dual-process theory**, which was proposed by Groves and Thompson (1970). The theory was based on neurophysiological studies of habituation and sensitization, but it can be described close to the level of a behavioral theory.

The dual-process theory is based on two underlying processes (a habituation process and a sensitization process) that are referred to by the same terms as the phenomena I described earlier. However, habituation and sensitization *processes* are distinct from habituation and sensitization *phenomena*. To avoid confusing the different terms, it is important to keep in mind that habituation and sensitization *phenomena* are performance effects; they are observable changes in behavior. In contrast, habituation and sensitization *processes* refer to the underlying events that are presumed to be responsible for the behavioral habituation and sensitization effects.

THE S-R SYSTEM AND THE STATE SYSTEM

According to the dual-process theory, habituation and sensitization processes are presumed to operate in different parts of the nervous system. For the purposes of the dual-process theory, the nervous system is conceptualized as consisting of two functional components, the S-R system and the state system.

The **S-R system** is the shortest path in the nervous system between an eliciting stimulus and the resulting elicited response. The S-R system corresponds to Descartes's reflex arc. It is the minimal physiological machinery involved in a reflex. Typically, the S-R system consists of three neurons, the **sensory** (or **afferent**) **neuron**, an **interneuron**, and a **motor** (or **efferent**) **neuron**. The eliciting or input stimulus activates the afferent neuron. The afferent neuron in turn activates the interneuron, which in turn activates the efferent neuron. The efferent neuron forms a synapse with the muscles involved in the elicited response and triggers the behavioral response.

The **state system** consists of all neural processes that are not an integral part of the S-R system but influence the responsivity of the S-R system. Spinal reflexes, for example, consist of an afferent neuron that ends in the spinal cord, an interneuron in the spinal cord, and an efferent neuron that extends from the spinal cord to the relevant muscle. That is the S-R system of a spinal reflex. However, the spinal cord also contains neural pathways that ascend to the brain and neural pathways that descend from the brain. These ascending and descending pathways serve to modulate spinal reflexes and make up the state system for spinal reflexes.

After one understands the categorization of the nervous system into the S-R and state components, the rest of the dual-process theory is fairly simple. As I noted earlier, the dual-process theory presumes the existence of separate habituation and sensitization processes. A critical aspect of the theory concerns the locus of action of these processes. The habituation process is assumed to take place in the S-R system, whereas the sensitization process is assumed to take place in the state system.

Habituation and sensitization processes are not directly evident in the behavior of the organism. Rather, observable behavior reflects the net effect of these processes. The habituation and sensitization processes serve as opponent mechanisms regulating reflex responsivity. Whenever the habituation process is stronger than the sensitization process, the net effect is a decline in behavioral output. This is illustrated in the left panel of Figure 3.6. The opposite outcome occurs if the sensitization process is stronger than the habituation process. In that event, the net effect of the two processes is an increase in behavioral output. This is illustrated in the right panel of Figure 3.6.

After being activated, both the habituation process and the sensitization process are assumed to decay with time. This temporal decay assumption is needed to explain the short-term nature of some habituation and sensitization effects.

IMPLICATIONS OF THE DUAL-PROCESS THEORY

Like Descartes's reflex arc, the S-R system is the minimal or most primitive mechanism of elicited behavior. Therefore, the S-R system is activated every time an eliciting stimulus is presented. Because the habituation process operates in the S-R system, each activation of the S-R system results

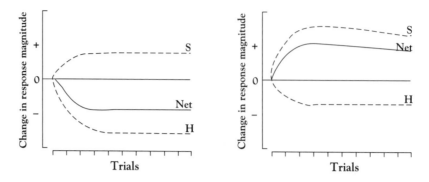

FIGURE 3.6 Mechanisms of the dual-process theory of habituation and sensitization.
The dashed lines indicate the strength of the habituation (H) and sensitization (S) processes across trials. The solid lines indicate the net (or combined) effects of these two processes. In the left panel, the habituation process becomes stronger than the sensitization process, and this leads to a progressive decrement in responding. In the right panel, the sensitization process becomes stronger than the habituation process, and this leads to a progressive increment in responding.

in some buildup of the habituation process. This makes habituation a universal feature of elicited behavior. According to the dual-process theory, the habituation process is activated whenever an eliciting stimulus is presented.

The universality of the habituation process does not mean that a habituation effect, or a decrement in responding, will always be observed. Whether a habituation effect is evident will depend on whether the habituation process is counteracted by activation of the sensitization process. Whether a habituation effect is observed will also depend on when the eliciting stimulus is presented relative to its previous occurrence. If two presentations of a stimulus are separated by a long rest interval, habituation created by the first stimulus will have a chance to decay completely before the stimulus is repeated, and a decrement in responding will not be observed. On the other hand, if the interval between stimulus presentations is too short to permit complete decay of the habituation process, a decrement in responding will occur.

In contrast to the habituation process, the sensitization process is not assumed to be universal. Sensitization occurs in the state system. The state system modulates responsivity of the S-R system, but it is not essential for the occurrence of elicited behavior. Elicited behavior can occur through the S-R system alone. Therefore, sensitization is not a universal property of elicited behavior.

When is the sensitization process activated? An informal way to think about this is that sensitization represents arousal. Sensitization or arousal occurs if the organism encounters a stimulus that is particularly intense or significant. You can become aroused by a loud unexpected noise, as well as by someone telling you in a soft voice that a close friend was seriously hurt in an accident. The state system and the sensitization process are activated by intense or significant stimuli.

The sensitization process can be activated by the same stimulus that is used to elicit the reflex response of interest. This is the case if an intense or significant stimulus is used as the eliciting stimulus. The right panel of Figure 3.6 illustrates such a situation. In that example, the eliciting stimulus produced a substantial degree of sensitization, with the result that the net behavioral effect was an increase in responding.

The sensitization process also can be activated by some event other than the eliciting stimulus. Because the state system is separate from the S-R system, the state system can be activated by stimuli that are not registered in the S-R system of the response that is being measured. This is a critical feature of the dual process theory and another respect in which sensitization is different from habituation. In contrast to habituation, sensitization is not necessarily produced by the eliciting stimulus of interest.

The fact that the sensitization and habituation processes can be activated by different stimuli permits the dual process theory to explain a number of key phenomenon, including the phenomenon of dishabituation. As I noted in Figure 3.5, the presentation of a dishabituating stimulus can result in recovery of a habituated response. In the example summarized in Figure 3.5, the presentation of a tone caused recovery of the habituated visual fixation response to a checkerboard pattern. According to the dual-process theory, this occurred because the tone activated the state system and produced enough sensitization to overcome the previous buildup of habituation to the visual stimulus. According to this interpretation, dishabituation is produced by the addition of the sensitization process to a behavioral situation rather than the reversal or weakening of the habituation process. Other evidence also supports this interpretation (see Groves & Thompson, 1970).

The dual-process theory is remarkably successful in characterizing short-term habituation and short-term sensitization effects. However, the theory is inconsistent with instances of long-term habituation and long-term sensitization. Explanations of long-term habituation and sensitization typically include mechanisms of associative learning, which I will discuss in upcoming chapters.

Summary

Reflexive or elicited behavior is commonly considered to be an automatic and invariant consequence of the eliciting stimulus. Contrary to this notion, however, repeated presentations of an eliciting stimulus may result in a monotonic decline in responding (a habituation effect), an increase in responding (a sensitization effect) followed by a decline, or a sustained increase in behavior. Thus, far from being invariant, elicited behavior is remarkably sensitive to different forms of prior experience. The magnitude of habituation and sensitization effects depends on the intensity and frequency of the eliciting stimulus. Responding elicited by one stimulus can also be altered by the prior presentation of a different event (as in the phenomenon of dishabituation).

Many findings concerning habituation and sensitization are characterized by a dual-process theory, wherein processes that produce decreased responding occur in the S-R system and processes that produce sensitization occur in the state system. The S-R system is activated every time an eliciting stimulus is presented, making habituation a universal property of elicited behavior. Sensitization, in contrast, occurs only when the organism encounters a stimulus that is sufficiently intense or significant to activate the state system. Through their additive effects, habituation and sensitization processes serve to regulate the vigor of elicited behavior.

Suggested Readings

GROVES, P. M., & THOMPSON, R. F. (1970). Habituation: A dual-process theory. *Psychological Review, 77,* 419–450.

KAPLAN, P. S., WERNER, J. S., & RUDY, J. W. (1990). Habituation, sensitization, and infant visual attention. In C. Rovee-Collier and L. P. Lipsitt (Eds.), *Advances in infancy research* (Vol. 6, pp. 61–109). Norwood, NJ: Ablex.

PEEKE, H. V. S., & PETRINOVICH, L. (Eds.) (1984). *Habituation, sensitization, and behavior.* Orlando, FL: Academic Press.

Technical Terms

Afferent neuron
Dishabituation
Dual-process theory
Efferent neuron
Flavor neophobia
Habituation effect
Homeostatic level
Interneuron
Long-term habituation
Long-term sensitization
Motor neuron

Opponent process
Orienting response
S-R system
Sensitization effect
Sensory neuron
Short-term habituation
Short-term sensitization
Spontaneous recovery
Startle response
State system
Stimulus generalization
    of habituation

CHAPTER FOUR

Pavlovian Conditioning and Extinction

DID YOU KNOW THAT:

- Pavlov viewed classical conditioning as a technique for studying the brain.
- Classical conditioning is not limited to glandular and visceral responses.
- The conditioned response is not always like the unconditioned response.
- Conditioned stimuli become part of the behavior system activated by the unconditioned stimulus.
- Pavlovian conditioning often involves S-S learning rather than S-R learning.
- Which stimulus can serve as a conditioned stimulus in classical conditioning depends on the unconditioned stimulus that is used.
- Associative learning is possible in the random control procedure.
- Extinction is not the opposite of acquisition; extinction does not involve "unlearning."

In Chapter 3, I described ways that behavior is changed by experience with individual stimuli. Habituation and sensitization may be considered to be instances of single-stimulus learning. We are now ready to consider how organisms learn about pairs of stimuli. Such learning is called **associative learning**. Associative learning is different from single-stimulus learning in that the change in behavior that occurs to one stimulus depends on when that event previously occurred in relation to a second stimulus. Associative learning represents what we learn about combinations of stimuli. The first form of associative learning I will describe is Pavlovian, or classical, conditioning.

Pavlov's Proverbial Bell

The basic elements of Pavlovian, or classical, conditioning are familiar to most of us. Accounts usually describe a hypothetical experiment in which Professor Ivan Pavlov rang a bell just before giving a bit of food powder to the dogs he was testing. The dogs were loosely held in a harness and were hooked up to an apparatus that enabled Pavlov to measure how much they salivated. At first the dogs salivated only when they were given the food powder. However, after several trials of having the bell paired with presentation of food, the dogs also came to salivate when the bell sounded.

The story of Professor Pavlov training his dogs to salivate to a bell is useful for introducing some important technical vocabulary. A stimulus like food powder that elicits the response of interest without prior training is called an **unconditioned stimulus**, or US. Salivation elicited by the food powder is an example of an **unconditioned response**, or UR. The bell is an example of a **conditioned stimulus**, or CS, and the salivation that develops to the bell is called the **conditioned response**, or CR.

Pavlov's proverbial bell illustrates associative learning because salivation to the bell depends on presenting the bell in combination with food powder. Ringing the bell each time the dog is about to receive a bit of food presumably results in an association of the bell with food. Once the bell has become associated with food, the dog starts to respond to the bell as if it were food; it starts to salivate when it hears the bell.

Some Common Misconceptions

Although Pavlov's proverbial bell is familiar and helpful in introducing technical terms used to describe Pavlovian, or classical, conditioning, several aspects of this example are misleading. First, Pavlov did not discover classical conditioning by ringing a bell just before presenting food powder. The basic elements of Pavlovian conditioning were well known in Pavlov's laboratory before he turned his attention to the study of classical conditioning (Boakes, 1984).

What Pavlov discovered was not the phenomenon of classical conditioning but the significance of this type of learning. In particular, he became interested in studying classical conditioning because he thought this would be a particularly powerful technique for studying how the nervous system works. Pavlov was a physiologist who pursued investigations of classical conditioning to better understand complex neural functions (Babkin, 1949).

Another misleading implication of the proverbial bell example is that classical conditioning primarily involves the conditioning of a response to a previously ineffective stimulus. In many descriptions, classical conditioning is presented as a mechanism for the learning of new responses. According to this interpretation, classical conditioning is a form of stimulus-response learning, or **S-R learning**. A more appropriate interpretation is that classical conditioning involves the learning of an association between the conditioned and unconditioned stimulus (Rescorla, 1988). According to this view, classical conditioning is a form of stimulus-stimulus learning, or **S-S learning**. Recent research has shown that classical conditioning usually involves stimulus learning (S-S learning) rather than response learning (S-R learning).

The proverbial example of salivary conditioning to a bell also suggests that classical conditioning is involved primarily in the modification of visceral and glandular responses. Skinner elevated this implication to an axiom. He postulated that classical conditioning can only modify glandular and visceral responses (Skinner, 1938). However, subsequent research has shown this to be an unwarranted assumption. Pavlovian conditioning can modify not just glandular and visceral responses but also skeletal responses (Hollis, 1997; Turkkan, 1989). A common example of the Pavlovian conditioning of skeletal behavior is the phenomenon of sign tracking. This refers to the fact that animals will move toward a conditioned stimulus that has been paired with a positive unconditioned stimulus such as food. (For more information on this phenomenon, see "Appetitive Conditioning," later in this chapter).

In the proverbial bell example, the conditioned response (salivation to the bell) is similar to the unconditioned response (salivation to food powder). This has encouraged another common misconception about Pavlovian conditioning, namely that the conditioned response is always similar to the unconditioned response. Contrary to this notion, in some cases the form of the conditioned response is opposite the form of the unconditioned response (Siegel, 1975). In yet other cases, the form of the conditioned response is entirely different from the form or topography of the unconditioned response (Holland, 1984).

Finally, the proverbial bell example has encouraged the view that the nature of the learning process does not depend on the specific conditioned and unconditioned stimuli that are used in an experiment. According to this view, Pavlov could have selected any detectable stimulus in place of the bell, with pretty much the same results. However, the assumption that conditioned and unconditioned stimuli can be selected arbitrarily has turned out to be incorrect. Contemporary research has shown that learning occurs slowly or rapidly depending on which CS is used with which US (e.g., LoLordo & Droungas, 1989). I will have more to say about such selectivity of associations later in this chapter.

Contemporary Pavlovian Conditioning Preparations

Although classical conditioning was discovered in studies of salivary conditioning with dogs, dogs are not used in such experiments any longer, and salivation is rarely the response that is measured. Instead, pigeons, rats, and rabbits commonly serve in the experiments, and several different responses are used to measure learning. In some contemporary Pavlovian conditioning situations, the unconditioned stimulus is a desirable, or appetitive, stimulus like food. These preparations are used to study **appetitive conditioning**. In other situations, an unpleasant, or aversive, event is used as the unconditioned stimulus. Such preparations are used to study **aversive conditioning**.

APPETITIVE CONDITIONING

Appetitive conditioning is frequently investigated with pigeons and laboratory rats. Pigeons that serve in appetitive conditioning experiments are usually mildly hungry and are tested in a small experimental chamber called a **Skinner box** (see Figure 4.1). The conditioned stimulus is a light projected on a small plastic disk or response key above the food cup. Pecks at the key are automatically detected by an electronic sensing circuit. The conditioning procedure consists of turning on the key light for a few seconds and then presenting a small amount of food.

After a number of pairings of the key light with food, the pigeons come to approach and peck the key as soon as it is lit (Hearst & Jenkins, 1974; Tomie, Brooks, & Zito, 1989). The conditioned approach and pecking behavior develops even if the key light is located some distance from the food cup (Boakes, 1979). The light becomes a signal for food, and the pigeons go where the light is located. Hence, one name for this type of conditioning is **sign tracking**. Because the procedure results in the pigeons pecking the response key without elaborate intervention by the experimenter, the procedure is also called **autoshaping**.

Laboratory rats are also used in Pavlovian conditioning with food as the unconditioned stimulus. Holland (1977), for example, presented a brief tone paired with pellets of food to laboratory rats. As conditioning proceeded, the tone came to elicit a sudden movement of the head, called a head-jerk response. In another group of rats, a light near the top of the experimental chamber served as the conditioned stimulus. As the light was re-

FIGURE 4.1 Pigeon in an autoshaping experiment.
A key light is periodically paired with food. As a result, the pigeon starts to peck the key when it is lit.

peatedly paired with food, the rats came to orient toward the ceiling and get up on their hind legs. These results indicate that rats can learn to associate both tones and lights with food, but different conditioned responses develop with the different conditioned stimuli (Holland, 1984).

AVERSIVE CONDITIONING

Laboratory rats are also often employed in studies of aversive conditioning. A common aversive procedure is called the **conditioned suppression** procedure. The conditioned suppression procedure was developed as a technique for the study of emotional learning and was originally called the **conditioned emotional response procedure**, or CER (Estes & Skinner, 1941).

The conditioned suppression or CER procedure takes advantage of the fact that animals tend to become motionless or freeze when they are afraid (Bouton & Bolles, 1980). In the conditioned suppression procedure, rats are first trained to press a small bar or response lever to obtain food (see Figure 4.2). Food is provided only some of the times the rats respond, which keeps them pressing the lever steadily. After lever-pressing is well established, aversive conditioning trials are introduced. On each of these trials, a tone or a light CS is presented for a minute or two, and the rats are then given a brief foot shock. Within a few conditioning trials, presentation of the CS results in suppression of the food-reinforced lever-press response. The degree of response suppression provides a measure of aversive conditioning of the CS.

FIGURE 4.2   Rat in a conditioned suppression experiment.
Pressing the response lever occasionally produces a pellet of food. Periodically a tone is presented ending in a brief shock through the grid floor. The rat comes to suppress lever-pressing during the tone.

Aversive conditioning has been also extensively investigated using the eye-blink response. The eye blink is an early component of the startle reflex. Eye-blink conditioning was first developed with human experimental participants (see Kimble, 1961, pp. 55–59). A mild puff of air to one eye served as the unconditioned stimulus, and a light served as the CS. After a number of pairings of the light with the air puff, the light came to elicit a conditioned eye-blink response. Subsequently, ways of studying eye-blink conditioning were also developed using albino rabbits and rats to facilitate investigations of the neurophysiology of learning. With these subjects, a mild electrical pulse to the skin near one eye serves as the US, and a brief visual or auditory cue serves as the CS. Pairings of the CS and US result in a conditioned eye-blink response when the CS is presented (Gormezano, Kehoe, & Marshall, 1983).

The Nature of the Conditioned Response

In Pavlov's salivary conditioning experiments, the conditioned response (salivation to a CS) was a glandular visceral response similar in form to the unconditioned response (salivation to food powder). These features of conditioned behavior were elevated to axiomatic status during much of the twentieth century. As I noted earlier, Pavlovian conditioning was considered to be primarily a mechanism for adjusting physiological and glandular responses to the environment through experience (Skinner, 1938), and the conditioned response was assumed to be always similar to the unconditioned response (e.g., Mackintosh, 1974). However, the common contemporary preparations used for the study of Pavlovian conditioning described earlier illustrate that there is no compelling empirical justification for either of these assumptions.

SKELETAL VERSUS GLANDULAR CONDITIONED RESPONSES

In none of the common contemporary procedures for the study of Pavlovian conditioning is the measured conditioned response a glandular or visceral response. In sign tracking or autoshaping, the conditioned response is approaching and pecking a key light. This response involves skeletal muscles, not the smooth musculature involved in visceral responses. Skeletal responses are also involved in the freezing behavior that is the basis for conditioned suppression. Conditioned eye-blink responses in aversive conditioning and head-jerk and rearing responses observed in appetitive conditioning in rats also involve skeletal rather than smooth musculature.

One might argue that the responses measured in contemporary Pavlovian conditioning procedures are only indirect reflections of what is being actually conditioned, and that the "true" conditioned response is in fact a visceral or glandular response. Such an argument has some validity in the case of the conditioned suppression procedure. Various physiological manifestations of fear and aversion no doubt become conditioned in the CER procedure. The response suppression that is elicited by the CS may be mediated by these visceral conditioned responses. However, it is less obvious what visceral conditioned responses might give rise to the skeletal responses involved in conditioned sign tracking in pigeons, the conditioned head-jerk and rearing responses of rats, or conditioned eye-blink responding. A more parsimonious characterization of the empirical evidence is that Pavlovian conditioning can result in the modification of skeletal responses.

SIMILARITY OF CONDITIONED AND UNCONDITIONED RESPONSES

What implications do the common contemporary Pavlovian conditioning preparations have for the traditional assumption that the conditioned response is similar in topography to the response elicited by the unconditioned stimulus? Here the evidence is mixed. In some conditioning preparations, the conditioned response does resemble the unconditioned response. This is the case, for example, in eye-blink conditioning, where both the CR and the UR involve blinking. However, in other cases the CR and the UR are distinctively different.

In the conditioned suppression procedure, the unconditioned stimulus is a brief mild shock to the grid floor on which the rat is standing. Because the rat detects the shock through its foot pads, the shock elicits sudden and

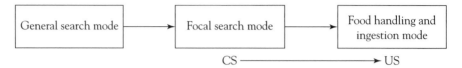

FIGURE 4.3 Behavior systems and Pavlovian conditioning.
Conditioning procedures with food as the US involve the feeding system. As a result of pairings of the CS with food, the CS becomes incorporated into the feeding system and comes to elicit food-related responses.

vigorous jumping. This vigorous jumping behavior contrasts dramatically with the lack of movement and response suppression that develops as the conditioned response in this situation.

THE BEHAVIOR SYSTEM APPROACH

If we cannot assume that the conditioned response will always be similar to the unconditioned response, how can we predict what kind of behavior will develop with Pavlovian conditioning? This question remains a major puzzle (e.g., Cunningham, 1997; Stewart & Eikelboom, 1987). Although a definitive answer is not yet available, a promising approach for analyzing the topography of behavioral conditioned responses has been developed in recent years based on the idea of behavior systems.

I previously introduced the concept of behavior systems in Chapter 2. The concept is relevant to the present discussion because the unconditioned stimulus in a Pavlovian conditioning procedure activates the **behavior system** relevant to that US. Presentations of food to a hungry animal activate the feeding system, and presentations of shock activate the defensive behavior system. The conditioned response that develops depends on how the conditioned stimulus becomes incorporated into the behavior system activated by the US.

The feeding system involves a sequence of response modes starting with general search, then moving on to focal search, and finally ingestive or consummatory behavior (see Figure 4.3). If a CS is presented before each portion of food the animal receives, the CS will become incorporated into one of the response modes of the feeding behavior system, and that in turn will determine what type of conditioned response the organism will perform (Timberlake & Lucas, 1989). If the CS becomes incorporated into the focal search mode, the conditioned response will consist of focal search responses such as approach and sign tracking (Wasserman, Franklin, & Hearst, 1974). In contrast, if the CS becomes incorporated into the ingestive, consummatory response mode, the conditioned response will involve handling and chewing the CS (Boakes, Poli, Lockwood, & Goodall, 1978).

In aversive conditioning, the nature of the conditioned response is determined by the defensive behavior system (Fanselow, 1997). Foot shock used in studies of conditioned suppression is an external source of pain, much like being bitten by a predator, and the response to shock is similar to the response to being bitten. Rodents have to cope with snakes and other predators. When a rat is bitten by a snake, it leaps into the air. Similarly, rats jump when they receive brief foot shock.

The rat's defensive response to an impending or possible attack is different from its response to the attack itself. If a rat sees or smells a snake that is about to strike, the rat freezes. In the conditioned suppression procedure, the conditioned stimulus signals impending attack. Therefore, the CS comes to elicit the freezing defensive behavior.

The Contents of Pavlovian Associations

As I noted earlier, a common belief about Pavlovian conditioning is that it involves primarily the learning of a conditioned response to a conditioned stimulus. In many cases, however, Pavlovian conditioning appears to involve stimulus-stimulus (S-S) learning rather than stimulus-response (S-R) learning. Whether Pavlovian conditioning results in an S-S or an S-R association concerns the contents of the learning. In this section we consider how investigators have distinguished between S-S and S-R learning.

According to the S-S learning mechanism, classical conditioning leads to the formation of an association between the conditioned and unconditioned stimuli. As a result of this association, presentation of the CS activates a neural representation of the unconditioned stimulus (see Figure 4.4). Expressed informally, this means that upon encountering the CS, the organism will be reminded of the unconditioned stimulus. What it will do when it is stimulated to "think" about the US will depend on its motivation to respond to the US.

EFFECTS OF US DEVALUATION

A powerful technique for differentiating between S-R and S-S mechanisms was popularized by Robert Rescorla (1973) and is basically a test of performance. The test involves evaluating the vigor of conditioned responding after the individual's motivation to respond to the unconditioned stimulus has been changed. In one type of experiment, motivation to respond to the US is reduced. This manipulation is called **US devaluation**.

Consider, for example, a study of sexual Pavlovian conditioning that was conducted with domesticated male quail (Holloway & Domjan, 1993). Brief exposure to a visual stimulus was paired with access to a female bird once a day. Initially, the visual CS did not elicit any significant behavior.

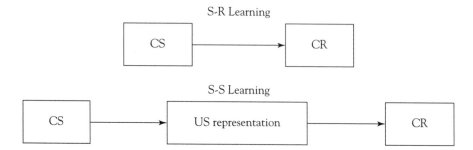

FIGURE 4.4 Distinction between S-R and S-S learning.
In S-R learning, a direct connection or association is established between the CS
and the CR. In S-S learning, the CS activates a representation of the US, which in
turn leads to the CR.

However, because the males were sexually motivated, they always readily
copulated with the female that was presented at the end of each conditioning trial. After 10 of these conditioning trials, the CS came to elicit a strong
approach response. Regardless of where they were in the test arena, the experimental birds rapidly approached the CS when it was presented.

According to the S-R learning mechanism, conditioned responding reflects the establishment of a direct connection between the CS and the
conditioned response, or CR. If such a direct connection has been established, then changing the animal's motivation to perform the unconditioned response should not influence its conditioned responding. An S-R
interpretation predicts that once the quail had learned the sexual conditioned approach response, presentation of the CS would elicit the CR even
if the birds were no longer sexually motivated.

Holloway and Domjan tested the S-R prediction by reducing the sex
drive of one group of birds. (This was done by changing the light cycle in
the laboratory to mimic winter conditions when the birds do not breed.)
The results of the experiment are summarized in Figure 4.5. Contrary to predictions of the S-R mechanism, a reduction in sexual motivation reduced
conditioned responding to the visual CS.

The results summarized in Figure 4.5 indicate that S-S learning had occurred in the experiment. S-S learning does not involve learning a specific
conditioned response. Rather, it involves learning an association between the
CS and the US. Once the CS-US association has been established, presentation of the CS activates a representation of the US. That in turn leads to conditioned responding, but only if the participants are motivated to respond to
the US. In the quail experiment, the opportunity to copulate with a female
was the unconditioned stimulus. After training, the CS elicited conditioned
approach behavior, but only if the birds were sexually motivated.

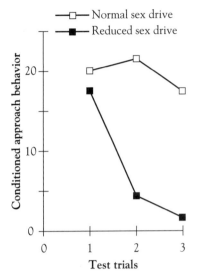

FIGURE 4.5 Effects of US devaluation on sexual approach conditioned behavior.

Three test sessions were conducted at 1-week intervals after two groups of quail had acquired a conditioned approach response. During the test phase, the sexual motivation of one group of birds was reduced. This US devaluation procedure resulted in a decrease in their conditioned responding. Adapted from Holloway & Domjan (1993).

EFFECTS OF US INFLATION

In the last example, motivation to respond to the unconditioned stimulus was reduced as a test for S-S learning. Another approach is to increase motivation to respond to the US. This is called **US inflation,** and it should result in increased conditioned responding according to S-S mechanisms.

In a particularly interesting application of the US inflation method, laboratory rats served as participants and the unconditioned stimulus was the taste of salt (Rescorla & Freberg, 1978, Experiment 3; see also Fudim, 1978). The preference for salt can be greatly increased in animals (including humans) by inducing a physiological sodium deficiency. Because creating a sodium deficiency substantially increases unconditioned responses to salt, this is a powerful US inflation procedure. The question addressed by Rescorla and Freberg was whether US inflation would also increase responding to a CS that had become associated with salt.

Two groups of laboratory rats were compared. Conditioning was carried out in the absence of sodium deficiency. A weak bitter taste (made by mixing a little quinine in water) served as the CS, and the taste of salt served as the US. For the experimental group, the bitter flavor was paired with the taste of salt (by adding the quinine to a mixture of salt and water). For the control group, the bitter flavor and the taste of salt were presented on alternate days. After these procedures, US inflation was created by inducing sodium deficiency in both groups. (Sodium deficiency causes an automatic increase in appetite for salt.) The rats were then tested for their response to the bitter flavor presented alone.

During the test, the animals in the experimental group drank much more of the quinine-flavored water than animals in the control group. This is a remarkable result because ordinarily rats hate to drink quinine. In this study, the taste of quinine had become associated with salt. After conditioning, sodium deficiency increased the value of salt, and that in turn increased the response to the salt-associated quinine flavor.

The Selectivity of Associations

The last traditional assumption about Pavlovian conditioning considered is that a stimulus (a brief tone, for example) that is effective as a CS in one conditioning situation will be equally effective as a CS in other conditioning situations as well. This is known as the **equipotentiality assumption**.

Investigators have known for a long time that animals do not learn about all conditioned stimuli equally rapidly. Pavlov (1927), for example, observed that a low-intensity CS becomes conditioned more slowly than a high-intensity CS. However, such differences do not contradict the equipotentiality assumption because a low-intensity CS is likely to be difficult to condition no matter what unconditioned stimulus is used.

The first clear evidence against the equipotentiality assumption was obtained in studies of aversion conditioning. The conditioned suppression phenomenon illustrates one type of aversion conditioning. Here a tone or a visual stimulus is paired with shock, with the result that the tone or light acquires aversive properties. Another type of aversion conditioning is **taste aversion learning**. In this case, a novel taste is followed by an unpleasant illness (a mild case of food poisoning, for example), and the organism learns an aversion to the novel taste as a result.

The conditioned suppression and taste aversion learning phenomena demonstrate that audiovisual cues and taste cues are both highly effective as conditioned stimuli. Interestingly, however, they are effective only in combination with their own particular unconditioned stimulus (see Figure 4.6). Rats do not easily learn an aversion to an auditory or visual cue paired with illness, and they do not easily learn an aversion to a taste cue paired with shock (Domjan & Wilson, 1972; Garcia & Koelling, 1966). Such results illustrate the phenomenon of **selective association**. The effectiveness of a con-

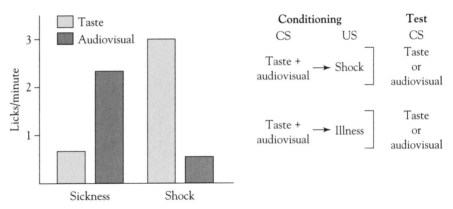

FIGURE 4.6 Procedure and results of the experiment by Garcia and Koelling (1966) demonstrating selective associations in aversion learning.

ditioned stimulus in a Pavlovian conditioning procedure depends selectively on the unconditioned stimulus that is used (LoLordo & Droungas, 1989).

Like laboratory rats, people also seem to learn aversions to stimuli selectively. People who experience some form of gastrointestinal illness are more likely to learn an aversion to a novel food they ate just before becoming sick than they are to learn an aversion to other types of stimuli they may have encountered. Consistent with selective associations, people do not report acquiring a food aversion if they hurt themselves in a physical accident or if they develop an irritating skin rash (Logue, Ophir, & Strauss, 1981; Pelchat & Rozin, 1982). Only illness experiences are effective in inducing a food aversion.

Since the initial demonstrations of selective association in aversion learning, such effects have been found in other forms of learning as well. For example, Shapiro, Jacobs, and LoLordo (1980) found that pigeons are more likely to associate a visual stimulus than an auditory stimulus with food. However, when the birds are conditioned with shock, the auditory cue is more likely to become conditioned than the visual cue.

In identifying selective associations, it is important to keep in mind that instances of selective learning are not absolute. For example, the fact that taste stimuli are more easily associated with gastrointestinal illness than audiovisual cues are does not mean that nontaste cues cannot become associated with illness. Such learning can occur but is more difficult and requires special procedures (e.g., Best, Batson, Meachum, Brown, & Ringer, 1985). Selective associations are instances in which the rate of learning depends on the combination of conditioned and unconditioned stimuli that is used, as opposed to the individual or independent features of the CS and US.

Although selective associations are well established, why such effects occur remains open to speculation. One factor that probably contributes to selective associations is the similarity of conditioned and unconditioned stimuli. Evidence indicates that similarity between a CS and US facilitates the establishment of associations (Rescorla & Gillan, 1980; Testa, 1974). However, the concept of similarity cannot explain all selective associations. It is unclear, for example, how similarity might encourage pigeons to associate auditory cues with shock more readily than they associate visual stimuli with shock. On the face of it, auditory cues do not seem any more like shock than visual cues.

The Control Problem in Pavlovian Conditioning

The critical feature of Pavlovian conditioning is that it involves the formation of an association between a conditioned stimulus and an unconditioned stimulus. Therefore, before any change in behavior can be attributed to Pavlovian conditioning, one must demonstrate that the effect depends on the establishment of an association between the CS and the US.

To promote the development of an association, the conditioned and unconditioned stimuli are presented in combination with one another in Pavlovian procedures. It is particularly effective, for example, to present the CS just before the presentation of the US on each conditioning trial. (I will have more to say about this in the next chapter.) In addition, a number of conditioning trials are usually needed to get a learning effect. Thus, a Pavlovian conditioning procedure involves repeated presentations of the conditioned and unconditioned stimuli. As we saw in Chapter 3, repeated presentations of stimuli can result in habituation and sensitization effects. Therefore, habituation and sensitization effects can occur during the course of Pavlovian conditioning.

Habituation and sensitization effects of repeated CS and US presentations do not depend on the formation of an association between the CS and the US and therefore do not constitute Pavlovian conditioning. Before a change in behavior can be interpreted as an instance of Pavlovian conditioning, it has to be distinguished from possible habituation and sensitization effects.

Habituation effects are typically of little concern because habituation results in decreased responding, whereas Pavlovian conditioning involves increased responding to the CS. Potential sensitization effects are much more troublesome. Increased responding to the CS can be caused by sensitization resulting from CS exposures, dishabituation or sensitization resulting from US presentations, or both. Control procedures have to be used to rule out such sensitization effects in studies of Pavlovian conditioning.

A universally applicable and acceptable solution to the control problem in Pavlovian conditioning is not available. Instead, various control procedures have been used, each with its advantages and disadvantages. In one procedure, CS sensitization effects are evaluated by repeatedly presenting the CS by itself. Such a procedure, called the **CS-alone control**, is inadequate because it does not take into account possible increased responding to the CS caused by dishabituation or sensitization effects of the US. Another control procedure involves repeatedly presenting the US by itself (the **US-alone control**) to measure US-induced sensitization. But the US-alone control does not consider possible sensitization effects of repeated CS presentations.

About 30 years ago, Rescorla proposed an ingenious solution, the **random control** procedure, which appeared to solve the problems of the CS-alone and US-alone controls (Rescorla, 1967). In the random control, both the CS and the US are presented repeatedly, but at random times in relation to each other. The random timing of the CS and US presentations is intended to prevent the formation of an association between them but should not interfere with sensitization processes.

The random control became popular soon after its introduction, but as investigators began to examine it in detail, they discovered some serious difficulties (Papini & Bitterman, 1990). Studies demonstrated that the random control is not ineffective in producing learning. Associative learning can develop in a random control procedure in two ways. First, random CS and US presentations permit occasional instances in which the CS is presented in conjunction with the US. Random procedures can result in nonrandom patterns in the short run. For example, flipping a coin five times occasionally yields five heads in a row. In an analogous fashion, random presentations of a CS and a US can result in occasional pairings of the CS and US. If such accidental CS-US pairings occur early in training, conditioned responding may develop (Benedict & Ayres, 1972).

Associative learning can also result from occasions when the US is presented without the CS in the random control procedure. In these instances the US is being presented in the presence of the background contextual cues of the experimental situation. The background contextual cues were ignored through much of the early development of Pavlovian conditioning theory. However, more recent research has shown that the repeated presentation of an unconditioned stimulus in the absence of an explicit CS can result in the conditioning of background cues (Balsam & Tomie, 1985; Kremer, 1974).

The conditioning of background cues creates problems for the random control procedure because conditioned contextual cues can provide an active source of interference for the conditioning of explicit conditioned stimuli. Organisms are less likely to associate a conditioned stimulus with food, for example, if the CS occurs in the presence of conditioned background stimuli (Tomie, Murphy, Fath, & Jackson, 1980). To the extent that the random control permits the conditioning of background cues, it

Time ———→

FIGURE 4.7 **Diagram of the discriminative control procedure for Pavlovian conditioning.**

Two types of trials occur in random alternation. In some trials, one conditioned stimulus, the CS$^+$, is paired with the US. In the remaining trials, another conditioned stimulus, the CS$^-$, is presented alone. Stronger conditioned responding to CS$^+$ than to CS$^-$ is evidence of associative learning rather than some form of sensitization.

---

does not provide a neutral nonassociative baseline for demonstrations of Pavlovian conditioning.

Although no entirely satisfactory control procedure for Pavlovian conditioning is available, the **discrimination control** procedure, summarized in Figure 4.7, is a reasonable compromise. Unlike the random control, the discrimination control involves two conditioned stimuli, a CS$^+$ and a CS$^-$. The two CSs may be a brief tone and a brief light. On half the trials the CS$^+$ is presented and paired with the US. (The "+" sign indicates that the US is presented with the CS.) On the remaining trials the CS$^-$ is presented and the US does not occur. (The "−" sign indicates that the US is omitted.) CS$^+$ and CS$^-$ trials are alternated randomly. For half the participants the tone serves as the CS$^+$ and the light serves as the CS$^-$; for the remaining participants these stimulus assignment are reversed.

What would happen if presentations of the US only sensitized responding to the light and tone CSs? Sensitization is not based on an association and therefore does not depend on the pairing of a stimulus with the US. Therefore, sensitization is expected to elevate responding to both the CS$^+$ and the CS$^-$. If only sensitization occurred in the discrimination control procedure, the participants would respond to the CS$^+$ and CS$^-$ in a similar fashion.

How about associative learning? In contrast to sensitization, associative learning should be specific to the stimulus that is paired with the US. Therefore, associative learning should elevate responding to the CS$^+$ more than the CS$^-$. Greater responding to the CS$^+$ than to the CS$^-$ in the discrimination control provides evidence of associative learning.

An issue that sometimes arises with the discrimination control is that differential responding to the CS$^+$ versus the CS$^-$ may occur in different ways. Responding to the CS$^+$ may be elevated by the training procedure, or responding to the CS⁻ may be inhibited. (The conditioning of inhibition will be discussed in Chapter 5.) The development of inhibition to the CS⁻ is not a common outcome, but if it is suspected, additional control procedures are required to reach an unambiguous conclusion.

Extinction of Pavlovian Conditioned Behavior

Once a conditioned response has been acquired through pairings of a CS with a US, does the behavior persist forever? In particular, does the organism continue to make the conditioned response if the CS is no longer paired with the US?

A procedure in which the CS is presented by itself after conditioning is called an **extinction procedure**. As one might suspect, repetitions of the CS without the US eventually result in a decline of the previously conditioned response. Such a decline in conditioned behavior is called an **extinction effect**.

The procedure for extinction of a Pavlovian conditioned response is very similar to the procedure for habituation that was discussed in Chapter 3. In both cases, a stimulus is repeatedly presented by itself, and the behavior elicited by that stimulus gradually declines. The critical difference is that habituation reflects the decline of a response that was not previously established through a special training procedure. In contrast, in extinction, the eliciting stimulus is a CS that was previously paired with a US in a Pavlovian conditioning procedure. Despite this difference, many Pavlovian extinction phenomena are similar to effects we previously encountered in studies of habituation.

EXTINCTION AND HABITUATION

One important similarity between habituation and Pavlovian extinction is that in both cases responding recovers after a period without stimulation. As we saw in Chapter 3, recovery of a habituated response following a period of rest is called **spontaneous recovery.** The recovery of extinguished responding that occurs after a period of rest is also called spontaneous recovery (Brooks & Bouton, 1993; Robbins, 1990).

Another similarity between habituation and Pavlovian extinction is that in both phenomena the presentation of a novel stimulus can cause a temporary recovery of the response. Habituated responding can recover temporarily because of the presentation of an arousing or sensitizing stimulus. As I pointed out in Chapter 3, this phenomenon is called dishabituation. The presentation of a novel stimulus can also result in the temporary recovery of a conditioned response following extinction (Pavlov, 1927). In this case, the phenomenon is called **external inhibition** or **disinhibition.**

To observe disinhibition, a previously conditioned stimulus is repeatedly presented by itself until conditioned responding declines. The CS is then

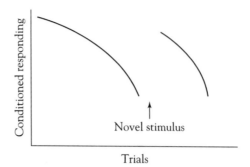

F I G U R E   4.8   Illustration of disinhibition in extinction.
During the course of extinction of a conditioned response, a novel stimulus is presented and produces temporary recovery of conditioned responding. (Note: Data are hypothetical.)

presented with a novel stimulus, and the conditioned behavior is observed to recover (see Figure 4.8).

Notice that the responding that occurs in the disinhibition effect cannot be attributed to the novel stimulus. Novel stimuli do not elicit conditioned responses. Rather, the novel stimulus releases the extinguished response from some sort of inhibitory influence.

EXTINCTION AS UNLEARNING

The phenomena of spontaneous recovery and disinhibition have important implications for theories of extinction. Superficially, extinction looks like the opposite of acquisition. During Pavlovian acquisition, conditioned responding progressively increases. In contrast, during extinction, responding progressively declines. This symmetry can lead to the erroneous conclusion that the processes of extinction are simply the opposite of the processes of acquisition. The assumption that extinction is the opposite of acquisition suggests that extinction involves the loss or unlearning of the CS-US association.

The phenomena of spontaneous recovery and disinhibition are important because they show that extinction is not the opposite of acquisition. If extinction were due to loss or unlearning of a CS-US association, then a period of rest could not produce recovery of the conditioned behavior. The presentation of a novel stimulus also could not reinstitute a conditioned response that had become lost through unlearning. Thus, the idea that extinction involves unlearning also cannot explain the phenomenon of disinhibition.

EXTINCTION AS A FORM OF INHIBITION

The phenomena of spontaneous recovery and disinhibition suggest that extinction involves some form of inhibition of the conditioned response. The inhibition dissipates with a period of rest, resulting in spontaneous recovery of the extinguished response. Presentation of a novel stimulus also disrupts the inhibition created by extinction, producing the phenomenon of disinhibition.

Yet another phenomenon that supports the idea that extinction involves some form of inhibition rather than unlearning is the **renewal effect** (e.g., Bouton, 1993). The renewal effect was discovered during research on transfer of training. The basic question in such studies is how the learning that occurs in one situation transfers to other circumstances or contexts. For example, if you learn something in a noisy dormitory lounge, will that learning transfer to a quiet classroom in which you have to take a test? An equally important question concerns the transfer of extinction. If extinction is conducted in one situation so that the conditioned stimulus no longer elicits conditioned responding there, will the CS be also ineffective in other situations?

Much of the research on the renewal effect has been conducted with laboratory rats. The animals were conditioned in an experimental chamber with a particular level of illumination and a particular odor. Let us call this conditioning chamber context A. The subjects were then moved to another chamber that had less lighting and a different odor and received an extinction procedure there. Let us call the second chamber context B. The reason for moving the participants to context B for extinction training was to see if the effects of extinction would transfer back to context A (see Figure 4.9).

If extinction involves the unlearning of a conditioned response, then returning the participants to context A after extinction in context B should not result in recovery of the conditioned behavior. Contrary to that prediction, the effects of extinction training in context B did not transfer to the original training context A. Rather, when participants were returned to context A, conditioned responding occurred again. Conditioned responding was "renewed" upon return to the context of original training. Hence, the phenomenon was called the renewal effect.

Spontaneous recovery, disinhibition, and the renewal effect illustrate that extinction does not result in the unlearning of conditioned behavior. Rather, extinction appears to involve some form of inhibition that results in the suppression of conditioned responding. Furthermore, the suppression of responding is not permanent but can be reversed by a period of rest, a novel stimulus, or return to the training context.

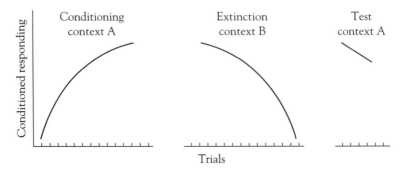

FIGURE   4.9   Illustration of the renewal effect.
Participants originally acquire the conditioned response in context A. They then receive extinction training in context B, which results in a decline of the conditioned response. In the third phase, they are returned to context A for testing. The conditioned response is "renewed" when the participants are returned to context A. (Note: Data are hypothetical.)

CLINICAL IMPLICATIONS

Spontaneous recovery, disinhibition, and the renewal effect have important implications for applications of extinction in therapeutic situations. The therapeutic goal of using an extinction procedure is to reduce an undesired conditioned response. Extinction may be used, for example, to reduce conditioned drug craving or pathological conditioned fear. Spontaneous recovery, disinhibition, and the renewal effect can all contribute to relapse after the therapeutic application of an extinction procedure.

The renewal effect in particular suggests that differences between the context in which a conditioned response is acquired and the context in which it is extinguished can determine the likelihood of relapse (Bouton & Swartzentruber, 1991). If therapeutic extinction is conducted in a context very different from the context in which the undesired response was originally acquired, returning the clients to the original learning situation may result in serious relapse of the pathological behavior.

Summary

Although studies of Pavlovian conditioning began with the conditioning of salivation and other glandular responses in dogs, contemporary investigations focus on conditioning skeletal responses in sign tracking, conditioned suppression, and eye-blink preparations. These investigations have shown that different types of conditioned responses can develop, depending on the nature of the conditioned stimulus and the behavior system activated by the unconditioned stimulus.

The vigor of the conditioned response depends not only on the CS but also on the current value of the US. Devaluation of the US causes a decline in the CR and inflation of the US causes an increase in the CR. These results indicate that Pavlovian conditioning typically results in S-S rather than S-R learning.

Because Pavlovian conditioning involves the learning of an association between a CS and a US, behavioral changes caused by mere repetition of the CS and US must be excluded. The random control procedure is not effective in this regard because it can result in associative learning. Although entirely satisfactory control procedures are not available, the discrimination control is a reasonable compromise. In this control procedure, one CS is paired with the US and another CS is presented without the US. Differential responding to the two CSs provides evidence of associative learning.

Following acquisition, a Pavlovian conditioned response will decline if the CS is no longer paired with the US. This is called extinction and is caused by active inhibition rather than "unlearning" of the CR. Several procedures, including a period of rest, a novel stimulus, and return to the context of original training, can reverse the effects of extinction and produce recovery of the conditioned behavior.

Suggested Readings

BOUTON, M. E. (1993). Context, time, and memory retrieval in the interference paradigms of Pavlovian learning. *Psychological Bulletin, 114,* 80–99.

HOLLAND, P. C. (1984). Origins of behavior in Pavlovian conditioning. In G. H. Bower (Ed.), *The psychology of learning and motivation* (Vol. 18, pp. 129–174). Orlando, FL: Academic Press.

HOLLIS, K. L. (1997). Contemporary research in Pavlovian conditioning: A "new" functional analysis. *American Psychologist, 52,* 956–965.

LOLORDO, V. M., & DROUNGAS, A. (1989). Selective associations and adaptive specializations: Taste aversions and phobias. In S. B. Klein & R. R. Mowrer (Eds.), *Contemporary learning theories: Instrumental conditioning and the impact of biological constraints on learning* (pp. 145–179). Hillsdale, NJ: Erlbaum.

PAPINI, M. R., & BITTERMAN, M. E. (1990). The role of contingency in classical conditioning. *Psychological Review, 97,* 396–403.

Technical Terms

Appetitive conditioning
Associative learning
Autoshaping
Aversive conditioning
Behavior system
Conditioned emotional
  response procedure
Conditioned response
Conditioned stimulus
Conditioned suppression
CS-alone control
Discrimination control
Disinhibition
Equipotentiality assumption
External inhibition
Extinction effect

Extinction procedure
Random control
Renewal effect
S-R learning
S-S learning
Selective association
Sign tracking
Skinner box
Spontaneous recovery
Taste aversion learning
Unconditioned response
Unconditioned stimulus
US-alone control
US devaluation
US inflation

CHAPTER FIVE

Stimulus Relations in Pavlovian Conditioning

DID YOU KNOW THAT:

- Delaying the US a bit after presentation of the CS produces stronger evidence of conditioning than presenting the CS and US simultaneously.

- A gap of just 0.5 sec between the CS and US can seriously disrupt excitatory fear conditioning.

- Taste aversions can be learned with a delay of several hours between the conditioned and unconditioned stimuli.

- Pavlovian conditioning depends not only on the temporal relation between the CS and the US but also on signal relations.

- Different CS/US contingencies produce different levels of conditioned responding because of differences in the conditioning of contextual cues.

- Extinction does not reduce responding through Pavlovian conditioned inhibition.

- The opposite of conditioned inhibition is facilitation or positive occasion setting—not conditioned excitation.

- In a facilitation procedure, one CS signals that a second CS will be paired with the unconditioned stimulus.

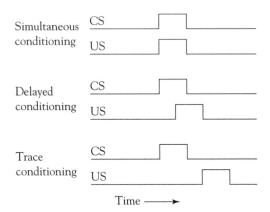

FIGURE 5.1 Procedures for simultaneous, delayed, and trace conditioning. One conditioning trial (involving a presentation of the CS and the US) is shown for each procedure.
In a typical experiment, the conditioning trial is repeated until evidence of learning develops.

In Chapter 4, I introduced Pavlovian conditioning as a type of learning that involves establishing an association between two stimuli, the conditioned and the unconditioned stimulus. For two stimuli or events to become associated with one another, they have to be related to each other in some way. In this chapter, I describe various relations that can exist between a conditioned and an unconditioned stimulus. I also describe how different stimulus relations determine what is learned in Pavlovian conditioning.

Temporal Relation between CS and US

Historically, the most prominent relation in Pavlovian conditioning is the temporal relation between the CS and US—when in time the stimuli occur relative to each other.

SIMULTANEOUS CONDITIONING

Perhaps the simplest temporal arrangement between a conditioned and an unconditioned stimulus is to present the two at the same time. Such a procedure is called **simultaneous conditioning** (see Figure 5.1). Because simultaneous conditioning brings the CS as close as possible to the US, it is reasonable to assume that simultaneous conditioning is the most effective temporal relation for associative learning. In many cases, however, simultaneous presentation of the CS and US does not yield strong evidence of learning (Bitterman, 1964; Smith, Coleman, & Gormezano, 1969).

DELAYED CONDITIONING

The best evidence for associative learning usually comes from a procedure in which the conditioned stimulus is presented slightly before the unconditioned stimulus on each trial (Schneiderman & Gormezano, 1964). Such a procedure is called **delayed conditioning** because the unconditioned stimulus is delayed after the presentation of the CS.

An example of a delayed conditioning trial is shown in the middle panel of Figure 5.1. The conditioned stimulus starts first and remains on until the unconditioned stimulus is presented. Notice that there is no gap between the CS and the US.

TRACE CONDITIONING

Introducing a gap between the CS and the US changes a delayed conditioning procedure into **trace conditioning**. A trace conditioning trial is presented in the bottom panel of Figure 5.1 for contrast with the delayed conditioning trial shown in the middle panel. The gap between the conditioned stimulus and the unconditioned stimulus is called the **trace interval**.

Introducing a gap or trace interval between the CS and the US can reduce drastically the degree of conditioned responding that develops. Kamin (1965), for example, compared fear conditioning in two groups of laboratory rats using the conditioned suppression procedure. One group received a delayed conditioning procedure in which a 3-min tone CS ended in a brief foot shock, without a gap between the tone and shock. For the second group, the tone also started 3 min before each presentation of shock, but ended 0.5 sec before the shock. Thus, the second group received a trace conditioning procedure with just a 0.5-sec gap or trace interval. The trace conditioning group showed much less conditioned suppression than the delay conditioning group.

Kamin's results indicate that having two events occur close together in time is important for Pavlovian conditioning. The CS and the US do not have to be presented simultaneously. In fact, having the CS start before the US is usually helpful. However, for best results, the CS should remain until the US occurs. There should not be a gap between the CS and the US.

EFFECTS OF THE CS-US INTERVAL

Another temporal relation that is critical for associative learning is how much time passes between the start of the CS and the presentation of the US. The interval between when the CS begins and when the US is presented is called the **CS-US interval** or **interstimulus interval**.

As I noted earlier, learning is usually not evident with simultaneous conditioning, where the CS-US interval is zero. More evidence of learning is seen with delayed conditioning procedures, in which the CS-US interval is greater than zero. However, the benefits of delaying the US after the start

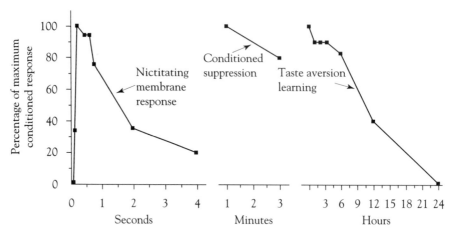

FIGURE 5.2   Strength of conditioned responding as a function of the CS-US interval in conditioning the nictitating membrane response, conditioned suppression, and taste-aversion learning.
Nictitating membrane adapted from Schneiderman & Gormezano (1964) and Smith, Coleman, & Gormezano (1969); conditioned suppression adapted from Kamin (1965); taste-aversion learning adapted from Smith & Roll (1967).

of the CS are rather limited. As the CS-US interval becomes longer and longer, evidence of learning declines. How rapidly responding declines depends on the response system that is being conditioned.

Figure 5.2 illustrates the effects of the CS-US interval in three different conditioning preparations. The left panel represents data from conditioning of the nictitating membrane response of rabbits. The nictitating membrane is a secondary eyelid present in many species. Like closure of the primary eyelid, closure of the nictitating membrane can be elicited unconditionally by a puff of air to the eye. Figure 5.2 shows that in conditioning of the nictitating membrane response, the best results are obtained with CS-US intervals of 0.2–0.5 sec. If the CS-US interval is shorter, less conditioned responding develops. In addition, conditioned responding drops off quickly as the CS-US interval is extended past 0.5 sec. Little, if any, learning is evident if the CS-US interval is more than 2 sec.

Conditioned suppression represents an intermediate case. Here strong learning can occur with CS-US intervals in the range of 2–3 min.

Learning over the longest CS-US intervals is seen in taste-aversion learning. A taste aversion is learned when the ingestion of a novel-flavored food (or drink) results in some form of illness or interoceptive distress (Braveman & Bronstein, 1985). The novel flavor is the conditioned stimulus, and the unconditioned stimulus is provided by the illness experience.

A taste aversion can be learned even if the illness experience is delayed several hours after ingestion of the novel flavor. This phenomenon was first documented by John Garcia and his associates (e.g., Garcia, Ervin, & Koelling, 1966) and is called **long-delay learning** because it represents learning with CS-US intervals that are a great deal longer than the intervals that will support eye-blink conditioning or conditioned suppression. However, as is illustrated in Figure 5.2, even with flavor-aversion learning, there is an inverse relation between conditioned responding and the CS-US interval.

TEMPORAL ENCODING OF US OCCURRENCE

The differences in learning that occur between simultaneous, delayed, and trace conditioning and the CS-US interval effects I described earlier illustrate that Pavlovian conditioning is highly sensitive to time factors. Recent research by Ralph Miller has provided even more impressive evidence that time is important in Pavlovian conditioning. With the use of complicated and clever experimental designs, Miller has shown that animals learn exactly when the US occurs relative to the CS in a conditioning procedure (e.g., Barnet, Grahame, & Miller, 1993; Cole, Barnet, & Miller, 1995).

Miller's research suggests that Pavlovian conditioning not only produces an association between the CS and the US but also teaches organisms when the US will occur. This type of learning is called **temporal encoding**. Pavlovian conditioning results in the establishment of a temporal code for when the US occurs in relation to the CS. Once the temporal code has been learned, it is activated whenever the CS is presented, and this enables the organism to predict the precise point in time when the US will occur.

Signal Relation between CS and US

In the previous section, I described some of the ways in which the temporal relation between CS and US is important in Pavlovian conditioning. Another important factor is the signal relation or informational relation between the CS and the US. In general, conditioned responding develops more rapidly with procedures in which the CS serves as a good signal for, or provides reliable information about, the occurrence of the US.

In the typical delayed conditioning procedure, each conditioning trial consists of the presentation of the CS, followed shortly by the presentation of the US. In addition, the US does not occur without being preceded by the CS. Thus, the US can be predicted perfectly from occurrences of the CS. The CS signals occurrences of the US perfectly, and an association between the CS and US develops quickly.

THE BLOCKING EFFECT

How might the signal relation between the CS and US be disrupted? One way is to present the CS with another cue that already predicts the US. In

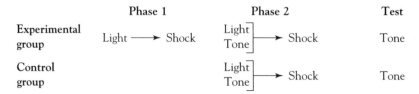

	Phase 1	**Phase 2**	**Test**
Experimental group	Light ⟶ Shock	Light⎤ Tone⎦ ⟶ Shock	Tone
Control group		Light⎤ Tone⎦ ⟶ Shock	Tone

F I G U R E 5.3   Diagram of the blocking procedure in a conditioned suppression experiment.
During Phase 1, a light CS is conditioned with foot shock in the experimental group until the light produces maximum conditioned suppression. The control group does not receive a conditioning procedure in Phase 1. In Phase 2 both groups receive conditioning trials in which the light CS is presented together with a novel tone CS, and the light-tone compound is paired with shock. Finally, during the test phase, responding is measured to the tone presented alone. Less conditioned suppression develops to the tone in the experimental group than in the control group.

this case the CS will be redundant, and little conditioned responding will develop. This idea was first developed experimentally by Kamin in what has come to be known as the **blocking effect** (Kamin, 1969).

Kamin studied the blocking effect using the conditioned suppression procedure with laboratory rats, but the phenomenon may be more effectively illustrated with a hypothetical example of human taste aversion learning. Let us assume that you are allergic to shrimp and get slightly ill every time you eat some. Because of these experiences, you acquire an aversion to the flavor of shrimp. However, you continue to eat shrimp on special occasions when you don't want to offend your host. On one such occasion, you are served shrimp with a steamed vegetable you don't remember eating before. To be polite, you eat some of the vegetable, as well as some of the shrimp. The vegetable tastes pretty good, but you end up feeling slightly ill after the meal.

To what will you attribute your illness, the shrimp or the new vegetable? Given your history of bad reactions to shrimp, you are likely to attribute your illness to the shrimp and may not acquire an aversion to the vegetable. In this situation, the presence of a previously conditioned flavor (shrimp) blocks the conditioning of a novel flavor (the vegetable) even though the novel flavor was just as closely paired with the illness US.

As this example illustrates, the blocking effect shows that what individuals learn about one CS is influenced by the presence of other cues that were previously conditioned with the same US. The conditioned stimuli Kamin used were a light and a tone (see Figure 5.3). For the blocking group, the light CS was first conditioned by pairing it with a foot shock often enough to produce strong conditioned suppression to the light. In the next phase of the experiment, the tone and light CSs were presented simultaneously immediately before the shock US. A control group received the same pairings of the tone-light compound with shock as the blocking group, but for the control group the light had not been conditioned earlier. The light and tone were both novel. The focus of the experiment was on how much fear became conditioned to the novel tone CS. Because of the prior conditioning of the light in the blocking group, less conditioned suppression developed to the tone in the blocking group than in the control group.

The blocking phenomenon is important because it illustrates that temporal contiguity between a conditioned and unconditioned stimulus is not sufficient for successful conditioned responding. A strong signal relation is also important. The temporal relation between the novel tone CS and the US was identical in the blocking and the control groups. Nevertheless, strong conditioned suppression developed only if the tone was not presented with the previously conditioned light CS. The prior conditioning of the light reduced the signal relation between the tone and shock and disrupted fear conditioning.

CS/US CONTINGENCY

Historically, an important approach to characterizing the signal relation between a CS and a US has been in terms of the **contingency** between the two stimuli (Rescorla, 1967). The contingency between two events refers to the extent to which the presence of one stimulus can serve as a basis for predicting the other. The CS/US contingency is defined in terms of two probabilities (see Figure 5.4). One of these is the probability that the US will occur given that the CS has been presented [p(US/CS)]; the other is the probability that the US will occur given that the CS has not happened [p(US/noCS)].

A situation in which the US always occurs with the CS and never by itself illustrates a perfect positive contingency between the CS and the US. In this case the presence of the US can be predicted perfectly from the presence of the CS. In contrast, a situation in which the US always occurs on trials when the CS is absent and never occurs on trials with the CS illustrates a perfect negative contingency. In this case, the CS signals the absence of the US. Finally, if the US occurs equally often with the CS and without the CS, the CS/US contingency is said to be zero. When the contingency between the CS and US is zero, the CS provides no useful information about whether the US will or will not occur.

Originally the contingency between a CS and a US was considered to determine the formation of CS-US associations directly. Since then, it has become more common to consider CS/US contingency as a procedural variable that predicts how much conditioned responding will develop. Contemporary analyses of contingency effects have focused on conditioning of the background cues that are present in any situation in which an organism en-

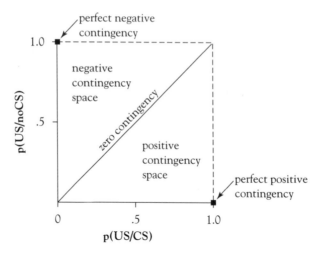

FIGURE 5.4 Contingency between a CS and a US is determined by the probability of the US given that the CS has occurred (horizontal axis) and the probability of the US given that the CS has not occurred (vertical axis). When the two probabilities are equal (45° line), the CS/US contingency is zero.

counters repeated presentations of discrete conditioned and unconditioned stimuli. Procedures involving different CS/US contingencies result in different degrees of context conditioning.

Consider, for example, a procedure involving a zero CS/US contingency. Such a procedure will involve presentations of the US by itself, presentations of the CS by itself, and occasional presentations of the CS together with the US. The US-alone trials can result in conditioning of the background or contextual cues in which the experiment is conducted. The presence of those conditioned background contextual cues can then block the future conditioning of the explicit CS on those few occasions when the CS is paired with the US (Tomie, Murphy, Fath, & Jackson, 1980) or disrupt performance of conditioned responding through other means (Miller & Matzel, 1989).

Higher-Order Relations in Pavlovian Conditioning: Conditioned Inhibition

In the examples of Pavlovian conditioning considered thus far, the focus of interest was on how a CS is directly related to a US. Now let us turn to more complex stimulus relations in Pavlovian conditioning. In higher-order stimulus relations, the focus of interest is not on how a CS signals a US but on how one CS provides information about the relation or pairing of a second

CS with a US. Thus, higher-order relations refer to the signaling or modulation of a simple CS-US pairing. The adjective "higher-order" is used because one of the elements of this relation is a CS-US associative unit. In considering higher-order stimulus relations, first I discuss conditioned inhibition or negative occasion setting. Then I turn to facilitation or positive occasion setting.

INHIBITORY CONDITIONING PROCEDURES

Conditioned inhibition was the first kind of higher-order signal relation that was extensively investigated. Concepts of inhibition are prominent in various areas of physiology. As a physiologist, Pavlov was interested not only in processes that activate behavior but also those that are responsible for the inhibition of responding. This led him to investigate conditioned inhibition. He considered the conditioning of inhibition to be just as important as the conditioning of excitation (Pavlov, 1927).

In excitatory conditioning procedures, the CS becomes a signal for the impending presentation of the US. In contrast, in inhibitory conditioning, the CS of interest becomes a signal for the absence of the US. However, this only occurs under special circumstances because ordinarily the absence of something has no particular psychological significance. If the absence of something is not meaningful, how can a CS become a signal for that non-event? For successful inhibitory conditioning, the absence of the US has to be made a salient event. How can that occur?

If a young woman's uncle tells her that he is not giving her $200 today, she is not likely to be disappointed if she didn't expect to get the money in the first place. However, if she is graduating from college and her uncle had promised her $200 when she graduated, she will be upset if he decides against the generous gift. The absence of something is psychologically meaningful only if the event is expected to occur.

The standard conditioned inhibition procedure.   As with the young lady I just described, in Pavlovian conditioning the absence of the US is significant if the US fails to occur when it is expected. This general principle is the basis of the standard Pavlovian conditioned inhibition procedure. The procedure involves two different conditioned stimuli (A and B) and a US (see Figure 5.5). For example, stimulus A might be a tone, stimulus B might be a light, and the US might be a few pellets of food. On some trials, stimulus A is presented by itself and is paired with the US. These trials are represented as A^+ (A plus), with the "+" sign indicating the presence of the US. Because of the A^+ trials, the organism comes to expect the US when it encounters stimulus A. This sets the stage for inhibitory conditioning.

On inhibitory conditioning trials, stimulus B is presented with stimulus A (forming the compound stimulus AB), but the US does not occur. These trials are represented as AB^- (AB minus), with the "−" sign indicating the

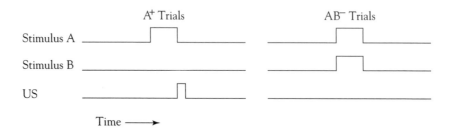

FIGURE 5.5 The standard procedure for conditioned inhibition.
On A⁺ trials, stimulus A is paired with the US. On AB⁻ trials, stimulus B is presented with stimulus A and the US is omitted. The procedure is effective in conditioning inhibition to stimulus B.

absence of the US. Because of the presence of stimulus A on the AB⁻ trials, stimulus B is encountered in the context of the expectancy of the US. This makes the absence of the US psychologically meaningful and serves to condition inhibitory properties to stimulus B.

Typically, A⁺ and AB⁻ trials are presented in an intermixed order. As training progresses with the two types of trials, A gradually acquires conditioned excitatory properties, and B becomes a conditioned inhibitor. The excitatory conditioning of A develops faster than the inhibitory conditioning of B.

Negative CS-US contingency. The standard inhibitory conditioning procedure (A⁺, AB⁻) is especially effective in making B a conditioned inhibitor, but there are other successful inhibitory conditioning procedures as well. In the **negative CS-US contingency** procedure, for example, only one explicit conditioned stimulus is used (a tone, for example), together with a US (see Figure 5.6). The tone and the US occur at irregular times, with the stipulation that the US is not presented if the tone has occurred recently. This stipulation establishes a negative contingency between the tone CS and the US. It ensures that p(US/CS) will be less than p(US/noCS) and serves to make the CS a conditioned inhibitor.

What provides the excitatory context for inhibitory conditioning of the tone CS in the negative contingency procedure? Because the US occurs when the CS is absent, the background contextual cues of the experimental situation become associated with the US. This then enables the conditioning of inhibitory properties to the CS. The absence of the US when the CS occurs in this excitatory context makes the CS a conditioned inhibitor.

Consider a child who periodically gets picked on when the teacher is out of the classroom. This is like periodically getting an aversive US and

CS

US

Time $\longrightarrow$

FIGURE 5.6   Negative contingency procedure for producing conditioned inhibition.
The US is presented at random times by itself but not if the CS has occurred recently.

serves to make the classroom a conditioned aversive environment. However, the harassment does not occur when the teacher is in the room. Under these circumstances the teacher will become a signal for the absence of harassment and will come to inhibit conditioned fear to the contextual cues of the classroom.

BEHAVIORAL MANIFESTATIONS OF CONDITIONED INHIBITION

The behavioral manifestations of excitatory conditioning are fairly obvious. Organisms come to make a new response, the conditioned response, to the CS. What happens in the case of conditioned inhibition? A conditioned inhibitory stimulus has behavioral effects that are opposite the behavioral effects of a conditioned excitatory stimulus. Thus, a conditioned inhibitory stimulus suppresses or inhibits excitatory conditioned responding. Unfortunately, suppression of responding is evident only under special circumstances.

Consider, for example, the eye-blink response of rabbits. Rabbits blink very infrequently, perhaps once or twice an hour. A conditioned inhibitory stimulus (CS^-) presumably actively suppresses blinking. But because rabbits hardly ever blink under ordinary circumstances, how can we tell when a CS^- actively inhibits their blinking?

Inhibition of blinking would be easy to determine if the baseline rate of blinking were elevated. If rabbits blinked 60 times an hour and we presented a conditioned inhibitory stimulus (CS^-), blinking should decline substantially below the 60/hr rate. Thus, the problem of measuring conditioned inhibition can be solved in principle by elevating the baseline rate of responding.

Summation test.   How can the baseline rate of responding be elevated? Perhaps the simplest way is to condition another stimulus as a conditioned excitatory cue (CS^+). Substantial responding should be evident when the CS^+ is presented by itself. Using this as a baseline, we can test the effects of

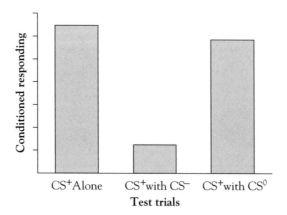

FIGURE 5.7 Procedure and hypothetical results of the summation test of conditioned inhibition.

On some trials a conditioned excitatory stimulus (CS⁺) is presented alone and a high level of conditioned responding is observed. On other trials CS⁺ is presented with a conditioned inhibitory stimulus (CS⁻) or a neutral stimulus (CS⁰). The fact that CS⁻ disrupts responding to CS⁺ much more than CS⁰ is evidence of the conditioned inhibitory properties of CS⁻.

a conditioned inhibitory stimulus (CS⁻) by presenting the CS⁻ at the same time as the CS⁺. Such a test strategy is called the **summation test** for conditioned inhibition.

Figure 5.7 presents hypothetical results of a summation test. Notice that considerable responding is observed when CS⁺ is presented by itself. Adding a conditioned inhibitory stimulus (CS⁻) to the CS⁺ results in much less responding than when the CS⁺ was presented alone. This outcome is what should happen if the CS⁻ has acquired conditioned inhibitory properties. However, presentation of the CS⁻ might disrupt responding simply by creating a distraction. That possibility is evaluated in the summation test by determining what happens to responding to the CS⁺ when a neutral stimulus without a history of either excitatory or inhibitory training is presented. Such a neutral stimulus is represented by CS⁰ in Figure 5.7.

In the results depicted in Figure 5.7, CS⁰ reduces responding to the CS⁺ a bit. This reflects the distracting effects of adding any stimulus to CS⁺. The reduction in responding is much greater, however, when the CS⁻ is presented with the CS⁺. That outcome shows that the CS⁻ has conditioned inhibitory properties.

Retardation of acquisition test.   The summation test is a performance-based test of inhibition. It is based on the assumption that the performance of excitatory conditioned behavior will be suppressed by a conditioned inhibitory stimulus. A second popular approach to the measurement of conditioned inhibition is an acquisition or learning test. This test is based on the assumption that conditioned inhibitory properties will interfere with the acquisition of excitatory properties to that stimulus. Hence, this is called the **retardation-of-acquisition test.**

The retardation-of-acquisition test involves comparing the rate of excitatory conditioning of two different groups of participants. The same conditioned stimulus (a tone, for example) is used for both groups. For the experimental group, the tone is first trained in an inhibitory conditioning procedure. For the comparison group, a control procedure is used that leaves the tone relatively "neutral." (For example, the tone may be presented alone a number of times in a nonexcitatory context.) Then, for both groups the tone is paired with the US, and the development of excitatory responding to the tone is observed. If inhibitory conditioning was successful in the first stage of the experiment, excitatory conditioned responding should develop more slowly in the experimental group than in the control group during the retardation-of-acquisition test.

STIMULUS RELATIONS IN CONDITIONED INHIBITION

In all of the procedures that are effective in producing conditioned inhibition, the US occurs on some occasions, but not when the inhibitory CS is presented. In the standard Pavlovian inhibition procedure, for example, the US occurs when stimulus A is presented alone (A^+) but does not occur when A is presented with stimulus B (in the AB^- compound), and B acquires inhibitory properties.

Direct versus higher-order inhibitory relations.   The inhibitory conditioning of stimulus B may be characterized in terms of a direct inhibitory relation between stimulus B and the US, according to which stimulus B becomes a signal for the absence of the US. This direct inhibitory relation may be represented as a "B–noUS" association. Alternatively, one might argue that a conditioned inhibitory stimulus is related to the US only indirectly. According to this indirect characterization, the critical feature of inhibitory conditioning procedures is that they enable the CS^- to provide information about how another stimulus is related to the US.

Consider, for example, the standard inhibitory conditioning procedure, which involves a mixture of A^+ and AB^- trials. In this procedure, B provides perfect information about whether or not stimulus A will be paired with the US on a particular trial. If stimulus B is present, A will not be paired with the US. In contrast, if stimulus B is absent, A will be paired with the US. This is a **higher-order stimulus relation** because in this situation B does not signal directly whether the US will (or will not) be presented. Rather, B signals whether A will (or will not) be paired with the US. The higher-order relation may be represented as B(A–noUS).

Extinction versus conditioned inhibition.   How can we tell whether in-hibitory conditioning results in a direct B–noUS association or a higher-order B(A–noUS) association? One possible strategy for answering this question involves comparing inhibitory conditioning to procedures in which only a B–noUS association could develop. One such procedure is **ex-tinction**, which was described in Chapter 4. In an extinction procedure, a CS is repeatedly presented without the US. Thus, an extinction procedure is one that might result in a CS–noUS association. However, given the sim-plicity of an extinction procedure, it could not result in a higher-order B(A–noUS) association.

Does an extinguished stimulus have the same behavioral effects as a conditioned inhibitory stimulus? Is an extinguished stimulus slower to acquire conditioned excitatory properties than a "neutral" stimulus in a retardation-of-acquisition test, and does an extinguish stimulus suppress re-sponding elicited by an excitatory CS in a summation test?

Extensive extinction can produce resistance to subsequent excitatory conditioning (Bouton, 1986). An extinguished stimulus is retarded in its subsequent acquisition of conditioned excitatory properties if the stimulus is presented in a context that reactivates memories of the extinction proce-dure (Bouton & Swartzentruber, 1989). Thus, an extinguished stimulus can pass the retardation-of-acquisition test of inhibition. However, even after extensive extinction training, an extinguished stimulus does not pass a sum-mation test of inhibition (Reberg, 1972). Only stimuli that have served in one of the inhibitory conditioning procedures we have described are ef-fective in suppressing responding in a summation test of conditioned in-hibition. These results suggest that an important aspect of inhibitory conditioning involves the opportunity to learn a higher-order relation in which the conditioned inhibitor provides information about occasions when another CS is not paired with the US.

Higher-Order Relations in Pavlovian Conditioning: Conditioned Facilitation

A **conditioned facilitation** procedure is similar to the standard inhibitory conditioning procedure in that it involves one unconditioned stimulus and two conditioned stimuli. As in inhibitory conditioning, the stimuli are arranged in such a way that the occasions when one CS (A) is paired with the US are perfectly predicted by a second CS (B). In conditioned inhibi-tion, B signals when A will not be paired with the US. In contrast, in con-ditioned facilitation, B signals when A will be paired with the US.

The differences between facilitation and inhibition are illustrated in Figure 5.8. In conditioned inhibition, stimulus B occurs on trials when A is not followed by the US (AB →noUS or AB⁻) and B is absent when A is paired with the US (A →US or A⁺). This arrangement is reversed in a fa-cilitation procedure. In conditioned facilitation, stimulus B occurs on trials

	Trials with the US	Trials without the US
Conditioned inhibition	A ⟶ US	AB ⟶ no US
Conditioned facilitation	AB ⟶ US	A ⟶ no US

FIGURE 5.8 Comparison of the types of trials that occur in procedures for conditioned inhibition and conditioned facilitation. A and B represent two different conditioned stimuli.

when A is reinforced (AB→US or AB⁺), and B is absent on trials when A is not reinforced (A →noUS or A⁻). The result of a facilitation procedure is that the participant responds to A when B is present but does not respond to A when B is absent (Holland, 1994).

Conditional relations like that represented by the facilitation procedure are not limited to experimental research. Consider the road sign "Slippery When Wet." Such a sign indicates that the road is ordinarily safe but can be dangerous when it is wet. These events exemplify the basic facilitation relation. The correspondence is evident if the roadway stimuli are represented by A, danger is considered to be the US, and wetness or rain is represented by B. Danger occurs only when cues of the road are encountered in combination with rain (AB →US). No danger is present when cues of the road are encountered without rain (A →noUS).

STIMULUS RELATIONS IN CONDITIONED FACILITATION

What kind of associations might produce responding in a facilitation procedure? As with inhibitory conditioning, there are two possibilities, one involving a direct relation of stimulus B with the US and the other involving an indirect or higher-order relation.

In a facilitation procedure, AB⁺ trials are intermixed with A⁻ trials. The US is only presented on trials when stimulus B occurs. This allows for the acquisition of a direct relation between stimulus B and the US (a B–US association).

A facilitation procedure also contains a higher-order relation. Stimulus B provides perfectly accurate information about the occasions when stimulus A will be paired with the US. Stimulus A is paired with the US on trials when stimulus B is present (AB⁺) but not on trials when stimulus B is absent (A⁻). Therefore, a facilitation procedure may result in the learning of a higher-order relation in which B comes to signal the pairing of stimulus A with the US. This higher-order relation may be represented as B(A–US). Because stimulus B signals the occasions when A is paired with the US, the facilitation procedure is also called **positive occasion setting** (e.g., Holland, 1986).

Trials with the US   Trials without the US

Noise present   Noise absent
Light ——→ Food   Light ——→ No food

FIGURE 5.9   Outline of the facilitation experiment by Rescorla et al. (1985).

DISTINGUISHING BETWEEN B–US AND B(A–US) RELATIONS

Conditioned response topographies.   How can we decide whether a facilitation procedure results in the learning of a B–US relation or a B(A–US) relation? One approach is to determine whether the conditioned responding is elicited by stimulus A or stimulus B. This approach has been used extensively in studies of facilitation in appetitive conditioning (Holland, 1992).

In one experiment (Rescorla, Durlach, & Grau, 1985), pigeons served as participants, a noise like static on the radio served as stimulus B, and a key light served as stimulus A. When the noise and key light stimuli were paired with food, they came to elicit different conditioned responses. The key light associated with food elicited conditioned pecking behavior. In contrast, the noise stimulus paired with food elicited increased locomotion but not pecking at the response key. Thus, any key pecks observed in this experiment could only be interpreted as conditioned behavior elicited by the key light, not as conditioned behavior elicited by the noise CS.

The procedure for the experiment is summarized in Figure 5.9. The key light was paired with food in the presence of the noise stimulus (AB →US). When the noise was absent, the key light did not end in food (A →noUS). The pigeons came to peck the key light when the noise was present but pecked much less when the noise was off. This outcome cannot be explained in terms of a direct association between the noise CS and food (a B–US association) because pigeons do not peck a noise stimulus associated with food. The results also cannot be explained in terms of a simple association between the key light and food (an A–US association) because such an association would have produced pecking of the key light whether or not the noise was present. The fact that the birds pecked the key light only when the noise was present suggests that they learned a B(A–US) relation, in which the noise set the occasion for responding to the key light.

Effects of extinction of stimulus B.   An alternative strategy for distinguishing between B–US and B(A–US) relations in a facilitation procedure involves testing the effects of extinguishing stimulus B. As was the case with conditioned inhibition, an extinction procedure is a powerful diagnostic tool here as well. Extinction of B involves repeatedly presenting stimulus B by itself (B–noUS). This experience is contrary to a B–US relation and should reduce responding that depends on the B–US relation. However, repeated presentations of stimulus B by itself is not contrary to a B(A–US) relation. The opposite of B(A–US) is B(A–noUS), not B–noUS. Therefore, extinction of stimulus B should not disrupt responding mediated by a B(A–US) relation. Results consistent with this prediction have been obtained repeatedly (e.g., Holland, 1989; Rescorla, 1985; Ross, 1983). Simple extinction of stimulus B does not weaken the ability of stimulus B to facilitate responding to A following training in a facilitation procedure.

Finally, I should point out that organisms do not invariably learn a B(A–US) relation as a result of a facilitation procedure. Sometimes procedures involving a mixture of AB–US trials and A–noUS trials result in the learning of only a B–US relation; in other cases participants learn both a B–US relation and a higher order B(A–US) relation. A number of factors beyond the scope of the present discussion determine whether a particular procedure favors the acquisition of a B–US relation or a B(A–US) relation (Holland, 1992; Schmajuk & Holland, 1998).

Summary

Pavlovian conditioning involves the formation of an association or linkage between two events. Typically, the events are individual stimuli, the CS and the US. However, in more complex cases, one of the events is a modulator CS and the other is a CS-US associative unit.

The development of conditioned responding is highly sensitive to the temporal relation between the CS and the US. Delayed conditioning procedures produce the most vigorous responding, but introducing a trace interval of as little as 0.5 sec between the CS and US can severely disrupt the development of conditioned behavior. Quantitative aspects of the CS-US interval function vary depending on the response system that is being conditioned.

Pavlovian conditioning is also highly sensitive to the signal relation between the CS and the US or the extent to which the CS provides information about the US. This is illustrated by the blocking phenomenon and by CS/US contingency effects. Originally, variations in the contingency between CS and US were considered to influence associative processes directly. More recent evidence suggests, however, that different degrees of context conditioning are responsible for CS/US contingency effects.

Higher-order relations in Pavlovian conditioning have been investigated within the context of conditioned inhibition and conditioned facilitation. In conditioned inhibition, a modulator stimulus (stimulus B) indicates when another CS (stimulus A) *is not paired* with the US. The outcome is that B comes to inhibit conditioned responding that normally occurs to stimulus A. In conditioned facilitation, the modulator stimulus B indicates when stimulus A *is paired* with the US. The outcome is that conditioned responding occurs only when stimulus B is present. Information concerning the topography of the conditioned response and the effects of extinguishing stimulus B is used to decide whether the results reflect learning a B(A–US) higher-order relation.

Suggested Readings

GORMEZANO, I., KEHOE, E. J., & MARSHALL, B. S. (1983). Twenty years of classical conditioning research with the rabbit. In J. M. Sprague & A. N. Epstein (Eds.), *Progress in psychobiology and physiological psychology* (Vol. 10, pp. 197–275). Orlando, FL: Academic Press.

HOLLAND, P. C. (1992). Occasion setting in Pavlovian conditioning. In G. Bower (Ed.), *The psychology of learning and motivation* (Vol. 28, pp. 69–125). Orlando, FL: Academic Press.

KAMIN, L. J. (1965). Temporal and intensity characteristics of the conditioned stimulus. In W. F. Prokasy (Ed.), *Classical conditioning* (pp. 118–147). New York: Appleton-Century-Crofts.

KAMIN, L. J. (1969). Predictability, surprise, attention, and conditioning. In B. A. Campbell & R. M. Church (Eds.), *Punishment and aversive behavior* (pp. 279–296). New York: Appleton-Century-Crofts.

PAPINI, M. R., & BITTERMAN, M. E. (1990). The role of contingency in classical conditioning. *Psychological Review, 97,* 396–403.

SCHMAJUK, N. A., & HOLLAND, P. C. (Eds.). (1998). *Occasion setting.* Washington, DC: American Psychological Association.

Technical Terms

Blocking effect	Long-delay learning
Conditioned facilitation	Negative CS-US contingency
Conditioned inhibition	Positive occasion setting
Contingency	Retardation-of-acquisition test
CS-US interval	Simultaneous conditioning
Delayed conditioning	Summation test
Extinction	Temporal encoding
Higher-order stimulus relation	Trace conditioning
Interstimulus interval	Trace interval

CHAPTER SIX

Instrumental or Operant Conditioning

DID YOU KNOW THAT:

- Learning a new instrumental response often involves putting familiar response components into new combinations.

- Variability in behavior can be an advantage in learning new responses.

- The deleterious effects of reinforcement delay can be overcome by presenting a marking stimulus immediately after the instrumental response.

- Thorndike's Law of Effect does not involve an association between the instrumental response and the reinforcer.

- Instrumental conditioning can result in the learning of three binary associations and one higher-order association.

- The various associations that develop in instrumental conditioning are difficult to isolate from each other, complicating studies of the neurophysiology of instrumental learning.

- Pavlovian associations in instrumental conditioning can disrupt performance of instrumental responses.

The various procedures that I have described so far (habituation, sensitiza-tion, and Pavlovian conditioning) all involve presentations of different types of stimuli according to various arrangements. The procedures produce changes in behavior—increases and decreases in responding—as a result of the stimulus presentations. Although they differ in important ways, a major common feature of habituation, sensitization, and Pavlovian conditioning procedures is that they are defined independently of the actions of the or-ganism. What the participants do as a result of the procedures does not in-fluence the stimuli they receive.

In a sense, studies of habituation, sensitization, and Pavlovian condi-tioning represent how organisms learn about events that are beyond their control. Adjustments to uncontrollable events are important because many aspects of the environment are beyond our control. When a class is sched-uled, how long it takes to toast bread, how far it is between city blocks, and when the local post office is open are but a few examples. Learning about uncontrollable events is important, but not all learning involves situations in which events are beyond the control of the organism. Another important category of learning involves situations in which the presentation of an un-conditioned stimulus depends on the individual's actions. Such cases in-volve **instrumental conditioning** or **operant conditioning**.

Instrumental conditioning procedures involve the periodic presentation of a significant stimulus or event. However, whether or not the event occurs depends on the behavior of the organism. Common examples of instrumen-tal behavior involve pulling up the covers to get warm in bed, putting ingre-dients together to make lemonade, changing the channel to find a particular television show, and saying "hello" to someone to get a greeting in return. In all of these cases, a particular response is required to obtain a specific stimu-lus or consequent outcome. Because the response is instrumental in produc-ing the outcome, the response is referred to as **instrumental behavior**. The consequent outcome (the warmth, the tasty lemonade, the television show, and the reciprocal greeting) is referred to as the **reinforcer**.

Sometimes instrumental behavior is called **operant behavior**. This is the case if the response is defined in terms of a particular operation or ma-nipulation of the environment. For example, we may define an operant re-sponse as turning a doorknob far enough to open a door. In this case, it does not matter what muscle movements are used to turn the door knob, pro-vided the knob gets turned far enough to release the door. The knob could be turned with a person's right hand, left hand, fingertips, or with a full grip of the knob. Such variations in response topography are ignored in studies of operant behavior.

A common example of operant behavior in animal research involves a laboratory rat pressing a response lever in a small experimental chamber (see Figure 6.1). (We previously encountered this example in discussions of conditioned suppression in Chapter 4.) Whether or not a lever-press re-sponse has occurred can be determined by placing a microswitch under the lever. A press of the lever with enough force to activate the microswitch is

FIGURE 6.1   A laboratory preparation for the study of operant behavior.
The Response lever and food cup are behind the rat.
Sniffy the Virtual Rat, Version 4.5 © 1996 University of Toronto. Brooks/Cole
Publishing Company. Used by permission.

counted as a response. Weak lever-presses that do not activate the switch
are ignored. In this case the lever press response "operates" on the environment by activating the microswitch.

Another common example of operant behavior in animal research is a
pigeon pecking a circular disc or response key on a wall (see Figure 4.1). A
microswitch behind the response key is used to detect instances of the key-
peck response.

The Traditions of Thorndike and Skinner

The intellectual traditions of classical conditioning were set by one dominant figure, Ivan Pavlov. In contrast, the intellectual traditions of instrumental or operant conditioning have their roots in the work of two
American giants of twentieth century psychology, Edward L. Thorndike and
B. F. Skinner (see Figures 6.2 and 6.3). The empirical methods as well as the
theoretical perspectives of these two scientists were strikingly different, but
the traditions started by each of them have endured to this day. I will first
consider the distinctive experimental methods used by Thorndike and
Skinner and then note some differences in their theoretical perspectives.

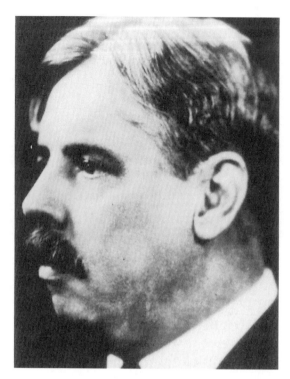

FIGURE 6.2   Edward L. Thorndike (1874–1949).
Courtesy of the Archives of the History of American Psychology.

METHODOLOGICAL CONSIDERATIONS

Thorndike was interested in studying animal "intelligence." To do this, he designed a number of escape tasks for young cats in a project that became his Ph.D. dissertation at Harvard University (Thorndike, 1898). Each task involved a box of some kind, a **puzzle box**. A different type of response was required to get released from each box. The puzzle was to figure out how to get out of the box.

Thorndike would put a kitten into a puzzle box on successive trials and measure how long the kitten took each time to escape and obtain a piece of fish. In some puzzle boxes, the kittens had to make just one type of response to get out (turning a latch, for example). In others, several actions were required and had to be performed in a particular order. Thorndike found that with repeated trials in a particular box, the kittens got quicker and quicker at escaping. Their escape latencies decreased.

The discrete-trial method.   Thorndike's experiments illustrate the **discrete-trial method** in the study of instrumental behavior. In the discrete-trial

FIGURE 6.3   B. F. Skinner (1904–1990).
Courtesy of the Bettman Archive.

method, the participant has the opportunity to perform the instrumental response only at certain times (during discrete trials), as determined by the experimenter. In the case of Thorndike's experiments, the kittens could only perform the instrumental escape response when they were placed in a puzzle box. When they made the required response, they were released from the box, and the next trial did not begin until Thorndike decided to put them back in.

The discrete trial method was subsequently adopted by investigators who used mazes of various sorts to study instrumental conditioning. Mazes are most commonly used with laboratory rats and were introduced into the investigative artillery of scientists by Willard Small, who built a maze in an effort to mimic the tunnel-like structures of the underground burrows in which rats live (Small, 1899, 1900).

A common type of maze is the **straight-alley runway** (see Figure 6.4). In a straight-alley runway, an animal is first placed in the start box. The start box door is then lifted to allow the animal to go to the goal box at the other end of the runway. Upon reaching the goal box, the animal is given a small piece of food and then removed until it is time to run the next trial.

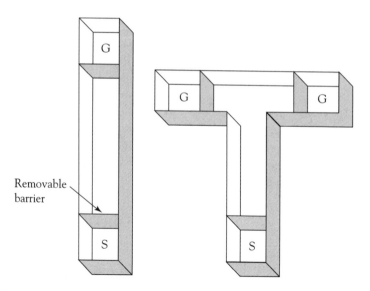

FIGURE 6.4   Top view of a runway and a T-maze.
S, start box; G, goal box.

The speed of running from the start box to the goal box is measured on each trial. Learning results in increased speeds of running.

The discrete-trial method requires numerous manipulations. The experimenter has to pick up the rat, place it in the start box, wait for it to reach the goal box, remove it from the goal box, and then put it in a holding area for the intertrial interval. Another distinction of the discrete-trial method is that how long the participant has to wait between trials is determined by the experimenter.

The free-operant method.   The major alternative to the discrete trial method for the study of instrumental behavior is the **free-operant method**. The free-operant method was developed by Skinner (1938). Skinner made numerous methodological and conceptual contributions to the study of behavior, and these two types of contributions were often interrelated. The free-operant method is a case in point.

Skinner's development of the free-operant method started with an interest in designing an automated maze for rats—a maze in which the rats would automatically return to the start box after each trial. Such an apparatus would have the obvious advantage that the rat would have to be handled only at the start and the end of a training session, freeing up the experimenter to do other things in the meanwhile. An automated maze would also permit the rat rather than the experimenter to decide when to start its next trial. That would enable the investigation of not only how rapidly the rat completed an instrumental response but how frequently it engaged in the instrumental behavior. Thus, an automated maze promised to provide new information that one could not obtain with the discrete-trial method.

Skinner tried several different approaches to automating the discrete-trial maze procedure. Each approach incorporated some improvements on the previous design, but as the work progressed the apparatus became less and less like a maze (Skinner, 1956). The end result was what has come be to known as the **Skinner box**.

We already encountered the Skinner box in discussing the definition of an operant response. For rats, the Skinner box is a small rectangular chamber. One wall has a small lever that the rat can press over and over again, and there is a food cup nearby, into which small pieces of food can be dropped by a pellet dispenser. Each lever-press response is electronically detected by the closure of a microswitch, and the apparatus can be programmed so that a piece of food is delivered each time the rat presses the lever.

In the Skinner box, the response of interest is defined in terms of the closure of a microswitch. The apparatus ignores whether the rat presses the lever with one paw or the other or with its tail. Another important feature of the Skinner box is that the operant response can occur at any time. The interval between successive responses is determined by the experimental participant rather than by the experimenter. Because the operant response can be made at any time, the method is called the free-operant method.

The primary conceptual advantage of the free-operant method is that it allows the participant to initiate the instrumental response. Skinner focused on this. How often a rat initiates the operant response can be quantified in terms of the frequency of the response in a given period of time, or the **rate of responding**. Rate of responding has come to serve as the primary measure of behavior in experiments using the free-operant method.

The Establishment of an Instrumental or Operant Response

People often think about instrumental or operant conditioning as a technique for training new responses. In what sense are the responses new? Does instrumental conditioning always establish entirely new responses, does it combine familiar responses in new ways, or does it establish a familiar response in a new situation?

LEARNING WHERE AND WHAT TO RUN FOR

Consider, for example, a hungry rat learning to run from one end of a runway to the other for a piece of food. An experimentally naive rat is slow to run the length of the runway at first. But this is not because it enters the experiment without the motor skill of running. Rats do not have to be taught to run, just as children don't have to be taught to walk. What they have to be taught is *where* to run, and what to run *for*. In the straight-alley runway, the instrumental conditioning procedure provides the stimulus control and the motivation for the running response. It does not establish the running response in the participant's repertoire.

CONSTRUCTING NEW RESPONSES FROM FAMILIAR COMPONENTS

The instrumental response of pressing a lever is a bit different from running. An experimentally naive rat probably has never encountered a lever before and has never performed a lever-press response. In this case, the required response is missing from the participant's repertoire at first. Unlike running, lever-pressing has to be learned in the experimental situation. But does it have to be learned from scratch? Hardly.

An untrained rat is not as naive about pressing a lever as one might think. Lever-pressing consists of a number of components: getting up on hind legs, raising one or both front paws, extending a paw forward over the lever, and then bringing the paw down with sufficient force to push down the lever. Rats perform responses much like these at various times while exploring their cages, exploring each other, or handling pellets of food. What they have to learn in the operant conditioning situation is how to put the various response components together to push down the lever and produce food.

Pressing a lever is a new response only in the sense that it involves a new combination of response components that already exist in the participant's repertoire. In this case, instrumental conditioning involves the construction or synthesis of a new behavioral unit from preexisting response components (Schwartz, 1981).

SHAPING NEW RESPONSES

Can instrumental conditioning also be used to condition entirely new responses, responses that the participant would never perform without instrumental conditioning? Most certainly. Instrumental conditioning is used to shape remarkable feats of performance in sports, ice skating, ballet, and musical performance—feats that almost defy nature. A police dog can be trained to climb a 12-foot vertical barrier, a sprinter can learn to run a mile in 4 minutes, and a golf pro can learn to drive a ball 200 yards in one stroke. Such responses are remarkable because they are unlike anything the participants are likely to do without special training.

In an instrumental conditioning procedure, the participant has to perform the required response before the outcome or reinforcer is delivered. Given this restriction, how can instrumental procedures be used to condition responses that never occur on their own? The learning of entirely new responses is possible because of the variability of behavior. Variability is perhaps the most obvious feature of behavior. Organisms rarely do the same thing twice in exactly the same fashion. Response variability is usually considered a curse because it makes predicting and controlling behavior difficult. However, for learning new responses, variability is a blessing.

The delivery a reinforcer does not result in repetition of the same exact response that produced the reinforcer the first time. If a rat, for example, is reinforced for pressing a lever with a force of 2 grams, it will not press the lever with exactly that force thereafter. Sometimes it will respond with less pressure; other times it will respond with more.

The first panel in Figure 6.5 shows what the distribution of responses might look like in an experiment where lever-pressing is reinforced only if a force greater than 2 grams is used. Notice that many, but not all, of the responses exceed the 2-gram criterion. A few of the responses exceed as much as 3 grams, but none exceeds 4 grams.

Because the variability in behavior includes responses as forceful as 3 grams, we can change the response criterion so that reinforcement is now only provided if the rat presses the lever with a force exceeding 3 grams. After several sessions on this new force requirement, the distribution of lever-presses will look something like what is represented in the second panel of Figure 6.5.

Responding remains variable after the shift in the response requirement. Increasing the force requirement shifts the force distribution to the right so that the majority of the lever presses exceed 3 grams. One consequence of this shift is that the rat occasionally presses the lever with a force exceeding 4 grams. Notice that these responses are entirely new. They did not occur originally.

Since we now have responses exceeding 4 grams, we can increase the response requirement again. We can change the procedure so that now the reinforcer is only given for responses that exceed 4 grams. This will result in a further shift of the force distribution to yet higher values, as shown in the third panel of Figure 6.5. Now most of the responses exceed 4 grams, and sometimes the rat presses the lever with a force exceeding 5 grams. Responses with such force are very different from what the rat started out doing.

This procedure is called **shaping**. Shaping is used when the goal is to condition instrumental responses that are not in the participant's existing behavioral repertoire. New behavior is shaped by imposing a series of response criteria. The response criteria gradually take the participant from its starting behavioral repertoire to the desired target response (e.g., Deich, Allan, & Zeigler, 1988; Galbicka, 1988; Pear & Legris, 1987).

In setting up a shaping procedure, the desired final performance must be defined clearly. This sets the goal or end point of the shaping procedure. Next, the existing behavioral repertoire of the participant has to be documented so that the starting point is well understood. Finally, a sequence of

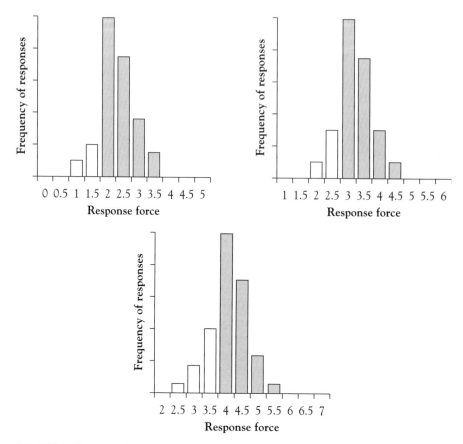

FIGURE 6.5   Frequency of lever-press responses involving various degrees of force.

In the first panel, only responses greater than 2 grams in force resulted in delivery of the reinforcer. In the second panel, only responses greater than 3 grams in force were reinforced. In the third panel, only responses greater than 4 grams in force were reinforced. (Note: Data are hypothetical.)

training steps have to be designed to take the participant from its starting behavior to the final target response. The sequence of training steps involves successive approximations to the final response. Therefore, shaping is typically defined as *the reinforcement of successive approximations.*

Shaping is useful not only in training entirely new responses but also in training new combinations of existing response components. Riding a bicycle, for example, involves three rather large response components, steering, pedaling, and maintaining balance. Children learning to ride usually start by learning to pedal. Pedaling is a new response. It is unlike anything a child is likely to have done before getting on a bicycle. To enable the child to learn to pedal without having to balance, parents usually start by giving a child a tricycle or a bicycle with training wheels. While learning to pedal, the child is not likely to pay much attention to steering and will need help to make sure she does not drive into a bush or off the sidewalk.

Once the child has learned to pedal, she is ready to combine this with steering. Only after the child has learned to combine pedaling with steering is she ready to add the balance component. Adding the balance component is the hardest part of the task. That is why parents often wait until a child is proficient riding a bicycle with training wheels before letting her ride without them.

The Importance of Immediate Reinforcement

Instrumental conditioning is basically a response selection process. The response (or unique combination of response components) that results in the delivery of the reinforcer is selected from the diversity of actions the organism performs in the situation. It is critical to this response selection process that the reinforcer be delivered immediately after the desired or target response. If the reinforcer is delayed, other activities are bound to occur between the target response and the reinforcer, and one of those other activities may be reinforced instead of the target response (see Figure 6.6).

Delivering a primary reinforcer immediately after the target response is not always practical. For example, the opportunity to go to a playground serves as an effective reinforcer for children in elementary school. However, it would be disruptive to allow a child to go outside each time he finishes a math problem. A more practical approach is to give the child a coin or token for each problem completed, and then allow those tokens to be exchanged for the opportunity to go to the playground. With such a procedure, the primary reinforcer (access to the playground) is delayed after the instrumental response, but the instrumental response is immediately followed by a stimulus (the token) that is associated with the primary reinforcer.

A stimulus that is associated with a primary reinforcer is called a **conditioned (or secondary) reinforcer**. The delivery of a conditioned reinforcer immediately after the instrumental response overcomes the ineffectiveness of delayed reinforcement in instrumental conditioning (e.g., Winter & Perkins, 1982).

The ineffectiveness of delayed reinforcement also can be overcome by presenting a **marking stimulus** immediately after the target response. A marking stimulus is not a conditioned reinforcer and does not provide information about a future opportunity to obtain primary reinforcement. Rather, it is a brief visual or auditory cue that distinguishes the target response from the other activities the participant is likely to perform during a delay interval. In this way the marking stimulus makes the instrumental response more

$$R_1 \ R_2 \ R_3 \ R_4 \ R_x \ S^* \qquad\qquad R_1 \ R_2 \ R_x \ R_3 \ R_4 \ S^*$$

Immediate reinforcement   Delayed reinforcement

FIGURE 6.6   Diagram of immediate and delayed reinforcement of the target response R_x.
R_1, R_2, R_3, etc., represent different activities of the organism. S^* represents delivery of the reinforcer. Notice that when reinforcement is delayed after R_x, other responses occur closer to the reinforcer.

memorable and helps overcome the deleterious effect of the reinforcer delay (Lieberman, McIntosh, & Thomas, 1979; Thomas & Lieberman, 1990).

Event Relations in Instrumental Conditioning

Methodologically, the most obvious events in instrumental conditioning are the instrumental response and the reinforcer. The response may be represented as R and the reinforcer as S^*. The relation between the response and reinforcer may be represented as **R-S^***. However, there is more to an instrumental conditioning situation than just the response and the reinforcer. Starting with the earliest theoretical efforts, investigators were aware that more than just the response and the reinforcer have to be considered in analyses of instrumental learning.

Thorndike pointed out that organisms experience a unique set of stimuli when they perform an instrumental response. In Thorndike's experiments these stimuli were provided by the puzzle box in which the participants were placed at the start of a training trial and the particular latch they had to manipulate to get out.

We don't know whether Thorndike's animals focused on the visual features of the puzzle box or the tactile cues of the latch they had to manipulate, but that does not matter for the theoretical analysis. Regardless of which particular stimuli a participant paid attention to, once it was assigned to a puzzle box, it experienced a unique set of cues whenever it performed the required escape response. The stimuli an organism experiences whenever it performs a required instrumental response may be represented by S.

These considerations suggest that an instrumental conditioning situation is made up of not just the response R and the reinforcer S^* but also the set of stimuli S in the presence of which the instrumental response occurs. The three components, S, R, and S^*, allow for the establishment of several event relations in instrumental conditioning in addition to the R-S^* relation.

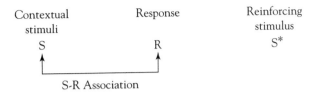

FIGURE   6.7   Diagram of the S-R association in instrumental conditioning.

THE S-R ASSOCIATION: THORNDIKE'S LAW OF EFFECT

Thorndike proposed that during the course of instrumental conditioning an association comes to be established between the response R and the environmental stimuli S (see Figure 6.7). In fact, Thorndike thought that the **S-R association** was the only thing learned in instrumental conditioning. He summarized his thinking in the **Law of Effect**. The Law of Effect states that instrumental learning involves the formation of an association between the instrumental response R and the stimuli S in the presence of which the response is performed. The reinforcer delivered after the response serves to strengthen or "stamp in" the S-R association, but the reinforcer is not one of the elements of that association.

According to the Law of Effect, instrumental learning does not involve learning to associate the reinforcer with the response. It does not involve the establishment of an R-S* association or learning about the reinforcer. Rather, instrumental conditioning only results in the establishment of an S-R association. The reinforcer S* is important just as a catalyst for the learning of the S-R association.

Assuming that organisms do not learn about the reinforcer in instrumental conditioning may seem counterintuitive. However, the Law of Effect was consistent with other theorizing early in the twentieth century. The Law of Effect is an adaptation of the Pavlovian concept of the conditioned response to instrumental learning. A Pavlovian CR is a response to a particular stimulus, the CS. In an analogous fashion, the Law of Effect considers the instrumental response R to be a response to the stimulus configuration S. Pavlovian conditioning was assumed to result in the establishment of a CS-CR association. Thorndike assumed that instrumental conditioning results in the establishment of an analogous S-R association.

S-S* AND S(R-S*) RELATIONS

Another event relation in instrumental conditioning that has received considerable theoretical and empirical attention is the relation between the antecedent stimuli S and the reinforcer S* (see Figure 6.8). Because the

FIGURE 6.8   Diagram of the S-S* association in instrumental conditioning.

instrumental response R results in delivery of the reinforcer S* in the presence of S, S is paired with S*. This is assumed to result in the learning of an **S-S* association** (Hull, 1930, 1931). The S-S* association is much like a Pavlovian CS-US association and presumably has the same behavioral consequences. For example, the establishment of the S-S* association presumably results in Pavlovian conditioned responses being elicited by S.

The three event relations we have considered thus far, R-S*, S-R, and S-S*, are binary or direct associations between pairs of elements of the instrumental conditioning situation. Another way that S, R, and S* may become related in instrumental conditioning is through a higher-order relation that is represented as **S(R-S*)** (see Figure 6.9). The first theoretician to recognize the S(R-S*) relation was Skinner (1938).

Skinner emphasized that in instrumental conditioning the reinforcer S* is presented contingent on the prior occurrence of the response R, not contingent on the prior occurrence of S. However, the R-S* contingency is in effect only in the presence of S. Based on these considerations, he suggested that a higher-order relation becomes established in which S signals the existence of the R-S* contingency or sets the occasion for the R-S* association. Skinner referred to this as a "three-part contingency." The three-part contingency may be represented as S(R-S*). The S(R-S*) relation in instrumental conditioning is analogous to the higher-order B(A-US) relation in Pavlovian conditioning described in Chapter 5.

Experimental investigations of the associative structure of instrumental conditioning have provided evidence for all four types of associations: R-S*, S-R, S-S*, and S(R-S*). Thorndike was the first to identify and emphasize the importance of the S-R association in instrumental conditioning. This association and the mechanisms of the Law of Effect were subsequently used in more elaborate neobehaviorist theories (e.g., Amsel, 1958; Hull, 1930, 1931; Spence, 1956). These theories, as well as subsequent so-called "two-factor" theories of learning (see Rescorla & Solomon, 1967), also emphasized the importance of the S-S* association in instrumental conditioning. More recently, investigators have turned their attention to the importance of the R-S* and S(R-S*) relations as critical components of instrumental learning (e.g., Colwill & Rescorla, 1986, 1990).

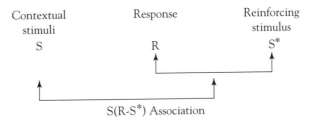

FIGURE 6.9   Diagram of the S(R-S*) association in instrumental conditioning.

IMPLICATIONS FOR NEURAL MECHANISMS

The complexity of the associative structure of instrumental learning that has been documented at the behavioral level presents serious challenges for scientists trying to discover the underlying neural mechanisms or neural circuitry of instrumental behavior. This is in contrast to the situation in Pavlovian conditioning. As we saw in Chapters 4 and 5, there are both simple and more complex forms of Pavlovian conditioning. Simple forms of Pavlovian excitatory conditioning are mediated by just an S-S association. More complex forms involve higher-order relations, B(A-US). Unfortunately, corresponding simple and complex associations cannot be isolated in instrumental conditioning.

Instrumental learning involves binary associations (S-R, S-S*, and R-S*), as well as the higher-order S(R-S*) relation. However, one cannot design an instrumental conditioning procedure that involves one of these factors to the exclusion of the others. For example, one cannot design an instrumental procedure that permits S-S* associations without allowing R-S* associations because the delivery of S* contingent on R is an inherent feature of instrumental conditioning. Because of this, investigators of the neural mechanisms of instrumental conditioning cannot isolate one associative component to the exclusion of others. This makes their job very difficult. Studies of the neural mechanisms of instrumental conditioning must consider multiple associative mechanisms (and their interactions) all at the same time.

IMPLICATIONS FOR CONSTRAINTS ON INSTRUMENTAL CONDITIONING

Understanding the associative structure of instrumental conditioning also provides insights into some enduring puzzles in instrumental learning. Thorndike (1911), for example, tested animals in a variety of different puzzle boxes. His young cats had to do different things in different boxes. In some boxes, the cats had to yawn or scratch themselves to be let out. Learning proceeded slowly in these boxes. Even after extensive training, the cats did not make vigorous and bona fide yawning responses. Rather, they performed rapid abortive yawns. Thorndike obtained similar results with the scratch response. The cats made rapid, half-hearted attempts to scratch themselves. These two examples illustrate the general finding that self-care and grooming responses are difficult to condition with food reinforcement.

Another category of instrumental behavior that is difficult to condition with food reinforcement is the release of a coin or token. Two of Skinner's graduate students, Keller and Marion Breland, became fascinated with the possibilities of animal training and set up a business that supplied trained animals for viewing in amusement parks, department store windows, and zoos. As a part of their business, the Brelands trained numerous species of animals to do various entertaining things (Breland & Breland, 1961).

For one display, they tried to get a pig to pick up a coin and drop it into a piggy bank to obtain food. Although the pig did what it was supposed to a few times, as training progressed, it became reluctant to release the coin and rooted it along the ground instead. This rooting behavior came to predominate, and the project had to be abandoned.

Several different factors are probably responsible for the **constraints on learning** evident in the difficulties that have been encountered in conditioning grooming and coin-release behavior (Shettleworth, 1975). One of the most important factors seems to be the development of S-S* associations in instrumental conditioning (Timberlake, Wahl, and King, 1982). In the coin release task, the coin becomes associated with the reinforcer and serves as stimulus S in the S-S* association. In instrumental reinforcement of grooming, stimulus S is provided by the contextual cues of the conditioning situation.

Because S-S* associations are much like Pavlovian associations between a CS and a US, Pavlovian conditioned responses related to the reinforcer come to be elicited by S. Pavlovian responses conditioned with food consist of approaching and manipulating the conditioned stimulus. These food-anticipatory responses are incompatible with self-care and grooming. They are also incompatible with releasing, and thereby withdrawing from, a coin that has come to signal the availability of food.

Analyses of the associative structure of instrumental conditioning indicate that Pavlovian associations develop during the course of instrumental conditioning. These Pavlovian associations can yield conditioned responses that are incompatible with the required instrumental response and can prevent increases in certain instrumental responses, such as grooming and coin-release responses.

Summary

In instrumental conditioning, the delivery of a biologically significant event or reinforcer depends on the prior occurrence of a specified instrumental or operant response. The instrumental behavior may be a preexisting response that the organism has to perform in a new situation, a set of familiar response components that the organism has to put together in an unfamiliar combination, or an activity that is entirely novel to the organism. Successful learning in each case requires delivering the reinforcer immediately after the instrumental response or providing a conditioned reinforcer or marking stimulus immediately after the response.

Instrumental conditioning was first examined by Thorndike, who developed discrete-trial procedures that enabled him to see how the latency of an instrumental response changes with training. Skinner's efforts to automate a discrete-trial procedure led him to develop the free-operant method, which allows measurement of the probability or rate of an instrumental behavior. Both discrete-trial and free-operant procedures consist of three components, contextual stimuli S, the instrumental response R, and the reinforcer S^*. Reinforcement of R in the presence of S allows for the establishment of S-R, $S\text{-}S^*$, $R\text{-}S^*$, and $S(R\text{-}S^*)$ associations. Because these associations cannot be isolated from one another other, investigating the neurophysiology of instrumental learning is much more difficult than studying the neurophysiology of Pavlovian conditioning. In addition, the $S\text{-}S^*$ association can create serious response constraints on instrumental conditioning.

Suggested Readings

COLWILL, R. M., & RESCORLA, R. A. (1986). Associative structures in instrumental learning. In G. H. Bower (Ed.), *The psychology of learning and motivation* (Vol. 20, pp. 55–104). San Diego: Academic Press.

COLWILL, R. M. (1994). Associative representations of instrumental contingencies. In D. L. Medin (Ed.), *The psychology of learning and motivation* (Vol. 31, pp. 1–72). San Diego: Academic Press.

RESCORLA, R. A., & SOLOMON, R. L. (1967). Two-process learning theory: Relationships between Pavlovian conditioning and instrumental learning. *Psychological Review, 74,* 151–182.

TIMBERLAKE, W., & LUCAS, G. A. (1989). Behavior systems and learning: From misbehavior to general principles. In S. B. Klein & R. R. Mowrer (Eds.), *Contemporary learning theories: Instrumental conditioning and the impact of biological constraints on learning* (pp. 237–275). Hillsdale, NJ: Erlbaum.

Technical Terms

Conditioned reinforcer
Constraint on learning
Discrete-trial method
Free-operant method
Instrumental behavior
Instrumental conditioning
Law of Effect
Marking stimulus
Operant behavior
Operant conditioning
Puzzle box

R-S* association
Rate of responding
Reinforcer
S-R association
S(R-S*) association
S-S* association
Secondary reinforcer
Shaping
Skinner box
Straight-alley runway

CHAPTER SEVEN

Schedules of Reinforcement

DID YOU KNOW THAT:

- Schedules of reinforcement determine rates and patterns of responding.
- Ratio schedules produce higher rates of responding than interval schedules.
- Schedule effects are related to the feedback function that characterizes each schedule of reinforcement.
- Training of a response chain does not have to begin with the last component of the chain.
- Reinforcement can be simultaneously available for two or more response alternatives.
- The Matching Law describes choice behavior.
- Extinction is slower following partial or intermittent reinforcement training than after continuous reinforcement training.
- Partial reinforcement promotes the learning of persistence mechanisms based on the memories and frustrative effects of nonreward.

Examples of instrumental conditioning were described in Chapter 6 with the implication that the reinforcer is delivered each time the required instrumental response occurs. Situations in nature in which there is a direct causal link between an instrumental response and a reinforcer come close to this ideal. Nearly every time you turn on the faucet, you get running water; nearly every time you pick up the phone, you hear a dial tone; and most of the time you buy an attractive piece of pastry, you end up with something good to eat. However, even in these cases, the relation between responding and the reinforcer is not perfect. The water main to your house may break, the phone may malfunction, and the pastry may be stale. In many instrumental conditioning situations, not every occurrence of the instrumental response is successful in producing the reinforcer.

Whether a particular occurrence of the instrumental response results in the reinforcer can depend on a variety of factors. Sometimes, the response has to be repeated a number of times before the reinforcer is delivered. In other situations, the response is only reinforced after a certain amount of time has passed. In yet other cases, both repetition and the passage of time are critical. The rule that specifies which occurrence of the instrumental response is reinforced is called a **schedule of reinforcement**.

Schedules of reinforcement have been of great interest because they determine many aspects of instrumental behavior. The rate and pattern of instrumental responding in free-operant situations are determined by the schedule of reinforcement. Seemingly trivial changes in a reinforcement schedule can produce profound changes in how frequently an organism responds and when it engages in one activity rather than another. Schedules of reinforcement also determine the persistence of instrumental behavior in extinction, when reinforcement is no longer available.

The Cumulative Record

The rate and pattern of responding produced by various schedules of reinforcement are typically investigated with the use of free-operant procedures. Microcomputers are programmed to record occurrences of the operant response (lever-pressing in rats, for example) and also determine which response is reinforced. Training sessions last about an hour each day, and numerous sessions typically are provided. After extensive experience with a particular schedule of reinforcement, the rate and pattern of responding stabilizes. The results are conveniently represented in terms of a **cumulative record**.

A cumulative record is a special kind of graph in which the horizontal axis represents the passage of time and the vertical axis represents the total or cumulative number of responses that have occurred up to a particular point in time (see Figure 7.1). If the participant does not respond for a while, its total or cumulative number of responses stays the same, and the

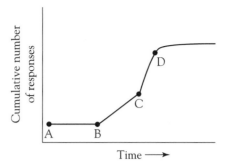

FIGURE **7.1** **An example of a cumulative record used to represent patterns of responding across time in free-operant studies of schedules of reinforcement.**
The section from point A to point B represents no responding. The section from point B to point C represents a low rate of responding. The section from point C to point D represents a high response rate. After point D, the rate of responding gradually declined to zero.

resultant curve on the cumulative record is a flat horizontal line, as between points A and B in Figure 7.1. Each response that is made is added to the previous total. Thus, each time the participant responds, the cumulative record goes up a bit. Because responses cannot be taken away, the cumulative record never goes down.

The slope of the cumulative record represents the participant's rate of responding. The slope is calculated by dividing the vertical displacement between two points on a graph by the horizontal displacement between those two points. Vertical displacement on a cumulative record represents a certain number of responses, and horizontal displacement represents time. Thus, the slope of a cumulative record represents responses per time or rate of responding. Low rates of responding produce a shallow slope on the cumulative record (e.g., from point B to point C in Figure 7.1) Higher response rates result in a steeper slope (e.g., from point C to point D in Figure 7.1).

Simple Schedules of Reinforcement

In simple schedules of reinforcement, which occurrence of the response is reinforced depends either on the number of responses that have been performed since the last reinforcer or how much time has passed since the last reinforcer. If the frequency of responses is the critical factor determining reinforcement, the procedure is called a **ratio schedule**. If the timing of the response since the last reinforcer is the critical factor, the procedure is called an **interval schedule**. In either case, the participant cannot obtain reinforcement unless it responds.

RATIO SCHEDULES

Fixed-ratio schedule of reinforcement.   In ratio schedules, the only thing that determines whether a response is reinforced is the number of responses the participant has performed since the last reinforcer. How much time it took to make those responses does not matter.

There are basically two types of ratio schedules, fixed and variable. In a **fixed-ratio schedule**, the participant has to perform a fixed number of responses for each delivery of the reinforcer. For example, each worksheet in a math class may have four problems on it, and students may receive a star for each worksheet they complete. This would be a fixed ratio 4 schedule of reinforcement, abbreviated as FR 4.

The number of responses required for reinforcement on a fixed-ratio schedule may be small or large. In some classes, each worksheet may have 4 problems on it; in other classes each sheet may have 15 problems. Regardless of the number, if each sheet has the same number of problems, a fixed-ratio schedule of reinforcement is in effect.

Figure 7.2 illustrates the stable pattern of responding that results from ratio schedules of reinforcement. The hatch marks in the records represent the delivery of the reinforcer. The typical result of reinforcing behavior on a fixed-ratio schedule is shown on the left side of the figure. Two features of this pattern are noteworthy. First, notice that after each hatch mark or reinforcer, the response rate is zero. The participant stops responding. This is called the **postreinforcement pause.** After the postreinforcement pause, a steady and high rate of responding occurs until the next delivery of the reinforcer. This is called the **ratio run**.

As illustrated in Figure 7.2, fixed-ratio schedules produce a break-run pattern of responding. Either the participant does not respond at all (in the postreinforcement pause) or it responds at a steady and high rate (in the ratio run). The duration of the postreinforcement pause is determined by the ratio requirement. As the ratio requirement is increased (from FR 10 to FR 20 to FR 40, for example), the duration of the postreinforcement pause will increase (Felton & Lyon, 1966).

Variable-ratio schedule of reinforcement.   A **variable-ratio schedule** is similar to a fixed ratio schedule in that the only factor that determines which repetition of the instrumental response is reinforced is the number of responses that have been performed. The difference between fixed- and variable-ratio schedules is that in a variable-ratio schedule the number of responses required varies from one reinforcer delivery to the next.

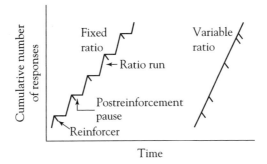

F I G U R E 7.2 Typical results of training on fixed-ratio and variable-ratio schedules of reinforcement.
The data were obtained with pigeons pecking a response key on an FR 120 and a VR 360 schedule of food reinforcement. The hatch marks indicate when the reinforcer was delivered. Adapted from Ferster and Skinner (1957).

When putting in golf, for example, reinforcement is provided by the ball going into the cup. On occasion, you may get the ball into the cup on the first try. More often, you will have to hit the ball several times before you succeed. Whether or not the ball gets into the cup depends only on your hitting the ball with the putter. How long you take between swings is irrelevant. Therefore, this is a ratio schedule. But the number of putting responses varies from one putting green to another. Therefore, this is a variable-ratio schedule.

A variable-ratio schedule is abbreviated as VR. If on average, you need to hit the ball three times to get it into the cup, you would be on a VR 3 schedule of reinforcement. The typical result of a variable ratio schedule is illustrated in the right panel of Figure 7.2. Unlike fixed-ratio schedules, variable-ratio schedules produce a steady and high rate of responding, with no predictable pauses.

INTERVAL SCHEDULES

In contrast to ratio schedules that are based on the number of responses the participant performs irrespective of time, when the responses occur is important in **interval schedules**. As with ratio schedules, there are basically two types of interval schedules, fixed and variable.

Fixed-interval schedule of reinforcement. In a **fixed-interval schedule**, a fixed amount of time has to pass before a response can be reinforced. Fixed-interval schedules occur in situations where it takes a certain amount of time for the reinforcer to be prepared or set up. Consider, for example, making a gelatin dessert (Jello, for example). After the ingredients are mixed, the Jello has to be cooled in the refrigerator for a certain amount of time (let's say an hour) before it is ready to eat. In this example, the reinforced response is taking the Jello out of the refrigerator to eat. If you take the Jello out too early, it will be watery, and your response will not be reinforced. Attempts to eat the Jello before the hour is up will not be reinforced. Another important feature of this example is that once the reinforcer is ready, it remains available until the individual responds to obtain it. Once the Jello is done, you don't have to eat it right away. It will be there for you even if you don't try eating it until the next day.

In a fixed-interval schedule of reinforcement, a fixed amount of time has to pass before the reinforcer becomes available. However, the reinforcer is not provided automatically at the end of the set interval. To obtain the reinforcer, the specified instrumental response has to be made. Early responses have no consequence. They do not produce the reinforcer early, nor do they result in a penalty. Finally, the reinforcer can be obtained any time after it has been set up. In a simple-interval schedule, the participant does not have to respond within a limited period once the reinforcer has become available.

Fixed interval schedules are abbreviated FI, with a number afterward indicating the duration of the fixed intervals during which responding is not reinforced. Figure 7.3 shows data obtained from a pigeon pecking a response key on a free-operant FI 4-min schedule of food reinforcement. On this schedule, delivery of the reinforcer at the end of one fixed interval starts the next fixed-interval cycle. Four minutes after the start of the cycle, the reinforcer becomes available and is delivered if the pigeon pecks the response key.

Responding on a fixed-interval schedule is similar to the pattern of responding that occurs on fixed-ratio schedules. There is little or no responding at the beginning of the fixed interval. Because the interval begins just after delivery of the previous reinforcer, the lack of responding here is called a postreinforcement pause. Responding increases as the end of the interval gets closer, with the participant responding at a high rate just as the fixed interval ends. The entire response pattern is called an *FI scallop* because it resembles the ridges on the shell of a scallop.

Variable-interval schedule of reinforcement.   **Variable-interval schedules** are similar to fixed-interval schedules except that the amount of time it takes to set up the reinforcer varies from trial to trial. The response of checking to see if a teacher has finished grading your paper is reinforced on a variable-interval schedule. It takes some time to grade a paper, but how long it takes varies from one occasion to the next. Checking to see if your paper has been graded is reinforced only after some time has passed since the start of the schedule cycle. Early responses (responses that occur before

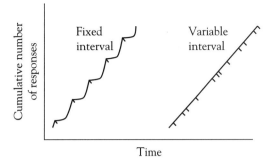

FIGURE 7.3   Typical results of training on a fixed-interval and variable-interval schedule of reinforcement.
The data were obtained with pigeons pecking a response key on FI 4-min and VI 2-min schedules of food reinforcement. The hatch marks indicate when the reinforcer was delivered. Adapted from Ferster and Skinner (1957) .

the paper has been graded) are not reinforced. In contrast, you can get your grade any time after the paper has been graded.

Variable-interval schedules are abbreviated VI, with a number afterward indicating the average duration of the intervals during which responding is not reinforced. Figure 7.3 shows data obtained from a pigeon pecking a response key on a free-operant VI 2-min schedule of food reinforcement. On this schedule, the reinforcer became available on average 2 min after the start of each schedule cycle.

Responding on variable-interval schedules is similar to responding on VR schedules of reinforcement. In both cases, a steady rate of behavior occurs, with no predictable pauses or changes in rate.

In simple interval schedules, once the reinforcer has become available it remains there until the organism responds and obtains the reinforcer. The cycle then starts over again. Picking up your letters from a mailbox, for example, is on a variable-interval schedule. Checking the mail before it is delivered doesn't speed up delivery of the mail, but once the letters have been placed in your mailbox, you don't have to pick them up right away. They will remain there even if you don't get them until the next day.

In some special cases, once the reinforcer has been set up, it remains available for just a limited period. For example, it takes a certain amount of time to bake a pan of cookies. But, once the required time has passed, if you don't take the cookies out of the oven, they will burn. This is an interval schedule with a **limited hold**. The reinforcer is "held" for a limited period after it becomes available, and the response has to occur during the hold period to be reinforced. Adding a limited hold to an interval schedule increases the rate of responding, provided the hold is not so short that the participant frequently misses the reinforcer altogether.

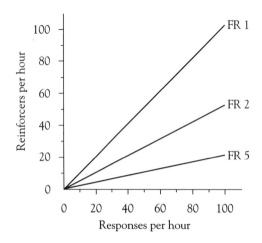

FIGURE 7.4   Feedback functions for ratio schedules of reinforcement.
Notice that each feedback function is a straight line. Because of that, every increase in the response rate results in a corresponding increase in the rate of
reinforcement.

Mechanisms of Schedule Performance

A key concept involved in analyses of the mechanisms of schedule effects
is the feedback function that characterizes the schedule. Reinforcement of
an instrumental response can be viewed as feedback for that response.
Schedules of reinforcement determine how this feedback is arranged. One
way to describe the arrangement is to show how the rate of reinforcement
obtained is related to the rate of responding. This relationship is the **feedback function**.

FEEDBACK FUNCTIONS FOR RATIO SCHEDULES

Feedback functions for ratio schedules are perhaps the easiest to understand.
In a ratio schedule, how soon (and how often) the organism gets reinforced
is determined only by how rapidly it completes the required number of responses. The faster the organism responds, the faster it obtains the reinforcer.

Figure 7.4 shows examples of feedback functions for several ratio schedules. On an FR 1 or continuous-reinforcement schedule, the participant is
reinforced for each occurrence of the instrumental response. Therefore, the
rate of reinforcement is equal to the rate of responding. This results in a
feedback function with a slope of 1.0.

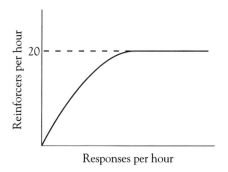

FIGURE 7.5   Feedback function for a VI 3-min schedule of reinforcement.
Responding is assumed to be distributed randomly in time. Notice that no matter how rapidly the organism responds, its maximum reinforcement rate is 20/hour.

If more than one response is required for reinforcement, the rate of reinforcement will be less than the rate of responding and the slope of the feedback function will be less than 1.0. For example, on an FR 5 schedule of reinforcement, the participant receives one reinforcer for every fifth response. Under these circumstances the rate of reinforcement is one-fifth the rate of responding, and the slope of the feedback function is 0.2.

Regardless of their slope, feedback functions for ratio schedules are always straight lines. Because of that, an increase in the rate of responding always yields an increase in the rate of reinforcement. This is true for both fixed- and variable-ratio schedules.

FEEDBACK FUNCTIONS FOR INTERVAL SCHEDULES

Interval schedules have feedback functions that differ markedly from those of ratio schedules. Figure 7.5 shows the feedback function for a VI 3-min schedule of reinforcement. On such a schedule, the reinforcer becomes available on average 3 min after the last time it was delivered. Therefore, no matter how often or how rapidly the organism responds, the maximum number of reinforcers it can obtain is limited to 20/hour.

As with ratio schedules, if the participant does not make any responses on an interval schedule it will not obtain any reinforcers. Increases in the rate of responding above zero will increase the chance of getting whatever reinforcers become available. Therefore, up to a point, increased responding is accompanied by higher rates of reinforcement. However, once the participant responds often enough to get all of the 20 reinforcers that can be obtained each hour, any further increase in response rate will have no further benefit. Thus, the feedback function for an interval schedule becomes flat once the maximum possible reinforcement rate has been achieved.

FEEDBACK FUNCTIONS AND SCHEDULE PERFORMANCE

One of the striking facts about instrumental behavior is that ratio schedules produce considerably higher rates of responding than interval schedules, even if the rate of reinforcement is comparable in the two cases (McDowell & Wixted, 1988; Peele, Casey, & Silberberg, 1984; Reynolds, 1975). Clues to explain why ratio schedules produce higher response rates may be gleaned from the feedback functions. Because the feedback function for an interval schedule reaches a maximum with a particular rate of responding, increases in response rate beyond that point provide no special benefit. Therefore, increases in response rate are not differentially reinforced beyond a particular point on interval schedules. In contrast, such a limit does not exist with ratio schedules. On ratio schedules, increases in response rate always result in higher rates of reinforcement. There is no limit to the differential reinforcement of higher rates of responding. Ratio schedules may produce higher rates of responding because such schedules differentially reinforce high response rates without limit.

Although feedback functions have been important in efforts to explain schedule performance, they have some conceptual limitations. One serious problem is that feedback functions are sometimes difficult to characterize. This is particularly true for interval-based schedules. In interval schedules reinforcement depends not only on the rate of responding but also on how the responses are distributed in time. The feedback function for the VI 3-min schedule presented in Figure 7.5 assumes that responses are distributed randomly in time. Other assumptions may alter the initial increasing portion of the feedback function. Despite such complications, however, many investigators believe that the nature of schedule performance is ultimately determined by how schedules of reinforcement provide feedback for instrumental behavior.

Chained Schedules of Reinforcement

In simple schedules of reinforcement, only one operant response is involved. The participant is allowed to repeat that response in the same situation, and the schedule determines which occurrence of the response is reinforced. In contrast, a **chained schedule** involves a sequence of responses. Each response constitutes a component of the chained schedule, and each response component has its own associated stimulus. The primary reinforcer is not provided until the participant has completed all of the components of the chain and has done so in the correct order.

HETEROGENEOUS CHAINS

The most familiar type of chained schedule involves a sequence of different responses, each of which is performed in the presence of a different stimulus. Consider, for example, putting on a pullover sweater. The goal or reinforcer is having the sweater on your body. To get to that point, first you have to put each of your arms into the arms of the sweater. Then you have to lift the sweater above your head and pull it over your head and neck. Finally, you have to pull the bottom of the sweater down around your waist.

Notice that putting on the sweater involves a series of different responses. In addition, each response occurs in the presence of a different stimulus. You start with the sweater in front of you. That is the stimulus for putting your arms into the sweater. Having the sweater on your arms is the stimulus for pulling the sweater over your head. Having the sweater around your neck is the stimulus for pulling the bottom of it down around your waist. The reinforcer is the enjoyment of wearing the sweater, and that is available only at the end of the chain of responses. No satisfaction or reinforcement is experienced if the response sequence is interrupted part way through, while the sweater is covering your head, for example.

Many activities can be analyzed as response chains: opening a can, doing your homework, or mowing the lawn. All of these cases involve a sequence of different activities, and each activity occurs in the presence of a different stimulus. If the response chain is made up of a sequence of different responses, it is called a **heterogeneous chain**.

HOMOGENEOUS CHAINS

Another type of chained schedule is called a **homogeneous chain**. In a homogeneous chain, the various components all involve the same response, but each component occurs in the presence of a different stimulus and involves a different schedule requirement. The example presented in Figure 7.6 involves two response components, FR 15 and FI 3 min, each with its associated stimulus, S_1 and S_2. During S_1 (which might be a red light), the participant has to respond 15 times to satisfy the FR 15 requirement. After the fifteenth response, S_2 (a green light, for example) is presented and the FI 3-min requirement comes into effect. On the FI 3-min schedule, the primary reinforcer is delivered for the first response that occurs after S_2 has been on for 3 min.

With a homogeneous chain, each component of the schedule produces a pattern of responding that is characteristic of the simple schedule in effect in that component. On an FR 15 - FI 3-min chained schedule, the participants would pause and then respond at a steady and high rate in the FR 15 component. They would then pause and show a scalloped pattern of responding in the FI 3-min component.

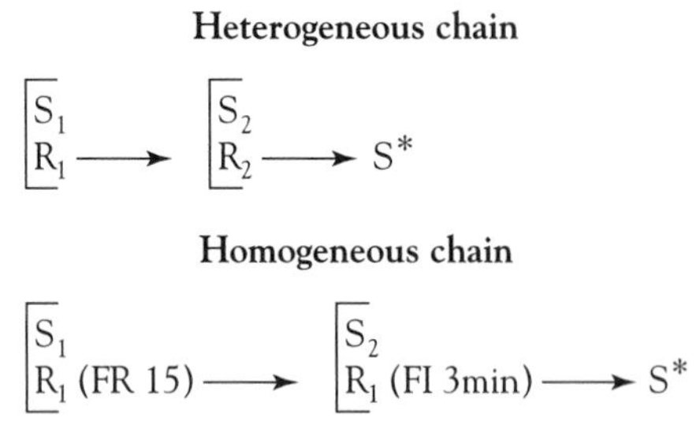

Heterogeneous chain

$$\boxed{\begin{array}{c}S_1\\R_1\end{array}} \longrightarrow \boxed{\begin{array}{c}S_2\\R_2\end{array}} \longrightarrow S^*$$

Homogeneous chain

$$\boxed{\begin{array}{c}S_1\\R_1\end{array}} \text{(FR 15)} \longrightarrow \boxed{\begin{array}{c}S_2\\R_1\end{array}} \text{(FI 3min)} \longrightarrow S^*$$

FIGURE 7.6   Difference between heterogeneous and homogeneous chains.

In a heterogeneous chain, the organism has to perform a sequence of different responses (R_1 followed by R_2) to obtain the reinforcer S^*. In a homogeneous chain, the organism has to perform the same response (R_1) on one reinforcement schedule (FR 15) followed by another (FI 3 min) to obtain the reinforcer S^*. In both cases, each response component has its own associated stimulus.

Homogeneous chain schedules are in effect when a person has to perform the same response under different contingencies during different parts of a task. Consider, for example, using screws to install two hinges and a latch on the lid of a storage chest. Each hinge requires four screws, and the latch requires two screws. The job is a homogeneous chain schedule with three components, two for the hinges and the third for the latch. Completing each component requires putting in a certain number of screws. Thus, each component involves a fixed ratio schedule in which putting in one screw constitutes a response. The sequence can be represented as S_1(FR 4) $\rightarrow S_2$(FR 4) $\rightarrow S_3$(FR $\rightarrow$2), where S_1 and S_2 represent the hinges and S_3 represents the latch.

TRAINING RESPONSE CHAINS

Techniques for the establishment of response chains are of great interest for teachers, especially if their students require extensive instruction. A while back, the conventional wisdom was that response chains are learned most readily with a **backward chaining** procedure (Ferster & Perrott, 1968). In backward chaining, the last response or response component of the chain is taught first because it is closest to the delivery of the reinforcer. Earlier response components are then added once the participant has mastered the end of the chain.

In the case of putting on a sweater, for example, the last response is pulling the sweater around the waist. To train this response, the teacher would place the sweater around the child's head and shoulders and encourage her to pull the sweater down. Once the child has mastered the last response, the response just before this one would be added. In our case, the sweater would be held above the child and she would be encouraged to pull it over her head and then over her body. Gradually, the earlier steps would be added until the child is able to perform all of the responses in the sequence.

The backward chaining method is intended to take advantage of the primary reinforcer to condition the terminal response of the chain. Through this training, the stimulus that signals the terminal component is presumed to become a conditioned or secondary reinforcer. Once that stimulus has acquired conditioned reinforcing properties, it can reinforce the response that occurs in the previous component and enable the previous stimulus to acquire conditioned reinforcing properties. This type of reinforcement of responses and conditioning of secondary reinforcers gradually works its way back to the start of the response chain, until the entire chain has been learned.

Backward chaining is an effective approach to training response sequences. However, response chains also can be effectively taught by starting from the beginning and initially reinforcing the first response in the chain. Once the first response has been learned, the second one can be added, and then the third and fourth. Such a forward chaining procedure can be as effective as backward chaining (see Sulzer-Azaroff & Mayer, 1991). However, in using a forward training sequence, each component of the chain has to be reinforced with the primary reinforcer initially.

Concurrent Schedules

In each of the schedules of reinforcement considered so far, the organism can either perform the specified instrumental response or not do so. These procedures are usually not considered to involve a choice, but in fact all instrumental conditioning situations involve a choice. With simple and chained schedules, the choice is to perform the response specified by the reinforcement schedule or do something else.

Investigators have become convinced that a complete understanding of instrumental behavior requires understanding why organisms choose to engage in one response rather than another. Unfortunately, simple and chained schedules of reinforcement are not good for analyzing how choices are made. In simple and chained schedules, the alternative to the instrumental response, the "something else" the participant might do, is poorly specified and not measured. These shortcomings are remedied in concurrent schedules. Concurrent schedules of reinforcement provide clearly defined and measured alternative responses and thereby permit studying more directly why organisms elect to engage in one activity rather than another.

As you might suspect, whether you do one thing or another depends on the benefits you derive from each activity. In the terminology of conditioning, how often you engage in activity A as compared to activity B will depend on the schedule of reinforcement in effect for response A, compared

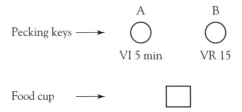

FIGURE 7.7 Diagram of a concurrent schedule of reinforcement.
Pecking the response key on the left is reinforced on a VI 5-min schedule of reinforcement. Pecking the response key on the right is reinforced on a VR 15 schedule of reinforcement.

---

with the schedule of reinforcement in effect for response B. On a playground, Joe could play with Peter, who likes to play vigorous physical games,
or Joe could play with Matt, who prefers to play quietly in the sand box. If
Joe is not getting much enjoyment from playing with Peter, he can go play
with Matt. Concurrent schedules are used to model this kind of situation in
the laboratory.

A concurrent schedule provides at least two response alternatives, A
and B (see Figure 7.7). Responding on alternative A is reinforced on one
schedule of reinforcement (VI 5 min, for example), and responding on B is
reinforced on a different schedule (VR 15, for example). Both response alternatives (and their corresponding reinforcement schedules) are available
at the same time, and the participant can switch from one activity to the
other at any time. Because the two choices are available at the same time,
the procedure is called a **concurrent schedule**.

Numerous factors determine how organisms distribute their behavior
between two response alternatives. These include the nature of each type
of response, the effort and time involved in switching from one response to
the other, the attractiveness of the reinforcer provided for each response,
and the schedule of reinforcement in effect for each response. Experiments
have to be designed carefully so that the effects of each of these factors can
be observed without being confounded with other features of the choice
situation.

Investigators of operant conditioning have been most interested in
how choice is determined by the schedule of reinforcement in effect for
each response alternative. In an effort to focus on this variable, they have
designed procedures that minimize the contribution of other factors. Studies of concurrent schedules are often carried out with pigeons. One wall of
the experimental chamber has two response keys positioned at about the
height of the bird's head. A feeder through which the bird can obtain grain
is centered below the two keys. This arrangement has the advantage that

the two responses require the same effort. Although pecks on the right and left keys are reinforced on different schedules, the reinforcer in each case is the same type of food. Another advantage is that the pigeon can easily switch from one response to the other because the left and right keys are located near each other.

If similar effort is required for the response alternatives, if the same reinforcer is used for both responses, and if switching from one side to the other is fairly easy, the distribution of responses between the two alternatives will depend only on the schedule of reinforcement in effect for each response. The results of numerous experiments fit the **Matching Law** (Herrnstein, 1970). According to the matching law, *the relative rate of responding on a response alternative is equal to the relative rate of reinforcement obtained with that response alternative.* For example, 70% of the responses will be made on the left side of a two-key chamber if 70% of all reinforcers are earned on the left side.

In a concurrent choice situation, organisms tend to match relative rates of responding to relative rates of reinforcement. Departures from matching occur if the response alternatives require different degrees of effort, if different reinforcers are used for each response alternative, or if switching from one response to the other is made more difficult (Davison & McCarthy, 1988; Williams, 1994).

Extinction of Instrumental Behavior

So far I have described what happens when instrumental behavior is reinforced periodically. An obvious related question is: What happens if the reinforcer is no longer provided? Once an instrumental response has been conditioned, does it persist if the reinforcer is no longer presented? Or do reinforcement procedures have to remain in effect to maintain conditioned responding?

The procedure of withholding the reinforcer for a previously conditioned instrumental response is called *extinction.* The participant is permitted to perform the instrumental response but the reinforcer is no longer presented. Organisms that have experienced instrumental conditioning continue responding for some time in extinction. However, the absence of reinforcement eventually results in a decline in behavior.

Extinction of instrumentally conditioned behavior has some of the same properties as extinction of Pavlovian conditioned responding. As in Pavlovian extinction, a period of rest after an extinction session can result in spontaneous recovery of the extinguished instrumental response. The phenomenon of disinhibition also occurs in the extinction of instrumental behavior. Presentation of a novel stimulus can result in a temporary recovery of the extinguished instrumental response. Another similarity between Pavlovian and instrumental extinction is the renewal effect. If extinction is provided in a situation that is distinctively different from the training context, the instrumental behavior will recover when the participant is returned to the training context.

Although extinction of instrumental behavior has some of the same characteristics as extinction of classically conditioned behavior, research on instrumental extinction has been pursued largely independently. In particular, investigators have focused on how various schedules of reinforcement influence the **persistence** of responding when extinction is introduced. Hundreds of experiments have been conducted to examine the effects of schedules of reinforcement on the persistence of instrumental behavior. Many of these studies have dealt with the partial reinforcement extinction effect.

THE PARTIAL REINFORCEMENT EXTINCTION EFFECT

As I described earlier, schedules of reinforcement can take many forms. There are ratio schedules, interval schedules, and concurrent schedules. How various schedules produce different patterns of behavior has been investigated in great detail in studies employing free-operant methods. In contrast, much of the research on how schedules of reinforcement determine extinction of instrumental behavior has been conducted with discrete-trial procedures in a straight-alley runway.

The most important factor that determines the persistence of responding in extinction is whether the instrumental response was initially trained on a continuous reinforcement (CRF) schedule or a partial reinforcement (PRF) schedule. In a continuous reinforcement schedule, the participant is reinforced each time it makes the instrumental response. By contrast, in a partial reinforcement schedule, the participant is reinforced only some of the times that it performs the response. In general, partial or intermittent reinforcement produces much more persistence in responding in extinction than continuous reinforcement (see Figure 7.8). This finding is known as the **partial reinforcement extinction effect**, or PREE.

The partial reinforcement extinction effect was first observed by Humphreys (1939), and for some time it was known as Humphreys's paradox. Before Humphreys's work, responding in extinction was considered to reflect the associative strength of the conditioned response, or how well the response had been learned. In addition, associative strength was assumed to be determined by how often the response had been reinforced. The assumption was that the more often a response is reinforced, the better it would be learned and the more persistent it would be in extinction.

Because the instrumental response is reinforced more often with continuous than with partial reinforcement, CRF was expected to yield more persistent responding in extinction than PRF. The partial reinforcement extinction effect is contrary to this prediction. In the PREE, more persistence occurs after partial reinforcement than after continuous reinforcement. Therefore, the PREE was considered a paradoxical finding.

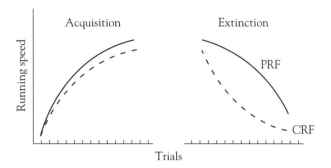

FIGURE 7.8   Illustration of the partial reinforcement extinction effect, or PREE.

During the acquisition phase, the instrumental response is conditioned on a partial reinforcement (PRF) schedule for one group and on a continuous reinforcement (CRF) schedule for the second group. During extinction, when responding is not reinforced for either group, group PRF shows more persistence than group CRF.

Since Humphreys's initial demonstration, the PREE has been documented in a wide variety of instrumental conditioning situations and species (e.g., Bitterman, 1975). The phenomenon may still be considered paradoxical, but it is not an anomaly. Rather, it is a common characteristic of instrumental behavior. Gamblers, aspiring actors, musicians, and research scientists are all on intermittent schedules of reinforcement, and all display considerable persistence in their behavior. They ardently pursue their goals even if they encounter a long string of failures or nonreinforcement.

EXPLANATIONS OF THE **PREE**

The discrimination hypothesis.   The first, and perhaps simplest, account of the partial reinforcement extinction effect was the **discrimination hypothesis**. The introduction of an extinction procedure after a period of training in which the instrumental response was reinforced represents a change in the contingencies of reinforcement—a change in the rules of the game, if you will. Proponents of the discrimination hypothesis pointed out that introducing extinction after continuous reinforcement involves a bigger or more noticeable change for the participant than introducing extinction after partial reinforcement.

During CRF, every occurrence of the instrumental response results in delivery of the reinforcer. This is dramatically different from extinction, where the reinforcer is never delivered. In contrast, the change from PRF to extinction is not as remarkable because responses are occasionally not reinforced during a partial reinforcement schedule. Thus, a partial reinforcement

	Acquisition phase 1	Acquisition phase 2	Extinction
Group C	CRF	CRF	no S*
Group P	PRF	CRF	no S*

F I G U R E   7.9   Design of experiments demonstrating the PREE despite interpolated continuous reinforcement before extinction.
Group C receives continuous reinforcement training in the first phase of acquisition, during which group P receives partial reinforcement. During the second phase of acquisition, responding for both groups is reinforced on a continuous reinforcement schedule. Then both groups receive extinction.

procedure is in some ways similar to extinction. According to the discrimination hypothesis, responding is more persistent after PRF than CRF because extinction is more difficult to detect following PRF training.

The Theios and Jenkins experiment.   Although the discrimination hypothesis is intuitively reasonable, it is too simplistic and has been shown to be incorrect. The hypothesis was definitively disproved by the results of an elegant experiment, independently conceived by Theios (1962) and Jenkins (1962). The design of the Theios and Jenkins experiment is shown in Figure 7.9.

The extinction performance of two groups was compared. As is true for all studies of the PREE, group C received CRF training initially, and group P received PRF training. In a second phase of acquisition, groups C and P both received continuous reinforcement training, and then both groups were shifted to extinction. The second acquisition phase, in which both groups received CRF training, was intended to make the change from reinforcement to extinction equivalent for both groups. Given the identical CRF training in Phase 2, introduction of the extinction procedure should have been just as noticeable for group P as it was for group C.

According to the discrimination hypothesis, the interpolated phase of CRF training for both groups should have eliminated the partial reinforcement extinction effect. Contrary to this prediction, however, both Theios and Jenkins observed greater persistence in group P than in group C during the extinction phase. The PREE was not eliminated by giving group P continuous reinforcement training just before extinction. The results of the Theios and Jenkins experiment are important because they show that persistence following partial reinforcement training does not result from possible perceptual difficulties in detecting the onset of extinction. The PREE does not reflect the nature of the transition from acquisition to extinction. Rather, the PREE results from something participants in group P learn long before extinction starts—something they learn during partial reinforcement training at the beginning of the experiment.

The Theios and Jenkins experiment showed that persistence created by partial reinforcement training is not erased by subsequent continuous reinforcement. A person who has become a habitual gambler because of occasional successes (partial reinforcement) will not change his habits after of an unbroken string of wins (continuous reinforcement).

Sequential theory and frustration theory.   What is learned during the course of partial reinforcement that creates persistence in extinction? What does a writer learn from the occasional article that is accepted for publication that makes her keep writing in the face of repeated rejection notices? There are two major explanations, sequential theory and frustration theory.

Sequential theory was developed by E. J. Capaldi (1967, 1971) and is based on the idea that memories of prior reward and nonreward can be an important source of the stimuli organisms encounter when their instrumental behavior is reinforced. According to sequential theory, persistence in extinction occurs if the instrumental response has become conditioned to cues of the memory of nonreward. Nonrewarded trials do not occur during the course of continuous reinforcement training. Therefore, the instrumental response cannot become conditioned to the memory of nonreward on a CRF schedule. In contrast, nonrewarded trials inevitably occur during partial reinforcement training. Furthermore, some of these nonrewarded trials are followed by a rewarded trial. When such a transition occurs, the memory of nonreward can become associated with the instrumental response and produce persistence during extinction. According to sequential theory, differences in association of the instrumental response with the memory of nonreward during PRF versus CRF training are assumed to be responsible for the partial reinforcement extinction effect.

Unlike sequential theory, **frustration theory**, which was developed by A. Amsel (1958, 1967, 1992), focuses on the emotional or frustrative effects of nonreward. The absence of reinforcement can be very upsetting. Consider, for example, losing money in a broken soft drink machine. We expect to get a soft drink when we put money in the machine and are therefore very annoyed if the machine malfunctions. As this example illustrates, nonreinforcement is especially upsetting when we anticipate being reinforced. Frustration theory considers persistence to be the result of learning to respond in the face of anticipated frustration. Such learning is produced by partial reinforcement training but not by continuous reinforcement. The nonreinforced trials that occur on a partial reinforcement schedule create the anticipation of frustration. Ordinarily, organisms are discouraged from responding when they anticipate being frustrated. But quitting does not make sense on a PRF schedule because if the organism quit responding it would miss the reinforcers that it could have obtained.

The occasional reinforcement that is available on a partial reinforcement schedule teaches organisms to keep going in the face of anticipated frustration. Thus, PRF training creates persistence by teaching organisms to continue to respond when they anticipate being frustrated.

Summary

Schedules of reinforcement are of interest because in many cases responding does not produce a reinforcer every time. A response may be reinforced after a fixed or variable number of responses have occurred (FR and VR schedules) or after a fixed or variable amount of time has passed since the last reinforcer (FI and VI schedules). Fixed but not variable schedules produce rapid responding just before delivery of the reinforcer and pauses just after reinforcement. In general, ratio schedules produce higher rates of responding than interval schedules, and this difference is related to the contrasting feedback functions for ratio and interval schedules.

Reinforcement may be also scheduled for a chain of responses or a choice of two or more activities. Response chains may consist of a series of components that involve the same type of activity (homogeneous chain) or a series of different activities (heterogeneous chain). A concurrent schedule is said to be in effect if reinforcement is available for two (or more) different activities at the same time. Responding on concurrent schedules tends to follow the Matching Law.

Schedules of reinforcement are also of interest because they determine the degree of response persistence that occurs in extinction, when reinforcement is no longer available. In general, partial or intermittent reinforcement leads to greater persistence in extinction than continuous reinforcement. Partial but not continuous reinforcement training promotes the learning of persistence mechanisms based on the memories and frustrative effects of nonreward.

Suggested Readings

AMSEL, A. (1992). *Frustration theory: An analysis of dispositional learning and memory.* Cambridge, England: Cambridge University Press.

BAUM, W. M. (1993). Performances on ratio and interval schedules of reinforcement: Data and theory. *Journal of the Experimental Analysis of Behavior, 59,* 245–264.

CAPALDI, E. J. (1971). Memory and learning: A sequential viewpoint. In W. K. Honig & P. H. R. James (Eds.), *Animal memory* (pp. 115–154). Orlando, FL: Academic Press.

FERSTER, C. B., & SKINNER, B. F. (1957). *Schedules of reinforcement.* New York: Appleton-Century-Crofts.

WILLIAMS, B. A. (1994). Reinforcement and choice. In N. J. Mackintosh (Ed.), *Animal learning and cognition* (pp. 81–108). San Diego: Academic Press.

Technical Terms

Backward chaining	Limited hold
Chained schedule	Matching Law
Concurrent schedule	Partial reinforcement
Cumulative record	extinction effect
Discrimination hypothesis	Persistence
Feedback function	Postreinforcement pause
Fixed-interval schedule	Ratio run
Fixed-ratio schedule	Ratio schedule
Frustration theory	Schedule of reinforcement
Heterogeneous chain	Sequential theory
Homogeneous chain	Variable-interval schedule
Interval schedule	Variable-ratio schedule

CHAPTER EIGHT

Theories of Reinforcement

DID YOU KNOW THAT:

- Reinforcers need not reduce a biological drive or need.
- Responses, not just stimuli, can serve as reinforcers.
- According to contemporary perspectives, reinforcement does not "strengthen" the instrumental response.
- Instrumental conditioning procedures not only increase the rate of the instrumental response but also decrease the rate of the reinforcer response.
- Instrumental conditioning procedures restrict how an organism distributes its behavior among its response alternatives.
- Reinforcement effects are a by-product of the new response choices an organism is forced to make when its activities are constrained by an instrumental conditioning procedure.

In Chapter 7, I discussed various types of instrumental conditioning procedures and their behavioral outcomes. There is no doubt that reinforcement procedures can produce dramatic changes in behavior. The issue I shall turn to next is how reinforcement causes these effects. That question is addressed by theories of reinforcement.

All good theories have to be consistent with the findings they are intended to explain. In addition, good theories should stimulate new research that serves to evaluate and increase the precision of the theory. Good theories also provide new insights and new ways of thinking about familiar phenomena.

The story of the development of theories of reinforcement is a marvelous example of creativity in science. The story is peppered with examples of small refinements in thinking that brought a particular theory in line with new data. The story also includes dramatic new departures and new ways of thinking about reinforcement. And there are interesting examples in which incremental changes in thinking culminated in major new perspectives on the problem.

A theory of reinforcement has to answer two questions about instrumental conditioning. The first question concerns the identity of reinforcers: What makes something a reinforcer, or how can we predict whether something will be an effective reinforcer? The second question concerns the mechanism of reinforcement effects: How does a reinforcer produce its effects, or how does a reinforcer produce an increase in the probability of the reinforced response?

Thorndike and the Law of Effect

The first systematic theory of reinforcement was provided by E. L. Thorndike, soon after his discovery of instrumental conditioning (Bower & Hilgard, 1981). According to Thorndike, a positive reinforcer is a stimulus that produces a "satisfying state of affairs." However, Thorndike did not go on to tell us why something was "satisfying." Therefore, his answer to our first question—"What makes something effective as a reinforcer?"—was not very illuminating.

One can determine whether a stimulus, such as a pat on the head for a dog, is a "satisfier" by seeing whether the dog increases a response that results in getting patted on the head. However, such evidence does not reveal why a pat on the head is a reinforcer. By calling reinforcers "satisfiers," Thorndike provided a label for reinforcers, but he did not give us an explanation for what makes something effective as a reinforcer.

Thorndike was a bit more forthcoming on the second question—"How does a reinforcer produce an increase in the probability of the reinforced response?" His answer was provided in the **Law of Effect**. As I noted in Chapter 6, according to the Law of Effect, a reinforcer establishes an association or

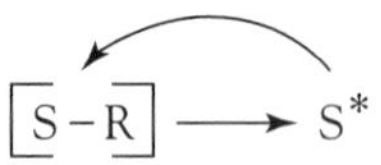

$$\boxed{S - R} \longrightarrow S^*$$

FIGURE 8.1 **Diagram of Thorndike's Law of Effect.**
The reinforcer S* acts retroactively to strengthen the S-R association.

---

connection between the instrumental response R and the stimuli S in the presence of which the response is performed. The reinforcer produces an S-R association (see Figure 8.1).

The Law of Effect explains how reinforcement increases the future probability of the instrumental response. Because of the S-R association that is established by reinforcement, stimulus S comes to produce the instrumental response R in much the same way that an elicited response is produced by its eliciting stimulus. The basic mechanism of the Law of Effect was considered a reasonable explanation for increased instrumental responding and was accepted by major behavioral theorists during the next 50 years. However, in hindsight, widespread acceptance of the Law of Effect is rather remarkable.

Although the Law of Effect predicts increased instrumental responding in the training environment, it does so by a bit of magic rather than by a well-established process. Thorndike did not say much about how a reinforcer after an instrumental response can act retroactively to strengthen an association between the response and the stimuli in the presence of which the response was made. That part of the Law of Effect had to be taken on faith. Furthermore, despite the widespread acceptance of the Law of Effect in the next 50 years, no one has filled the gap left by Thorndike. The mechanisms whereby a reinforcer acts backward in time to strengthen an S-R association remain to be specified.

In summary, Thorndike provided little more than a name in answer to the first question—"What makes something effective as a reinforcer?" His answer to the second question—"How does a reinforcer produce an increase in the probability of the reinforced response?"—was successful in that it accurately predicted the behavioral effect of reinforcement. But the answer was superficial because it simply stated that an S-R association was formed without specifying exactly how this came about.

Hull and Drive Reduction Theory

The next major theorist we will consider is Clark Hull. (For a review of Hullian theory, see Amsel & Rashotte, 1984.) Hull accepted the S-R mech-

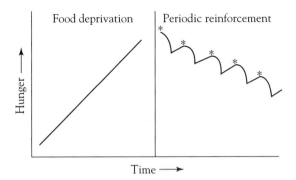

FIGURE 8.2 Illustration of the mechanisms of drive reduction reinforcement using hunger as an example.
Deliveries of the food reinforcer are indicated by asterisks.

anism of the Law of Effect and concentrated instead on the question that Thorndike had pretty much ignored, "What makes something effective as a reinforcer?" To answer this question, Hull made use of the concept of **homeostasis** that had been developed to explain the operation of physiological systems.

According to a homeostatic model, organisms defend a stable state with respect to certain biologically critical factors. Consider, for example, food intake (see Figure 8.2). For survival, organisms have to maintain a stable or optimal supply of nutrients. Food deprivation creates a challenge to the nutritional state of the organism. It creates a need for food. The psychological consequence of this is the motivational or drive state of hunger, which can be reduced by the ingestion of food. According to Hull, food is an effective reinforcer because it reduces the hunger drive. More generally, Hull proposed that what makes a stimulus reinforcing is its effectiveness in reducing a drive state. Hence, his theory is called the **drive reduction theory** of reinforcement.

PRIMARY REINFORCERS

Common laboratory examples of instrumental reinforcement are consistent with Hull's drive reduction theory. Mild food deprivation is routinely used to make food an effective instrumental reinforcer for rats and pigeons in laboratory situations. Similarly, mild water deprivation makes water an effective reinforcer. Rats will respond to obtain heat when they are in a cold environment, and they will respond to obtain cold air in a hot environment. Deprivation procedures and other circumstances that challenge a biological homeostatic system create drive states, and stimuli that reduce those drive states are effective reinforcers for instrumental behavior.

Hull's drive reduction theory provides a successful account of reinforcers such as food and water. Stimuli that are effective in reducing a biological need without prior training are called **primary reinforcers**. However, if Hull's theory could only characterize reinforcers that reduce primary biological drives, it would be rather limited. Many effective reinforcers do not satisfy a biological drive or need. You may find the smell of Italian food reinforcing, but the smell of food does not reduce hunger. A $20 bill also does not reduce a biological drive or need but is a highly effective reinforcer.

SECONDARY REINFORCERS AND ACQUIRED DRIVES

Hull's theory has been successfully extended to stimuli like the smell of food by adding the principle of Pavlovian conditioning. As one repeatedly eats spoonfuls of a particular food, the smell of that food becomes associated with the reduction of hunger through Pavlovian conditioning. That makes the food's aroma a **conditioned** (or **secondary**) **reinforcer**. The concept of conditioned reinforcers extended Hull's theory to stimuli that do not reduce a drive state directly but gain their reinforcing properties through association with a primary reinforcer.

Another way that Hull's theory has been extended beyond events that involve primary biological drives is through the concept of a conditioned drive state. Stimuli that become associated with a primary drive state are assumed to elicit a **conditioned** (or **acquired**) **drive**. Reduction of a conditioned or acquired drive is assumed to be reinforcing in the same manner as the reduction of a primary or biological drive state.

The concept of conditioned or acquired drive has been used most extensively in the analysis of aversively motivated behavior. You can lose your balance and fall on a moving escalator. If the fall is severe enough, you will become afraid of escalators. Such conditioned fear is an example of a conditioned or acquired drive. According to Hull's drive reduction theory, a reduction in the intensity of the acquired drive will be reinforcing. Therefore, any response that enables you to escape from the conditioned fear of escalators will be reinforced. Walking away from the escalator and using an elevator will be reinforced by reduction of the conditioned fear elicited by the escalator. (I will have more to say about fear conditioning in Chapter 10).

SENSORY REINFORCEMENT

Although Hull's theory was successfully extended to situations that do not involve primary biological drives, the theory has not been able to explain all instances of reinforcement. For example, investigators have found that rats kept in the dark will press a response lever to turn on a light, and rats kept in an illuminated chamber will press a response lever to produce periods of darkness. Chimpanzees have been found to perform instrumental responses that are reinforced by nothing more than the opportunity to watch an electric toy train move around a track. These are all examples of **sensory reinforcement**. In many situations, sensory stimulation with no apparent relation to a biological need or drive state can serve as an effective reinforcer (see Berlyne, 1969). Music, beautiful paintings, and other works of art are examples of sensory reinforcers for human beings.

The growing weight of evidence of sensory reinforcement, along with the success of alternative conceptualizations of reinforcement, led to abandonment of Hull's drive reduction theory. As we will see, the theories that emerged were highly creative and involved radical new ways of thinking about instrumental reinforcement.

Reinforcers as Responses

The modern era in reinforcement theory was ushered in by the work of David Premack, who considered reinforcement from an entirely different perspective than Hull. Like Hull, Premack considered situations like a rat pressing a response lever for food. However, instead of thinking about the reinforcer as a pellet of food, he thought about the reinforcer as the act of eating the food. For Premack, the question was not what made food a reinforcing stimulus, but what made eating a reinforcing response. Premack (1965) stated the issues of reinforcement in terms of responses, not in terms of stimuli.

THE PREMACK PRINCIPLE

What makes eating different from pressing a response lever in a standard Skinner box? Many answers are possible. The rat has to learn to press the lever but it does not have to learn to eat. Eating can occur not just in the Skinner box but anywhere the rat finds food. Eating involves a special set of muscles and activates digestive processes. Another difference is that a food deprived rat in a Skinner box is much more likely to eat than it is to press the lever if it is given free access to both activities. Premack focused on this last difference and elevated it to a general principle.

According to Premack, the critical precondition for reinforcement is not a drive state. Rather, it is the existence of two responses that differ in their likelihood of occurrence when the organism is given free access to both activities. Given two such responses, Premack proposed that the opportunity to perform the higher probability response will serve as a reinforcer for the lower probability response.

This general claim is known as the **Premack principle**. A more descriptive name for it is the **differential probability principle**. According to the differential probability principle, the specific nature of the instrumental and reinforcer responses does not matter. Neither of them has to involve eating or drinking, and the organism need not be hungry or thirsty. The only requirement is that one response be more likely than the other. Given such a differential response probability, the more likely response can serve as a reinforcer for the less likely response.

THE PREMACK REVOLUTION

The Premack principle took the scientific community by storm. It was a radical departure from previous ways of thinking about reinforcers. For the first time, scientists started thinking seriously about reinforcers as responses rather than as special stimuli. And, for the first time, the distinction between conditioned and unconditioned reinforcers became irrelevant.

For Hull, all reinforcers were ultimately related to unconditioned biological needs or drives. Secondary or conditioned reinforcers were effective only through association with primary reinforcers. In contrast, Premack was unconcerned with how one response might have come to be more likely than another. For him, the only thing that mattered was that the reinforcer response be more likely than the instrumental response.

The Premack principle was important because it liberated psychologists from the grip of stimulus views of reinforcement and views of reinforcement rooted in biological needs and drives. In addition, the Premack principle provided a convenient tool for the application of instrumental conditioning procedures in a variety of educational settings, including homes, classrooms, psychiatric hospitals, centers for the mentally retarded, and correctional institutions.

APPLICATIONS OF THE PREMACK PRINCIPLE

In all educational settings, students are encouraged to learn and perform new responses. The goal is to get the students to do things that they did not do before and things they would not do without special encouragement. In other words, the goal is to increase the likelihood of low-probability responses. Instrumental conditioning procedures are ideally suited to accomplish this task, but the teacher first has to find an effective reinforcer. Withholding a student's lunch so that food may be used as a reinforcer is not socially acceptable and would create a great deal of resentment. Candy and other food treats are effective reinforcers for young children without food deprivation but are not good for them nutritionally.

The Premack principle provides a way out of this dilemma (Homme, deBaca, Devine, Steinhorst, & Rickert, 1963). According to Premack, a reinforcer is any activity the participant is more likely to engage in than the instrumental response. Some students may like to watch television a lot; others may enjoy some time on the playground; still others may enjoy helping the teacher. Whatever the high-probability response may be, the

Premack principle suggests that one can take advantage of it in encouraging the student to engage in a less likely behavior. All one has to do is to provide access to the high-probability response only if the student first performs the lower-probability behavior (Charlop, Kurtz, & Casey, 1990).

Consider, for example, a mentally retarded student who enjoys playing on swings and is a messy eater, ending up with food all over his clothes after each meal. The goal is to teach this student to eat more carefully. The Premack principle suggests that an effective instrumental conditioning procedure could be set up in which eating neatly is reinforced by the opportunity to play on a swing after the meal.

The Premack principle facilitated the application of instrumental conditioning to a variety of educational settings. It enabled teachers to use a variety of activities rather than food items as reinforcers, and it encouraged taking advantage of each student's unique set of preferred activities. In this way, training procedures could be tailor-made to fit a student's unique likes and dislikes.

THEORETICAL PROBLEMS

The Premack principle continues to be used in educational settings. However, it has been superseded by other concepts in theoretical analyses of reinforcement. The differential response probability principle has two major shortcomings. One problem is the measurement or calculation of response probabilities. We all have an intuitive sense of what it means to say that one response is more likely than another, but assigning a precise numerical value to the probability of a response can be difficult. Furthermore, the likelihood of a given response may change unexpectedly. A youngster may enjoy swimming one morning but not later in the day.

There is no satisfactory solution to the theoretical problems posed by the fact that response probabilities fluctuate and are difficult to measure. However there are ways to get around such problems in practical applications of the Premack principle. For example, a system can be set up in which students are given points for performing the target instrumental response correctly. The students could then be permitted to exchange their points for various response opportunities (watching television, reading a comic book, going out to the playground, getting some crayons and paper, etc.) depending on what they wanted to do at the moment. Such systems are called **token economies** and have been instituted in a variety of behavioral settings (Kazdin, 1985). If a wide enough range of reinforcer activities are provided, one does not have to obtain precise measurements of the probability of each reinforcer response or worry about fluctuations in reinforcer preferences.

The second major theoretical problem of the Premack principle is that it is just a formula or rule for finding reinforcers. It does not tell us how reinforcers work. It answers our first question—"What makes something effective as a reinforcer?"—but it does not answer our second question—"How does a reinforcer produce an increase in the probability of the reinforced response?"

The Response Deprivation Hypothesis

The next major development in theories of reinforcement was the **response deprivation hypothesis**, proposed by Timberlake and Allison (1974). The response deprivation hypothesis was designed to solve some of the theoretical problems that were left unresolved by the Premack principle.

Timberlake and Allison followed in Premack's footsteps in thinking about reinforcers as responses rather than as stimuli, and their starting point was also to think about the difference between an instrumental response and a reinforcer response. However, their consideration of this question led them down a different path. Timberlake and Allison suggested that the critical difference between instrumental and reinforcer responses is that the participant has free access to the instrumental response but is restricted in performing the reinforcer response.

In a typical Skinner box, for example, the rat can press the response lever any time, but it is not at liberty to eat pellets of food any time. Eating can occur only after the rat has pressed the lever, and even then the rat can only eat the small portion of food that is provided. Timberlake and Allison suggested that these restrictions on the reinforcer response are what makes eating an effective reinforcer. In their view, instrumental conditioning situations deprive the participant from free access to the reinforcer response. That is why the Timberlake-Allison proposal is called the response deprivation hypothesis.

RESPONSE DEPRIVATION AND THE LAW OF EFFECT

The response deprivation hypothesis captures an important idea. The idea is obvious if one considers what would happen if there were no restriction on eating for a rat in a Skinner box. Imagine a situation in which the rat receives a week's supply of food each time it presses the response lever. According to Thorndike's Law of Effect, a week's worth of food should be a highly satisfying state of affairs; therefore, it should result in a strong S-R bond and should produce a large increase in lever-pressing. But that hardly seems sensible from the rat's point of view. A more sensible prediction is that if the rat received a week's supply of food for each lever-press, it would press the response lever about once a week, when its food supply was depleted.

According to the response deprivation hypothesis, what makes food an effective reinforcer is not that food satisfies hunger or that eating is a high-probability response. Rather, the critical factor is that an instrumental conditioning procedure places a restriction on eating. It is this response deprivation that makes eating reinforcing. If the response deprivation is removed (by providing a week's supply of food), instrumental responding will not increase; the instrumental response will not be reinforced.

RESPONSE DEPRIVATION AND RESPONSE PROBABILITY

Notice that the response deprivation hypothesis does not require computing response probabilities. Thus, the response deprivation hypothesis avoids the computational problem that undermined the Premack principle. To apply response deprivation, one just has to determine the rate of a response during a baseline period in the absence of any restrictions and then limit access to the reinforcer response below the baseline level.

An interesting prediction of the response deprivation hypothesis is that even a low-probability response can be made into a reinforcing event. According to the response deprivation hypothesis, the opportunity to perform a low-probability response can be used to reinforce a higher probability behavior if access to the low probability response is restricted below its already low baseline rate. Such a prediction is contrary to the Premack principle but has been confirmed by experimental evidence (Allison & Timberlake, 1974; Eisenberger, Karpman, & Trattner, 1967).

RESPONSE DEPRIVATION AND THE LOCUS OF REINFORCEMENT EFFECTS

In addition to avoiding the problems involved in computing response probabilities, the response deprivation hypothesis shifted the locus of the explanation of reinforcement. In earlier theories, reinforcement was explained in terms of factors that were outside the instrumental conditioning procedure itself. With drive reduction theory, the external factor involved procedures that established a drive state. With the Premack principle, the external factor involved the differential baseline probabilities of the reinforcer and instrumental responses. In contrast, with the response deprivation hypothesis, the locus of reinforcement rests with how the instrumental conditioning procedure constrains the organism's activities. This is a new idea. Never before had someone suggested that reinforcement effects are determined by the response restrictions that are inherently involved in all instrumental conditioning procedures.

The response deprivation hypothesis moved our understanding of reinforcement forward in that it avoided some of the problems of the Premack principle. However, as was true of the Premack principle, the response deprivation hypothesis only provided an answer to our first question—"What makes something effective as a reinforcer?" The answer to our second major question—"How does a reinforcer produce an increase in the probability of the reinforced response?"—had to await development of the behavioral regulation approach.

The Behavioral Regulation Approach

In many ways the **behavioral regulation** approach is similar to the response deprivation hypothesis. Like its predecessor, the behavioral regulation approach rejects the assumption that reinforcers are special kinds of stimuli or special kinds of responses. In addition, the behavioral regulation approach accepts that reinforcement effects are determined by how an instrumental conditioning procedure restricts an organism's activities. In fact, the behavioral regulation approach builds on this idea in its answer to the second question about reinforcement—"How does a reinforcer produce an increase in the probability of the reinforced response?" (Allison, 1989; Timberlake, 1980, 1984).

The behavioral regulation approach borrowed the concept of homeostasis from physiology and drive reduction theory and extended it to response choice. Behavioral homeostasis is analogous to physiological homeostasis in that both involve defending the optimal or preferred level of a system. Physiological homeostatic mechanisms exist to maintain physiological parameters (blood levels of oxygen and glucose, for example) close to an optimal or ideal level. The homeostatic level is "defended" in the sense that deviations from the target blood levels of oxygen or glucose trigger compensatory physiological mechanisms that return the systems to their respective homeostatic levels.

THE BEHAVIORAL BLISS POINT

In behavioral regulation, what is defended is the organism's preferred distribution of activities, its **behavioral bliss point**. The behavioral bliss point refers to how an organism distributes its activities among available response options in the absence of procedural restrictions. The bliss point is the participant's preferred response choices before an instrumental conditioning procedure is imposed.

Consider, for example, a teenager named Kim. Left to her own devices, during the course of a 24-hour day, Kim might spend 3 hours a day talking to friends on the telephone, 1.5 hours eating, 4 hours driving around, 10 hours sleeping, 2 hours watching television, 3 hours listening to music, and a half hour doing school work. This distribution of activities would constitute the behavioral bliss point for Kim. Notice that at the bliss point, Kim devotes only half an hour each day to doing school work.

IMPOSING AN INSTRUMENTAL CONTINGENCY

Kim's parents may want to introduce an instrumental conditioning procedure to increase the amount of time Kim devotes to school work. They could do this by restricting her access to music. For example, they could require that Kim spend a minute doing school work for every minute that she gets to listen to music.

Before the instrumental contingency, listening to music and doing homework were independent activities for Kim. How much time she spent on one activity had little to do with how much time she spent on the other. This characterized the bliss point. The behavioral bliss point for listening to music and studying is illustrated in the upper left quadrant of Figure 8.3.

Requiring Kim to spend a minute on homework for every minute of music listening ties the two activities together in a special way. Now time spent on homework has to equal time spent on music. This relationship is illustrated by the 45° line in Figure 8.3. This is also called the **schedule line**. With the instrumental conditioning procedure in effect, studying is no longer independent of listening to music. The two activities are tied together and restricted to the schedule line.

The contingency between studying and listening to music illustrated by the schedule line in Figure 8.3 restricts Kim's behavior so that she can no longer distribute her responses as she did at the behavioral bliss point. The schedule line does not go through the behavioral bliss point. Because of that, the instrumental contingency is a challenge to the behavioral bliss point, analogous to how a drive state is a challenge to physiological homeostasis.

The behavioral regulation approach is similar to physiological homeostatic models in that deviations from the preferred level are assumed to trigger mechanisms of adjustment that move the system back toward the preferred level. In the case of behavioral regulation, these mechanisms of adjustment involve moving the participant's response choices or her distribution of activities back toward the behavioral bliss point.

Once the instrumental conditioning procedure has been put into effect for Kim (one minute of music listening for one minute of school work), she can never get all the way back to her preferred response allocation. Every possible route for returning to the behavioral bliss point involves some cost or disadvantage. If Kim elects to listen to music for as long as she would like (ideally 3 hours a day), she would have to do much more school work than she likes. On the other hand, if she spent as little time doing school work as she prefers (half hour a day), she would have to settle for much less music than she likes.

Instrumental conditioning procedures constrain response options. They disrupt the free flow of behavior and interfere with how an organism selects among its available response alternatives. Furthermore, most cases are like Kim's in that the instrumental conditioning procedure does not allow the participant to return to the behavioral bliss point. The best that can be achieved is to approach the bliss point under the constraints of the instrumental conditioning procedure.

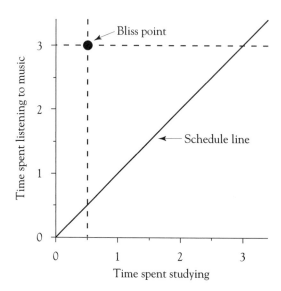

FIGURE 8.3   Illustration of the behavioral regulation approach to instrumental conditioning.

The bliss point represents how much time a person spends studying and listening to music in the absence of an instrumental conditioning procedure or schedule constraint. The schedule line represents how much time the person can devote to each activity when she is required to spend one minute studying for each minute spent listening to music.

RESPONDING TO SCHEDULE CONSTRAINTS

How an organism goes about moving back toward its behavioral bliss point after an instrumental contingency has been imposed depends on the costs and benefits of various strategies. If doing school work is much more unpleasant for Kim than the potential loss of music listening time, then she will not increase her school work much but will give up time spent listening to music. In contrast, if the potential loss of music time is much more aversive for Kim than increased effort devoted to school work, she will adjust to the constraint imposed by the instrumental conditioning procedure by substantially increasing her time doing school work.

A particularly important factor determining how an individual responds to schedule constraints is the availability of substitutes for the reinforcer activity (Green & Freed, 1993). Instrumental conditioning procedures are powerful if no substitutes are available for the reinforcer activity. However, if the participant has something that it can substitute for the reinforcer, restricting access to the reinforcer will not increase instrumental responding.

If Kim loves music and cannot derive the same satisfaction from any other type of activity (if Kim has no substitute for music), music will be a very powerful reinforcer. In this case, Kim will adjust to the instrumental procedure with a large increase in schoolwork. Quite a different outcome would occur if Kim did not like music any more than watching television. If watching television were a good substitute for listening to music, the instrumental contingency would have little effect on how much schoolwork Kim did In this case, she would respond to the schedule constraint by substituting watching television in place of listening to music, without any increase in time spent on school work.

CONTRIBUTIONS OF BEHAVIORAL REGULATION

The behavioral regulation approach has advanced our understanding of instrumental behavior because it has encouraged thinking about instrumental conditioning and reinforcement within the context of the participant's entire behavioral repertoire. Behavioral regulation focuses attention on the fact that instrumental conditioning procedures do not operate in a behavioral vacuum. Rather, instrumental conditioning procedures disrupt the free flow of behavior; they disrupt how the participant allocates its behavior among available response options. Behavioral regulation also focuses attention on the fact that constraints on response choices can have effects not only on the instrumental and the reinforcer responses. Schedule constraints can also result in changes in related or substitutable responses that are not directly a part of the instrumental procedure.

The behavioral regulation approach encourages us to think about instrumental behavior from a broader perspective than we did with previous conceptualizations. It encourages us to consider all of the activities of a participant, how those activities are organized, and how that organization determines the effects of schedule constraints. These ideas are a far cry from the more limited stimulus-response perspective that dominated earlier theories of reinforcement.

Summary

A theory of reinforcement has to tell us: (1) what makes something a reinforcer and (2) how a reinforcer produces its effects. Early theories assumed that reinforcers were special types of stimuli. According to the most influential of these theories, a stimulus will be reinforcing if it is effective in reducing a drive state. Drive reduction theory was prominent for several decades but ran into some difficulties (it could not explain sensory reinforcement, for example) and was supplanted by response views of reinforcement. A prominent response view was Premack's differential response probability principle. According to this principle, a reinforcer is not a drive-reducing stimulus but is the opportunity to make a response that has a higher baseline probability than the baseline probability of the instrumental response.

The Premack principle formed the basis of numerous applications of reinforcement in clinical and educational settings. However, difficulties with measuring response probabilities stimulated the next theoretical development, the response deprivation hypothesis. According to this hypothesis, the opportunity to perform a response will be an effective reinforcer if the instrumental conditioning procedure restricts access to that activity below its baseline rate. The response deprivation hypothesis shifted the focus of attention from reinforcers as special stimuli or responses to how an instrumental conditioning procedure constrains the organism's activities. This idea was developed further in the behavioral regulation approach.

According to the behavioral regulation approach, organisms have a preferred or optimal distribution of activities in any given situation. The introduction of an instrumental conditioning procedure disrupts this optimal response distribution or behavioral bliss point. Typically, the adjustment to the disruption is that the rate of the instrumental response increases whereas the rate of the reinforcer response decreases. The extent of this response reallocation is governed by the schedule of reinforcement imposed and the availability of substitutes for the reinforcer response.

Suggested Readings

ALLISON, J. (1983). *Behavioral economics*. New York: Praeger.
PREMACK, D. (1965). Reinforcement theory. In D. Levine (Ed.), *Nebraska symposium on motivation* (Vol. 13, pp. 123–180). Lincoln: University of Nebraska Press.
TIERNEY, K. J. (1995). Molar regulatory theory and behavior therapy. In W. O'Donohue and L. Krasner (Eds.), *Theories of behavior therapy* (pp. 97–128). Washington, DC: American Psychological Association.
TIMBERLAKE, W., & FARMER-DOUGAN, V. A. (1991). Reinforcement in applied settings: Figuring out ahead of time what will work. *Psychological Bulletin, 110*, 379–391.

Technical Terms

Acquired drive
Behavioral bliss point
Behavioral regulation
Conditioned drive
Conditioned reinforcer
Differential probability principle
Drive reduction theory
Homeostasis

Law of Effect
Premack principle
Primary reinforcer
Response deprivation hypothesis
Schedule line
Secondary reinforcer
Sensory reinforcement
Token economy

CHAPTER NINE

Punishment

DID YOU KNOW THAT:

- Punishment does not have to involve physical pain.

- When properly applied, punishment can produce permanent suppression of behavior in a single trial.

- The effectiveness of punishment is substantially reduced by delivering punishment intermittently or with a delay.

- Mild punishment for an initial offense may immunize the individual to further punishment.

- Severe punishment for an initial offense may sensitize the individual to further punishment.

- The effectiveness of punishment is greatly increased by positive reinforcement of alternative behavior.

- Punishment facilitates responding if it signals positive reinforcement or if the punished response is a form of escape behavior.

- When one person punishes another out of anger or frustration, the parameters of effective punishment are usually violated, and no constructive changes in behavior are produced.

- The successful application of response-suppression procedures requires considering not only the undesired response but also the individual's other activities and sources of reinforcement.

In discussing instrumental conditioning up to this point, I relied primarily on examples of positive reinforcement—examples in which the instrumental response results in the delivery of an appetitive, or "pleasant," event. It is common knowledge that instrumental behavior can be also controlled by aversive, or "unpleasant," events. Perhaps the simplest aversive control procedure is **punishment**. In a punishment procedure, an aversive event is delivered contingent on the performance of an instrumental response. The expected or typical outcome is suppression of the punished behavior. However, the degree of response suppression depends on numerous factors, many of which are not intuitively obvious.

Punishment is the most controversial topic in conditioning and learning. It conjures up visions of cruelty and abuse, and it is the only conditioning procedure whose application is regulated by law. However, punishment need not involve unusual forms of physical cruelty or pain. A variety of aversive events has been effectively used for punishment, including verbal reprimands, monetary fines, placement in a time-out corner or a time-out room, loss of earned privileges or positive reinforcers, demerits, various restitution procedures, and even water mist or a squirt of lemon juice in the mouth. Electric shock is rarely used as a punisher with people, but it is common in animal research because its intensity and duration can be controlled more precisely than with other types of aversive events.

The stage for the punishment debate was set by Thorndike early in the twentieth century. Thorndike (1932) claimed that punishment is an ineffective procedure for producing significant and lasting changes in behavior and therefore should not be used. Based on his own studies, Skinner (1953) adopted a similar point of view. He argued that we should make every effort to eliminate the use of punishment in society because punishment is cruel and ineffective. Whether punishment is cruel cannot be decided by empirical evidence. However, the other aspect of the argument—that punishment is ineffective—can be tested experimentally. Contrary to the early claims of Thorndike and Skinner, such tests have indicated that punishment can be very effective in suppressing behavior, provided the punishment is properly applied.

Effective and Ineffective Punishment

Casual observation suggests that Thorndike's and Skinner's claims that punishment is ineffective may be correct. Violations of traffic laws are punished by fines and other unpleasant consequences. Nevertheless, we often see people driving through red lights and driving faster than the posted speed limit. Students scolded by a teacher for not having their homework completed do not necessarily finish their next assignment on time. A drug dealer apprehended for selling cocaine or heroin is likely to return to selling drugs once he is released from jail.

In contrast to these examples, sometimes punishment is remarkably effective. A child who accidentally gets shocked while playing with an electric outlet is unlikely to poke his fingers into the outlet ever again. A person who falls and hurts herself rushing down a slippery staircase will slow down next time she has to negotiate those stairs. Someone who tips over a canoe by leaning too far to one side the first time out will be much more careful about staying in the middle of the canoe after that.

Why is punishment highly effective in suppressing behavior in some cases and ineffective in other instances? Let us first consider the cases in which punishment fails.

WHEN PUNISHMENT FAILS

Why do drivers often exceed the speed limit even though speeding can result in a fine? Punishment in the enforcement of traffic laws is similar to punishment in much of the criminal justice system and in many social situations. In all of these cases, punishment is administered by an individual rather than as an automatic environmental consequence of a response. A police officer has to detect whether a driver is going too fast, and an officer of the court has to judge the severity of the offense and decide on what penalty to apply. Requiring people to detect the punished response and administer the aversive stimulus can make punishment ineffective for a variety of reasons.

One consequence of requiring a police officer to detect speeders is that drivers are not caught every time they exceed the speed limit. In fact, the chances of getting caught are pretty slim. A driver may exceed the speed limit 50 times or more undetected for each time his speed is recorded by a patrol officer. Thus, *punishment is highly intermittent.*

On the rare occasion that a driver is detected speeding, chances are that he is not detected right away but only after he has been going too fast for some time. Therefore, *punishment is delayed* after the initiation of the behavior targeted for punishment. Further delays in punishment occur because typically fines do not have to be paid right away. Fines also can be appealed, and an appeal may take several months.

If the appeal is unsuccessful, punishment for the first offense is likely to be fairly mild. The driver will probably just have to pay a fine. More severe penalties are imposed only if the driver is repeatedly ticketed for speeding. Thus, *punishment is initially mild and is increased in severely only after repeated offenses.* This kind of gradual escalation of the severity of punishment is a fundamental aspect of societal uses of punishment. Someone who does something undesirable is first given a warning and a second chance. We get serious about punishing him only after repeated offenses.

Another reason punishment is not effective in discouraging speeding is that drivers can often tell when they are about to be clocked by a patrol officer. In some cities, the location of radar check points is announced on the radio each morning. The presence of traffic police is also obvious from the distinctive markings of patrol cars. Many drivers have radar detectors in their cars that signal the presence of a radar patrol. Patrol cars and radar detectors provide discriminative stimuli for punishment. Thus, *punishment is often signaled by a discriminative stimulus.*

WHEN PUNISHMENT SUCCEEDS

Compared to the ineffectiveness of punishment in discouraging speeding, why does punishment work well in discouraging a child from poking his fingers into an electric outlet? A child shocked while playing with an electric outlet is unlikely to ever do that again and may develop a strong fear of outlets. What are the critical differences in the punishment contingencies involved in driving too fast and playing with an electric outlet?

First, *punishment occurs consistently* for sticking your fingers into an electric outlet. Every time you do that, you will get shocked. If you touch an outlet and come in contact with the electrodes, you are sure to get shocked. The physical configuration of the outlet guarantees that punishment is delivered every time.

Second, *punishment is immediate.* As soon as you make contact with the electrodes, you get shocked. There is no elaborate detection or decision process involved to delay delivery of the aversive stimulus.

Third, *punishment is intense for the first transgression.* The outlet does not give you a warning the first time you touch the electrodes. The first offense is treated the same way as the tenth one. Each time you make the response, you get an intense shock.

Finally, punishment is not limited to times when a police officer or observer is watching. Thus, *punishment is not signaled* by a discriminative stimulus. No matter who is present in the room, sticking your fingers in the outlet will get you shocked. Severe and immediate punishment is always in effect for each occurrence of the target response.

Characteristics of effective and ineffective punishment are listed in Table 9.1.

Research Evidence on Punishment

All of the factors that characterize the punishment for touching the electrodes in an electric outlet have been found to be important in carefully conducted experimental work. In addition, research has identified several additional factors that strongly determine the effectiveness of punishment. Ironically, much of the research was done under the leadership of one of Skinner's former students, Nathan Azrin (Azrin & Holz, 1966). Complementary studies were performed in a research program conducted by Church

TABLE 9.1   Characteristics of Punishment

For Driving too Fast	For Poking Fingers into an Electric Outlet
Occurs intermittently	Occurs every time
Delayed	Immediate
Low intensity aversive stimulus at first	High intensity aversive stimulus every time
Signaled by a discriminative stimulus	Not signaled

(1969). Azrin used pigeons for much of his research, whereas Church used laboratory rats. Contrary to the early claims of Thorndike and Skinner, these experiments demonstrated that punishment can be a highly effective technique for producing rapid and long-term changes in behavior.

RESPONSE-REINFORCER CONTINGENCY

Punishment is similar to positive reinforcement in that it involves a positive contingency between the instrumental response and the reinforcer. The reinforcer is delivered only if the organism previously performed the target response. The primary difference between punishment and positive reinforcement is that in punishment the reinforcer is an aversive stimulus.

As with other instrumental conditioning procedures, a fundamental variable in punishment is the response-reinforcer contingency. This refers to the extent to which delivery of the aversive stimulus depends on the prior occurrence of the target response. If an aversive stimulus is administered independently of the target response, the procedure is a form of Pavlovian aversive conditioning rather than punishment. As we saw in Chapter 4, Pavlovian aversive conditioning results in the conditioning of fear, and this is evident in freezing or the general suppression of ongoing behavior.

Some general suppression of ongoing behavior can result from punishment procedures as well. However, punishment also produces behavioral suppression specific to the target response (Camp, Raymond, & Church, 1967; Goodall, 1984). The specificity of the behavioral suppression depends on the contingency between the target response and the aversive reinforcer. The stronger the response-reinforcer contingency, the more specific the response suppression produced by punishment.

RESPONSE-REINFORCER CONTIGUITY

As I previously described for positive reinforcement, the response-reinforcer contingency is just one aspect of the relation between an instrumental response and a reinforcer. Another important factor is the interval between the target response and delivery of the reinforcer. In a punishment procedure, this is the interval between the target response and the aversive consequence.

Response-reinforcer contiguity is just as important with punishment as it is with positive reinforcement. Punishment is most effective if the aversive stimulus is presented without delay after the target response (Camp et al., 1967). If punishment is delayed after the target response, some suppression of behavior may occur. However, the response suppression will not be specific to the punished response.

INTENSITY OF THE AVERSIVE STIMULUS

As one might suspect, the response-suppressing effects of punishment are directly related to the intensity of the aversive stimulus. Low intensities of punishment produce only mild suppression of behavior. In contrast, dramatic suppressions of behavior can result from the use of intense aversive stimuli (Azrin, 1960). More importantly, the effects of the intensity of punishment depend largely on the participant's prior experience with punishment. In general, individuals tend to respond to a new level of punishment similarly to how they responded during earlier encounters with punishment.

The historical effects of exposure to punishment can lead to somewhat unexpected results. Consider, for example, individuals who are initially exposed to a low intensity of punishment. Weak aversive stimuli produce only mild, if any, suppression of responding. Animals exposed to low-intensity punishment learn to continue to respond with little disruption in their behavior. Furthermore, their persistent responding in the face of mild punishment generalizes to higher intensities of aversive stimulation (Azrin, Holz, & Hake, 1963; Miller, 1960). As a result, the animals continue to respond when the intensity of punishment is increased. In a sense, exposure to mild aversive stimulation serves to immunize individuals against the effects of more intense punishment (see Figure 9.1).

Interestingly, a history of exposure to intense punishment can have just the opposite effect. Initial exposure to intense punishment can increase the impact of subsequent mild punishment (see Figure 9.2). High-intensity aversive stimulation produces dramatic suppression of the punished response, and this severe suppression of responding persists when the intensity of the aversive stimulus is subsequently reduced (Church, 1969). Thus, mild punishment produces much more severe suppression of behavior in individuals who previously received intense punishment than in individuals that were not punished previously. Exposure to intense punishment sensitizes the participant to subsequent mild aversive stimulation.

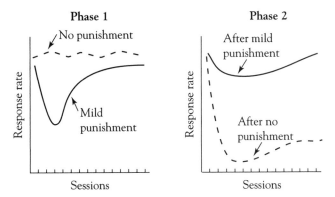

FIGURE 9.1   Immunizing effects of prior experience with mild punishment.
During Phase 1, one group of subjects is exposed to mild punishment while another group is permitted to respond without punishment. During Phase 2, both groups receive intense punishment. (Note: Data are hypothetical.)

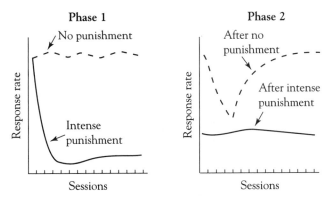

FIGURE 9.2   Sensitizing effects of experience with intense punishment.
During Phase 1, one group of subjects is exposed to intense punishment while another group is permitted to respond without punishment. During Phase 2, both groups receive mild punishment. (Note: Data are hypothetical.)

SIGNALED PUNISHMENT

Some punishment contingencies are always in effect. However, more commonly (particularly in the case of punishment administered by a teacher or patrol officer), the punishment contingency is only in effect in the presence of particular stimuli. If punishment is signaled by a distinctive stimulus, the procedure is called **discriminative punishment**. A child, for example, may be reprimanded for running through the living room when her parents are home but not when her grandparents are in charge. In this case, punishment would be signaled by cues associated with the presence of the child's parents. The parents would be discriminative stimuli for punishment.

As you might suspect, a child reprimanded by her parents but not by her grandparents will avoid running through the living room when her parents are home but will not show such restraint when the grandparents are in charge. Discriminative punishment procedures result in discriminative suppression of behavior (Dinsmoor, 1952). Responding becomes suppressed in the presence of the discriminative stimulus but continues unabated when the discriminative stimulus is absent.

Discriminative control of a punished response can be problematic. A parent may try to get a child not to use foul language by punishing her whenever she curses. This may discourage the child from cursing in the presence of the parent but will not stop her from cursing around her friends. The suppression of foul language will be under discriminative control and the parent's goal will not be achieved.

In other cases, discriminative punishment is not problematic. If a child starts talking loudly during a religious service, he is likely to be reprimanded. If the punishment procedure is effective, the child will cease talking during the service, but this will not stop him from talking boisterously elsewhere. Having the response suppressed only under the discriminative stimulus control of the church service is not a problem.

PUNISHMENT AND MECHANISMS MAINTAINING THE PUNISHED RESPONSE

Punishment procedures are applied to responses that already occur for one reason or another. Typically, punished responses are maintained by some form of positive reinforcement. This turns out to be very important because the effects of punishment depend on the type of reinforcement and schedule of reinforcement that supports the target response.

A child may talk during a church service to attract attention or to enjoy the camaraderie that comes from talking with a friend. If the child is reprimanded for talking, the aversiveness of the reprimand is pitted against the enjoyment of the attention and camaraderie. The outcome of the punishment procedure depends on how the individual solves this cost-benefit problem. In general, punishment will be less effective if the target response is reinforced often than if the target response is reinforced only once in a while (Church & Raymond, 1967).

The outcome of punishment also depends on the particular schedule of positive reinforcement that maintains the target response. With variable- and fixed-interval schedules, punishment reduces the overall level of responding but does not change the temporal distribution of behavior (e.g., Azrin & Holz, 1961). In contrast, if the instrumental response is maintained on a fixed ratio schedule of reinforcement, punishment tends to increase the postreinforcement pause (Azrin, 1959; Dardano & Sauerbrunn, 1964).

PUNISHMENT AND REINFORCEMENT OF ALTERNATIVE BEHAVIOR

As we saw in the preceding section, the outcome of punishment procedures can be analyzed in terms of the relative costs and benefits of performing the target response. This cost-benefit analysis involves not only the punished response but also other activities the individual may perform. A powerful technique for increasing the effects of punishment is to provide positive reinforcement for some other behavior (Perry & Parke, 1975). Effective parents are well aware of this principle. Punishing children on a long car ride for quarreling among themselves is relatively ineffective if the children are not given much else to do. Punishment of quarreling is much more effective if it is accompanied by an alternative reinforced activity, such as listening to a story or playing with a new toy.

PARADOXICAL EFFECTS OF PUNISHMENT

The factors described so far determine the extent to which punishment will suppress the target response. Punishment will not be very effective if the punished response is maintained by a powerful schedule of positive reinforcement, if there is no positive reinforcement for alternative behavior, and if the punishment is mild, delayed, and involves a weak response-reinforcer contingency. Weak punishment parameters make punishment ineffective. Under some circumstances, punishment can even produce the opposite of what is intended—facilitation rather than suppression of responding.

Punishment as a signal for positive reinforcement.   Paradoxical facilitation of responding can occur when punishment serves as a signal for positive reinforcement (Holz & Azrin, 1961). Attention, for example, is a powerful source of reinforcement for children. A child may be ignored by his parents most of the time as long as he is not doing anything dangerous or disruptive. If he starts playing with matches, he is severely reprimanded and sent to his room. Will punishment suppress the target response in this case? Not likely. Notice that the child receives attention from his parents only after he does something bad and is being punished. Under these circumstances, punishment can become a signal for positive reinforcement, with the outcome that the child will seek out punishment as a way of obtaining attention.

Punishment of escape behavior.   Paradoxical effects can also occur if punishment is applied to an escape response. An escape response serves to terminate an aversive stimulus. The termination or removal of an aversive stimulus is called escape or **negative reinforcement**. (I will have more to say about negative reinforcement in Chapter 10).

Negative reinforcement is a bit unusual because before an organism can escape from an aversive stimulus, the aversive stimulus has to be presented or turned on. Therefore, a negatively reinforced escape response is performed in the presence of an aversive stimulus (see Figure 9.3). That makes the presence of the aversive stimulus a discriminative cue for the escape response.

Punishment of an escape response facilitates rather than suppresses responding (e.g., Dean & Pittman, 1991). This paradoxical effect often occurs because the aversive stimulus used to punish the response preserves the conditions that motivated the behavior in the first place. Hence, the escape response persists even though it is being punished.

Paradoxical effects of punishment are not common, and they should not encourage us to jump to the conclusion that punishment produces unpredictable results. Rather, if a paradoxical effect of punishment is observed, one should examine the situation carefully to determine whether punishment had come to serve as a signal for positive reinforcement. If that does not seem likely, perhaps the target response was previously reinforced as an escape response.

Can and Should We Create a Society Free of Punishment?

As I noted at the outset, both Thorndike and Skinner advocated that punishment not be used because they regarded punishment as ineffective in producing significant and lasting changes in behavior. Their recommendation was fine, but their reasoning was wrong. Research has shown that punishment can be highly effective in decreasing undesired behavior. Does this mean that we should go ahead and use punishment whenever we are interested in discouraging some activity? Or should we work to try to build a society entirely free of punishment? Answers to these questions depend in part on what one considers to be just and ethical human conduct. Ethical issues are outside the scope of this discussion. We can, however, consider how empirical evidence about the effectiveness of punishment may inform the decisions we make about societal uses of punishment.

First, can we create a punishment-free society? Unlikely. Punishment is an inevitable consequence of various aspects of the physical and biological environment. If you mishandle a cat, the cat will scratch you. If you don't hold your glass steady as you pour from a pitcher, you will spill and get your clothes wet. If you lift a pot out of the oven without a pot holder, you will burn yourself. It would be impossible to redesign our environment so as to eliminate all sources of punishment.

Given that punishment cannot be eliminated entirely, what kinds of punishment should we try to get rid of, and would doing that be sensible? The kind of punishment that people in our culture find most objectionable

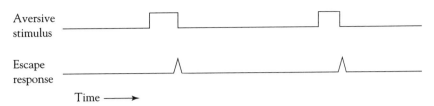

FIGURE 9.3   **Diagram of an escape or negative reinforcement procedure.**
The escape response occurs during the aversive stimulus and results in termination
of the aversive stimulus.

---

is physical pain inflicted by one person in an effort to suppress an undesired
response on the part of someone else. We have laws against the use of cor-
poral punishment in schools. We also have laws against child abuse and
spousal abuse in the home. Such laws are justified on moral and ethical
grounds. Do such laws also make sense from the perspective of empirical
principles of punishment? I think so.

Interpersonal interactions involving punishment require one individual
to inflict pain on another. An important factor is the willingness of the person administering the punishment to hurt the recipient. A parent may
claim to be punishing a child for having received a poor grade in school,
and a husband may say that he is punishing his wife for getting home late.
However, whether or not the punishment takes place is often related to the
emotional state of the person who administers the punishment. People are
likely to administer punishment if they are frustrated and angry, and under
those circumstances, effective principles of punishment are probably far-
thest from their mind.

If punishment is administered out of frustration and anger, it is not
likely to be closely related to an undesired response. A poor grade on a
school assignment will not aggravate a parent every time. Therefore, the
punishment is likely to be intermittent. Frustrative punishment is also likely
to occur some time after the target response has taken place. A parent may
become abusive when a child brings home a poor report card, even though
the responses that contributed to the poor grades occurred over a period of
weeks earlier.

Frustrative punishment is also often under discriminative stimulus control, and the discriminative stimulus is unrelated to the punished behavior.
A parent may become upset by a poor report card when his or her emotional
resources are strained by events entirely unrelated to the child's behavior.
The parent may be irritable because of stresses at work, ill health, or drug
abuse. Under these circumstances, the likelihood of punishment will be signaled by the parent's irritability, and the child will learn that she can get her
report card signed without being punished if she just waits until the next
day or the weekend.

Another shortcoming of frustrative punishment is that it is rarely accompanied by positive reinforcement of alternative behavior. When a parent punishes a child out of irritability and anger, the parent is not likely to have the presence of mind to accompany the punishment with a programmatic effort to provide positive reinforcement for more constructive activities.

Punishment as an act of aggression and frustration violates many of the parameters of effective punishment and therefore does not produce constructive changes in behavior. Because punishment out of frustration is poorly related to the targeted behavior, frustrative punishment is abusive and cannot be justified as a systematic behavior modification procedure. To avoid administering punishment out of frustration, a reasonable rule of thumb is not to administer punishment on impulse.

Alternatives to Punishment

Abusive punishment cannot be justified on either ethical or empirical grounds. But undesired responses are bound to occur in homes, classrooms, and other settings. What are we to do about them? What alternatives are there to abusive punishment? Unfortunately, there are no easy solutions. It has become clear that whatever procedure is adopted to suppress undesired responses, the procedure has to be applied as a part of a systematic intervention program that considers not only the response to be suppressed but also the other activities of the individual and other sources of reinforcement.

TIME-OUT

A popular alternative to physical punishment in educational settings is the **time-out** procedure. In fact, many classrooms have a time-out chair where a student has to sit if he is being punished. In a time-out procedure, the consequence of making an undesired response is not a physically aversive event but time away from sources of positive reinforcement. A teenager who is "grounded" for a week for having taken the family car without permission is experiencing a form of the time out procedure. Time-out is also being used when a child is told "go to your room" as a form of punishment.

As with other instrumental conditioning procedures, the effectiveness of time-out depends on the delay between the target response and the time-out consequence. The effectiveness of the procedure also depends on how consistently it is applied. In addition, time-out involves some special considerations. To be effective, the procedure has to result in a substantial reduction in the rate of positive reinforcement.

Whether a substantial reduction in reinforcement is experienced in time-out depends on how much reinforcement was available beforehand

and how much reinforcement is available in the time-out situation. Time-out is not likely to suppress behavior if the individual is not getting much positive reinforcement anyway. A child who is not enjoying any aspect of being in a classroom will not experience much of a loss of reinforcement when he is put in time-out. One also has to make sure that the time-out situation is actually devoid of reinforcement. A child who has many fun things to do in her room will not be discouraged by being sent to her room as a form of time-out.

DIFFERENTIAL REINFORCEMENT OF OTHER BEHAVIOR

Another alternative to abusive punishment is **differential reinforcement of other behavior**, or DRO. A DRO procedure involves a negative contingency between a target response and a reinforcer. I previously discussed learning produced by a negative contingency in connection with inhibitory Pavlovian conditioning. There the negative contingency was between a conditioned and an unconditioned stimulus. The inhibitory CS indicated that the US would not occur. In a DRO procedure, the negative contingency is between a target instrumental response and presentations of a reinforcing stimulus. Occurrence of the target response leads to the omission of the reinforcer.

In a DRO procedure, the reinforcer is scheduled to be delivered periodically, every 30 sec, for example. Occurrence of the target response causes cancellation of these scheduled reinforcers for a specified period. Thus, the target response may result in reinforcement being cancelled for the next 20 sec. This serves to suppress the target response.

DRO is different from the time-out procedure described in the preceding section in several respects. One important difference is that reinforcers are not cancelled by having the individual go to a specific time-out chair or time-out room. In a DRO procedure, previously scheduled reinforcers are simply omitted for a certain amount of time after the target response. Another important difference is that in the DRO procedure reinforcers are explicitly provided when the target response does not occur. Thus, activities other than the target behavior are explicitly reinforced. This is why the procedure is called differential reinforcement of *other* behavior. It does not matter what those "other" behaviors are. But, because organisms are always doing something, alternatives to the target response are reinforced in a DRO procedure.

A DRO procedure is more difficult to administer than the more common time-out procedure because it requires providing a reinforcer periodically when the target response is not made. To use a DRO procedure, a convenient reinforcer has to be identified and arrangements have to be made to deliver the reinforcer over long periods of time. Thus, the DRO procedure requires interacting with the organism for long periods even if the response of interest does not occur.

Summary

In a punishment procedure, an aversive stimulus is presented contingent on the instrumental response. Punishment is highly effective in suppressing the target response if it is administered without delay, at a high intensity from the beginning, and each time the target response is made. The effectiveness of punishment can be further increased by providing positive reinforcement for alternative activities. Initial exposure to mild punishment can result in learned resistance to the suppressive effects of more intense punishment, and signaling punishment can limit the response suppression to the presence of the signal. Punishment can cause a paradoxical increase in responding if it serves as a signal for positive reinforcement or is applied to escape behavior which is aversively motivated.

In daily life, the use of punishment is often related to the emotional state of the person who administers the aversive stimulus. People are likely to use punishment when they are frustrated and angry. Under these circumstances many of the parameters of effective punishment are violated, with the result that no constructive changes in behavior develop. Problems with the use of punishment have encouraged consideration of alternatives such as time-out and differential reinforcement of other behavior. Successful application of any response-suppression procedure requires considering not only the undesired response but also the individual's other activities and other sources of reinforcement.

Suggested Readings

AZRIN, N. H., & HOLZ, W. C. (1966). Punishment. In W. K. Honig (Ed.), *Operant behavior: Areas of research and application* (pp. 380–447). New York: Appleton-Century-Crofts.

CHURCH, R. M. (1969). Response suppression. In B. A. Campbell & R. M. Church (Eds.), *Punishment and aversive behavior* (pp.111–156). New York: Appleton-Century-Crofts.

REPP, A. C., & SINGH, N. N. (Eds.). (1990). *Perspectives on the use of non-aversive and aversive interventions for persons with developmental disabilities*. Sycamore, IL: Sycamore.

Technical Terms

Differential reinforcement
    of other behavior
Discriminative punishment

Negative reinforcement
Punishment
Time-out

CHAPTER TEN

Avoidance Learning

DID YOU KNOW THAT:

- Avoidance is a form of instrumental conditioning in which the instrumental response prevents the delivery of an aversive stimulus.

- No major theory assumes that avoidance behavior is reinforced by the absence of the avoided aversive stimulus.

- Although avoidance is a form of instrumental behavior, theories of avoidance learning rely heavily on concepts of Pavlovian conditioning.

- In many situations, avoidance learning is assumed to involve learning about internal temporal cues and proprioceptive or feedback cues.

- Avoidance behavior is strongly determined by the preexisting defensive behavior of the organism.

Punishment is just one of the major forms of instrumental conditioning that involve aversive stimuli. Another form of aversive control is avoidance conditioning. In punishment procedures, performance of the instrumental response results in the presentation of an aversive stimulus. In avoidance conditioning, performance of the instrumental response prevents or blocks the presentation of the aversive event.

We do a lot of things that prevent something bad from happening. Putting out one's hand when approaching a door prevents the discomfort of walking into a closed door; grabbing a handrail prevents the discomfort of slipping on a flight of stairs; slowing down while driving prevents a collision with the car in front of you; putting on a coat prevents you from catching a chill. All of these are avoidance responses.

As with other forms of instrumental conditioning, avoidance procedures involve a contingency between an instrumental response and a motivating or reinforcing stimulus. Avoidance conditioning differs from instances of positive reinforcement in two ways. First, the motivating or reinforcing stimulus is an unpleasant or **aversive stimulus**. Second, the contingency between the instrumental response and the motivating stimulus is negative. With a negative contingency, if the organism performs the instrumental response, the aversive event is not delivered. Thus, by responding, the participant prevents the delivery of the aversive reinforcer.

Since I have already discussed various instrumental conditioning procedures and since people are highly familiar with avoidance learning from personal experience, one might suppose that analyses of avoidance conditioning would be fairly straightforward, if not self-evident. Unfortunately, that is not the case. In fact, avoidance learning has been one of the most difficult forms of learning to analyze and explain. Because of thorny conceptual problems involved in avoidance learning, much of the research has been motivated by theoretical rather than practical considerations. This is in sharp contrast to research on punishment, which has been dominated by practical considerations

Dominant Questions in the Analysis of Avoidance Learning

Avoidance procedures are clear enough: The participant performs an instrumental response that prevents the delivery of an aversive stimulus. However, it is not clear what aspect of the avoidance procedure reinforces the instrumental response. A successful avoidance response prevents the delivery of the aversive stimulus. Therefore, a successful avoidance response is followed by nothing. Mowrer and Lamoreaux (1942) pointed out that this raises a major theoretical question in the analysis of avoidance learning: How can "nothing" reinforce behavior and produce learning?

Various hypotheses and theories have been offered to explain how "nothing" can reinforce avoidance responding. The hypotheses and theories differ in many ways. However, all of the major explanations reject the common sense idea that avoidance responses occur because they prevent the delivery of the aversive event. As we will see, a number of ingenious proposals have been offered in an effort to explain avoidance learning without relying on the theoretically vacuous idea that "nothing" serves as a reinforcer.

The second major question in analyses of avoidance behavior is: How are Pavlovian conditioning processes involved in avoidance learning? As we have seen, Pavlovian conditioning processes have also been discussed in analyses of positively reinforced instrumental behavior (see Chapter 5). However, Pavlovian conditioning concepts have not dominated thinking about positively reinforced instrumental behavior as much as they have dominated analyses of avoidance learning. Historically, avoidance learning was regarded as a special case of Pavlovian conditioning. In fact, to this day some accounts of avoidance learning regard avoidance behavior as entirely the product of Pavlovian conditioning mechanisms.

Origins of the Study of Avoidance Learning

Avoidance learning was first investigated by the Russian scientist Bechterev (1913), who set out to study Pavlovian conditioning in people. For obvious reasons, Bechterev did not want to use the salivary fistula methods that Pavlov and his students developed with dogs. The alternative procedure Bechterev devised was fairly simple. He asked people to place a finger on metal electrodes resting on a table. Mild current could be passed through the electrodes, and this caused the participant to lift his finger. Thus, the unconditioned response was finger withdrawal. To turn the situation into one involving classical conditioning, Bechterev presented a brief warning stimulus immediately before the shock on each trial. As you might suspect, the participants quickly learned to lift their fingers when the CS was presented, and this was measured as the conditioned response.

Although Bechterev considered his finger-withdrawal technique to be a convenient way to study Pavlovian conditioning, more careful consideration of his procedure shows that in fact it was an instrumental rather than a Pavlovian procedure. Recall that the electrodes rested on the surface of a table; they were not attached to the participant's finger. Therefore, by lifting his finger in response to the CS, the participant could entirely avoid getting shocked. This differs from standard Pavlovian conditioning procedures in which the occurrence of the conditioned response does not alter the delivery of the US. Bechterev had inadvertently given his participants control over presentation of the unconditioned stimulus. This made the finger-withdrawal technique an instrumental rather than a Pavlovian conditioning procedure.

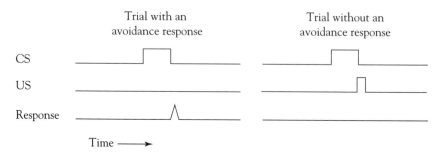

FIGURE   10.1   **Diagram of the discriminated, or signaled, avoidance procedure.**
If the organism responds during the warning signal or CS, the conditioned stimulus is turned off and the aversive US is not delivered. In contrast, if the organism fails to respond during the warning signal or CS, the CS continues to be presented for its full duration and ends in the presentation of the aversive US.

Contemporary Avoidance Conditioning Procedures

Two types of avoidance conditioning procedures are commonly used in contemporary research: the discriminated avoidance procedure and the nondiscriminated or free-operant avoidance procedure.

DISCRIMINATED AVOIDANCE

Without knowing it, Bechterev invented what has come to be known as the **discriminated avoidance** procedure. In a discriminated avoidance procedure, the response-reinforcer contingency is not always in effect. Rather, responding prevents delivery of the reinforcer only during discrete periods or trials when a conditioned stimulus is presented. As illustrated in Figure 10.1, what happens during these trials depends on the participant's behavior. If the participant responds, the conditioned stimulus is turned off and the aversive US is not delivered. In contrast, if the participant fails to respond during the conditioned stimulus, the CS continues to be presented for its full duration and ends in the presentation of the aversive US. Thus, a discriminated avoidance procedure involves two types of trials, response trials and no-response trials, and the aversive US only occurs in no-response trials. Because the aversive stimulus occurs at the end of the CS in no-response trials, the CS is also called the **warning stimulus** or **warning signal**.

Since Bechterev's research, the discriminated avoidance procedure has been adapted for use with laboratory animals. In fact, most of the research on the theoretical mechanisms of avoidance learning has been done with

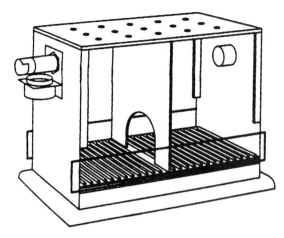

FIGURE 10.2. Shuttle box used in studies of avoidance learning.
The animal has to cross from one compartment to the other to avoid mild shock through the grid floor.

laboratory animals, primarily rats. Typically the aversive unconditioned stimulus has been mild electric shock because stimulus intensity and duration can be controlled more easily with shock than with other aversive stimuli. In addition, shock is unlike any other aversive stimulus the animals are likely to have encountered (or learned about) before participating in the experiment.

In some experiments, rats have to press a response lever during the CS to avoid receiving the shock. In other experiments, they have to run from one side of a **shuttle box** to the other. Figure 10.2 illustrates a typical shuttle box. It consists of two compartments set side-by-side. The rat is allowed to move from one compartment to the other through an open doorway. Mild shock is administered through a grid floor. Each trial starts with presentation of a CS, a light or a tone, on one side of the apparatus. If the rat moves to the other side before the end of the CS, the shock does not occur. If the shuttle avoidance response is not made, the mild shock is turned on and remains on until the rat escapes to the other side.

The shuttle box can be used to implement either a one-way or a two-way avoidance procedure In a **one-way avoidance** procedure, the participant is always placed in the same compartment at the start of each trial (the left side, for example). Because each trial starts on the same side (left), the avoidance response involves always going in the same direction (left to right).

Notice that in a one-way avoidance procedure, the side the organism starts on is always potentially dangerous because if the rat doesn't run to the other side it gets shocked. In contrast, the other side is always safe. The animal never gets shocked on the other side. Thus, a one-way avoidance procedure has a consistently safe side and a consistently dangerous side. This makes the one-way avoidance task rather easy to learn.

In a **two-way avoidance** procedure, trials can start either on the left side or the right side, depending on which compartment the animal happens to occupy. If the rat starts on the left, it has to go to the right to avoid shock. If the rat starts on the right, it has to go to the left side to avoid shock. Because trials can start on either side, both sides of the shuttle box are potentially dangerous. The lack of a consistently safe side makes the two-way avoidance task more difficult to learn than the one-way procedure (Theios, Lynch, & Lowe, 1966).

NONDISCRIMINATED OR FREE-OPERANT AVOIDANCE

In discriminated avoidance procedures, responding is effective in preventing the aversive stimulus only if the response occurs during the trial period, when the warning stimulus is presented. Responses made during the intertrial interval have no effect. In fact, in many studies the participants are removed from the apparatus during the intertrial interval. In contrast to such traditional discrete trial procedures, Sidman (1953) devised a **nondiscriminated avoidance** or **free-operant avoidance** procedure.

Sidman's free-operant procedure was developed in the Skinnerian or operant tradition. In this tradition, trials are not restricted to periods when a discrete stimulus is present, and the participant can repeat the instrumental response at any time. On a fixed-ratio schedule in a Skinner box, for example, responses made at any time count toward completion of the ratio requirement. Sidman extended these features of operant methodology to the study of avoidance behavior.

In the free-operant avoidance procedure, an explicit warning stimulus is not used and there are no discrete trials. The avoidance response can be performed at any time, and responding always provides some measure of benefit. A brief shock is programmed to occur periodically, with different schedules of shock presentation in effect depending on whether (or not) the avoidance response is made. For example, a brief shock may be scheduled every 15 sec if the participant does not respond. This specifies the shock-shock interval, or **S-S interval**. Performance of the avoidance response creates a period of safety, during which no shocks are given. The safe period may be 30 sec. This is the response-shock interval, or **R-S interval** (see Figure 10.3).

An important aspect of free-operant avoidance procedures is that the R-S interval is reset and starts over again each time the avoidance response occurs. Thus, if the R-S interval is 30 sec, each response resets the R-S interval and starts the 30-sec period of safety all over again. Because of this feature, each occurrence of the avoidance response provides some benefit. However, the degree of benefit depends on exactly when the response is made.

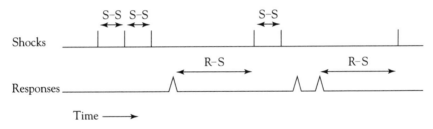

FIGURE   10.3   Diagram of a nondiscriminated, or free-operant, avoidance procedure.
As long as the animal fails to respond, a brief shock is scheduled to occur periodically, as set by S-S interval. Each occurrence of the avoidance response creates a period without shock, as set by the R-S interval.

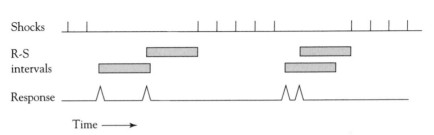

FIGURE   10.4   Effect of repeating the avoidance response early or late in an R-S interval in a free-operant avoidance procedure.
The R-S intervals are indicated by the shaded horizontal bars. On the left, the response was repeated late in an R-S interval; on the right, the response was repeated early in an R-S interval. Notice that the total time without shocks is longer if the response is repeated late in an R-S interval.

If the participant responds when the R-S interval is already in effect, the R-S interval will start over again and time left on the R-S clock will be lost. The net benefit of responding will depend on whether the response occurs early or late in the R-S interval (see Figure 10.4). If the participant responds late in the R-S interval, it will lose little time remaining on the R-S clock, and the net benefit of responding will be substantial. In contrast, if the participant responds early in the R-S interval, it will lose a lot of time remaining on the R-S clock, and the net benefit of responding will be much smaller. In either case, however, if the individual manages to respond before the end of each R-S interval, it will reset all of the R-S intervals and thereby successfully avoid all shocks.

Theoretical Approaches to Avoidance Learning

Because research on avoidance learning emerged from investigations of Pavlovian conditioning, Pavlovian concepts have been important in the analysis of avoidance learning. In fact, avoidance learning initially was considered to be entirely caused by Pavlovian conditioning. As I noted earlier, Bechterev considered his finger-withdrawal task to be a Pavlovian conditioning procedure. In keeping with that interpretation, he considered the avoidance response to be a classically conditioned response to the warning signal, much like salivation conditioned to a visual cue paired with food. According to this interpretation, the fact that the avoidance response prevented the delivery of the aversive US was considered to be irrelevant to the acquisition of avoidance behavior.

TEST OF THE ROLE OF THE INSTRUMENTAL CONTINGENCY

The idea that the instrumental contingency is entirely irrelevant to avoidance learning is counterintuitive and has been found to be wrong. A powerful test of the idea was conducted by Brogden, Lipman, and Culler (1938), who studied the avoidance conditioning of guinea pigs in a running wheel apparatus. Each trial started with a tone CS or warning signal. One group of subjects received a strictly Pavlovian conditioning procedure. For them, the warning signal always ended in a brief shock through the grid floor of the running wheel. A second group (the instrumental group) received a conventional discriminated avoidance procedure. If they rotated the wheel during the warning signal, the CS was turned off and the shock scheduled on that trial was omitted.

Notice that from the perspective of Pavlovian conditioning, the instrumental group received a rather poor conditioning procedure. For the instrumental group, pairings of the warning signal with shock occurred only on trials when they did not respond. In contrast, for the Pavlovian group the warning signal ended in shock on every trial. Therefore, if Pavlovian conditioning had been entirely responsible for avoidance learning, the Pavlovian group should have shown higher rates of responding than the instrumental group.

The results turned out just the opposite. The Pavlovian group responded significantly less often than the instrumental group. Within six sessions, the subjects given the instrumental procedure were responding on 100% of the trials. In contrast, the Pavlovian group responded on just 20–30% of the trials even after extensive training (see Figure 10.5).

The results of the study by Brogden et al. indicated clearly that the instrumental contingency makes a significant contribution to avoidance learning. Although the empirical result was unambiguous, the two dominant questions about avoidance learning remained unresolved. The experi-

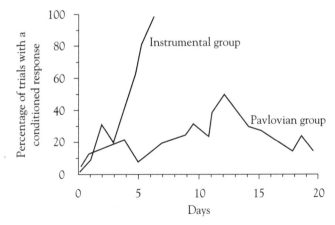

FIGURE   10.5   Results of the experiment by Brogden et al. (1938).
The Pavlovian group received a pure Pavlovian conditioning procedure. The instrumental group received a discriminated avoidance procedure.

ment left no doubt that response consequences are important, but the reinforcer for avoidance responding remained unidentified. Successful avoidance responses were followed by nothing, and the experiment provided no hints about how "nothing" could serve as an effective reinforcer. The experiment also did not clarify what role Pavlovian conditioning might have in avoidance learning. Was Pavlovian conditioning entirely irrelevant? If Pavlovian conditioning was not irrelevant, how was it involved?

Two-Factor Theory of Avoidance

The questions left unresolved by the Brogden et al. experiment were answered by the **two-factor theory** of avoidance behavior that was proposed about 10 years later by O. H. Mowrer (Mowrer, 1947; see also Miller, 1951). According to this theory, avoidance learning involves both Pavlovian and instrumental conditioning processes (hence the name "two-factor" theory). However, Mowrer did not describe either of these processes in ways that are intuitively obvious.

Let us consider first the Pavlovian conditioning process in two-factor theory. Instead of thinking about the Pavlovian process as being directly responsible for the avoidance response (as Bechterev had thought), Mowrer proposed that the Pavlovian process resulted in the conditioning of a hypothetical emotional state called "fear." On trials when the avoidance response does not occur, the CS or warning stimulus is paired with the aversive US, and this is assumed to result in the conditioning of fear to the warning stimulus.

Conditioned fear presumably is an unpleasant or aversive state. Therefore, the reduction or elimination of fear is assumed to be reinforcing. Fear reduction brings into play the second process in two-factor theory. On trials when the avoidance response is made, the response turns off the warning stimulus and prevents the delivery of the US. Turning off the warning stimulus is assumed to result in the reduction of conditioned fear, and this fear reduction is assumed to provide reinforcement for the avoidance response. Thus, the second factor in the two-factor theory of avoidance is instrumental reinforcement of the avoidance response through fear reduction.

Notice that according to two-factor theory, avoidance behavior is not reinforced by "nothing" occurring after the avoidance response. Rather, avoidance behavior is reinforced by fear reduction. Fear reduction is a form of negative reinforcement (removal of an aversive stimulus contingent on behavior). In two-factor theory, the instrumental response is considered to be an escape response—a response that escapes fear. Instead of focusing on the fact that avoidance behavior prevents delivery of the aversive US, two-factor theory treats avoidance behavior as a special type of escape behavior. (For a discussion of escape behavior, see Chapter 9.)

Interactions between the Pavlovian and instrumental factors. Two-factor theory provides answers to many questions about avoidance learning. The answers were innovative when they were first proposed and have shaped the course of research on avoidance conditioning ever since. According to the theory, both Pavlovian and instrumental processes contribute to avoidance learning. Furthermore, the two processes are interdependent in various ways.

Before fear reduction can provide instrumental reinforcement for the avoidance response, fear first has to become conditioned to the warning stimulus. Thus, the Pavlovian conditioning of fear is a prerequisite for the instrumental component of two-factor theory. The instrumental process depends on the integrity of the Pavlovian process.

The Pavlovian process is in turn influenced by the instrumental contingency, but in this case the influence is disruptive. Each time the avoidance response occurs, the aversive US is omitted, and the warning stimulus ends up being presented without the US. According to the principles of Pavlovian conditioning, this should result in extinction of the fear that had been conditioned to the warning stimulus. Thus, frequent avoidance responding should result in Pavlovian extinction of conditioned fear.

Extinction of fear in turn undermines the effectiveness of fear reduction as a source of instrumental reinforcement. If the instrumental avoidance response is no longer followed by fear reduction, the response will undergo extinction. As the avoidance response becomes extinguished, the warning stimulus will again end in presentation of the aversive US. This in turn should reactivate conditioning of fear to the warning signal. Once fear has become reconditioned to the warning stimulus, fear reduction can again serve as an effective reinforcer for instrumental responding. Thus, according to two-process theory, avoidance behavior is determined by a continually changing dynamic interaction of Pavlovian and instrumental processes.

Challenges to two-factor theory.   Many predictions of two-factor theory have been substantiated. Despite these successes, however, the theory has been challenged by several striking results. One set of findings that has been challenging (but not impossible) for two-factor theory is free-operant avoidance behavior. As I noted earlier, in a free-operant avoidance procedure, shocks occur periodically without an explicit warning stimulus, and each occurrence of the avoidance response initiates a period of safety (the R-S interval). Since the mechanisms of two-factor theory seem to require a warning stimulus, it is not obvious how two-factor theory can explain free-operant avoidance behavior.

Another challenging phenomenon for two-factor theory is the common observation that once well learned, avoidance responding persists at high levels for long periods of time even though shocks are no longer delivered. As noted earlier, a long string of avoidance responses should result in Pavlovian extinction of fear, which in turn should result in extinction of the instrumental avoidance response. This does not seem to happen (Solomon, Kamin, & Wynne, 1953).

A third major finding that has been challenging for two-process theory is that after participants become proficient in avoiding the aversive US, they do not seem to be very fearful. In fact, levels of conditioned fear often decline with increased proficiency in avoidance responding (Mineka & Gino, 1980). Common experience also suggests that not much fear exists once an avoidance response becomes well learned. Steering a car so that it does not drift off the road is basically avoidance behavior; a competent driver avoids having the car get too close to the side of the road or another lane of traffic. Yet proficient drivers show no fear under normal traffic conditions.

CONDITIONED TEMPORAL CUES

Findings that are difficult to explain in terms of the two-factor theory of avoidance have encouraged modifications and additions to the theory. Efforts to integrate new findings with two-factor theory have often involved postulating internal stimuli and ascribing important functions to those internal cues. For example, one approach to explaining nondiscriminated or free-operant avoidance behavior in terms of two-factor theory involves assuming that internal cues related to the passage of time (temporal cues) acquire conditioned aversive properties (Anger, 1963).

Recall that in a nondiscriminated avoidance procedure, explicit warning stimuli are not provided before each shock. However, shocks occur at predictable times. Free-operant avoidance procedures are constructed from two types of intervals (S-S intervals and R-S intervals), both of which are of fixed duration. Therefore, the passage of time is predictive of when the next shock will occur. With both S-S and R-S intervals, shock occurs when the intervals have been completed.

Free-operant avoidance learning can be explained in terms of two-factor theory by assuming the existence of internal **temporal cues**. Temporal cues characteristic of the end of the S-S and R-S intervals are presumably different from temporal cues characteristic of the beginning of these intervals. At first, participants probably do not distinguish between the beginning and the end of the S-S and R-S intervals. However, they soon learn the difference because early and late temporal cues have different consequences. Temporal cues that characterize the beginning of the S-S and R-S intervals are never paired with shock. If shock occurs, it always occurs at the end of these intervals. Because of this differential reinforcement, participants presumably learn to distinguish the early and late temporal cues.

Temporal cues characteristic of the end of an S-S or R-S interval are paired with shock and presumably acquire conditioned aversive properties. Each avoidance response starts a new R-S interval and thereby reduces the conditioned aversiveness created by temporal cues characteristic of the end of the S-S and R-S intervals (see Figure 10.6). In this way, an avoidance response can result in reduction of conditioned fear and satisfy the tenets of two-factor theory.

SAFETY SIGNALS IN AVOIDANCE LEARNING

The next explanation of avoidance learning that we will consider—the **safety signal** hypothesis—also originated from a consideration of internal cues that participants may experience during the course of avoidance conditioning. However, instead of focusing on cues that predict danger, the safety signal hypothesis focuses on signals for the absence of shock or signals for safety (Dinsmoor, 1977).

In an avoidance procedure, periods of safety are best predicted by the occurrence of the avoidance response. After all, avoidance behavior is defined as responding that cancels the delivery of an aversive stimulus. We know from biology that the movements of muscles and joints that are involved in making responses can give rise to internal **proprioceptive cues**. Such cues are also called response feedback cues or just **feedback cues**. The feedback cues that are produced by an avoidance response are followed by a predictable period without the aversive US, or a predictable period of safety. As we saw in Chapter 5, stimuli that reliably predict the absence of a US can acquire Pavlovian conditioned inhibitory properties. Therefore, feedback cues generated by avoidance responses may also acquire Pavlovian conditioned inhibitory properties.

The safety signal explanation of avoidance learning is based on these ideas. According to the safety signal hypothesis, feedback cues from the

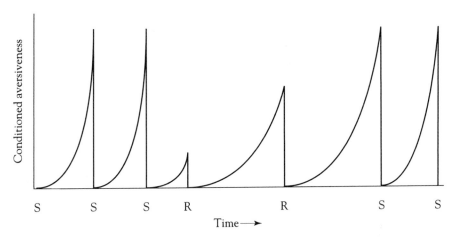

FIGURE 10.6 The presumed conditioned aversiveness of temporal cues during R-S and S-S intervals in a free-operant avoidance procedure.
R, occurrence of the avoidance response; S, occurrence of a brief shock. Notice the low levels of conditioned aversiveness at the beginning of each S-S and R-S interval and high levels of aversiveness at the end of these intervals. Each occurrence of the response always reduces the conditioned aversiveness of temporal cues because each response starts a new R-S interval.

avoidance response acquire Pavlovian conditioned inhibitory properties and thereby become signals for safety. In a situation involving potential danger, safety signals are assumed to be reinforcing. According to the safety signal hypothesis, avoidance behavior is positively reinforced by conditioned inhibitory safety signals.

Although the safety signal hypothesis is similar to the temporal cue hypothesis in relying on stimuli internal to the organism, it has been more accessible to experimental verification. The safety signal hypothesis has been evaluated by introducing an external stimulus (a brief tone, for example) at the time the interoceptive feedback cue is presumed to occur. That is, a brief tone is presented when the participant performs the avoidance response. If the safety signal hypothesis is correct, such an exteroceptive cue should acquire conditioned inhibitory properties. In addition, these conditioned inhibitory properties should make the feedback stimuli effective as a positive reinforcer for instrumental behavior. Both of these predictions have been confirmed (e.g., Morris, 1974, 1975; Weisman & Litner, 1972).

A less obvious prediction is that avoidance learning should be facilitated by increasing the salience of safety signal feedback cues. Consistent with that prediction, the introduction of an external response feedback stimulus (which is presumably more salient than internal proprioceptive cues) substantially facilitates avoidance learning (e.g., D'Amato, Fazzaro, & Etkin, 1968).

The safety signal hypothesis is not incompatible with two-factor theory and need not be viewed as an alternative to that theory. Rather, positive reinforcement through a conditioned inhibitory safety signal may be considered a third factor in avoidance learning that operates in combination with Pavlovian conditioning of fear and instrumental reinforcement through fear reduction.

AVOIDANCE LEARNING AND UNCONDITIONED DEFENSIVE BEHAVIOR

As I noted in Chapter 2, learning procedures are superimposed on an organism's preexisting behavioral tendencies, and learned responses are the product of the interaction between conditioning procedures and that preexisting behavioral structure. Two-factor theory and safety signal mechanisms are based on a simple view of the organism's preexisting behavior structure. For these learning mechanisms to operate, all we have to presume is that organisms find some stimuli aversive. Given an aversive stimulus, fear can become conditioned to stimuli that predict the aversive event, safety can become conditioned to stimuli that predict the absence of the aversive event, and fear reduction and safety can serve as reinforcers for any instrumental behavior.

Starting about 30 years ago, it became evident that the preexisting behavioral tendencies organisms bring into an avoidance conditioning situation are a lot more complex than is presumed by two-factor theory and the safety signal hypothesis. Organisms come into an avoidance conditioning situation not only with certain stimuli they find aversive but also with a rich behavioral repertoire for dealing with aversive situations. The existence of this unconditioned behavioral repertoire was first emphasized by Bolles (1970).

Bolles suggested organisms could not survive with just the ability to detect aversive stimuli and the ability to learn about them through the Pavlovian and instrumental conditioning mechanisms presumed by traditional theories. The mechanisms of two-factor theory and safety signal learning require extensive training to generate avoidance responses. An animal first has to learn about signals for danger and signals for safety. It then has to learn what instrumental responses are required to turn off the danger signals and produce the safety signals.

Bolles pointed out that in their natural habitat, animals may not have time to learn about danger and safety signals. An animal being pursued by a predator has to avoid the danger successfully the first time because it may not be alive for a second or third attempt. Because dangerous situations require effective coping mechanisms without much opportunity for practice,

Bolles suggested that organisms respond to aversive situations with a hierarchy of unconditioned defensive responses. Bolles called these **species-specific defense reactions,** or SSDRs.

The SSDR theory of avoidance.   Because SSDRs are unconditioned responses to aversive stimuli, they are assumed to predominate during the initial stages of avoidance training. SSDRs are responses such as freezing, fleeing, and fighting. Bolles suggested that which particular SSDR occurs depends on the nature of the aversive stimulus and the response opportunities provided by the environment. If a familiar and effective means of escape is available, the animal is most likely to try to flee when it encounters the aversive stimulus. Without a familiar escape route, freezing will be the predominant defensive response. In social situations, fighting may predominate.

In addition to describing what animals are likely to do initially in an aversive situation, the SSDR theory also specified how an avoidance conditioning procedure can shape the future actions of the organism. In contrast to the negative and positive reinforcement mechanisms of earlier theories, SSDR theory presumed that defensive responses were shaped and selected by punishment.

If the particular SSDR that occurred during the first few trials of an avoidance conditioning procedure was not effective in preventing the aversive US, the aversive stimulus would be applied and the SSDR would end up being punished. Suppression by punishment of the first SSDR the animal made was assumed to result in a switch to the next most likely SSDR in that situation. If that response also turned out to be ineffective in preventing delivery of the aversive US, it would be punished and suppressed as well. This in turn would result in switching to the third SSDR in the response hierarchy.

According to SSDR theory, the participant would eventually end up performing the required avoidance response as its ineffective SSDRs became suppressed by punishment. The required avoidance response was assumed to emerge not because it was reinforced by shock avoidance, fear reduction, or safety signals. Rather, the required avoidance response presumably emerged because it was the only response that was not followed by the aversive US and therefore the only response not suppressed by punishment.

The SSDR theory advanced our knowledge of avoidance learning a great deal because it emphasized that avoidance learning is influenced by the preexisting defensive behavior of the organism. However, details of the SSDR theory have not survived subsequent empirical scrutiny. Punishment has not been found to be effective in suppressing SSDRs (e.g., Bolles & Riley, 1973). In addition, SSDRs appear to be organized by the imminence of injury rather than by response opportunities provided by the environment.

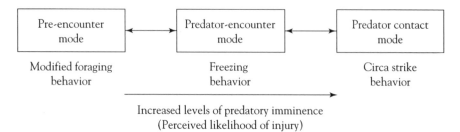

FIGURE 10.7   The predatory imminence continuum.
Different modes of defensive behavior are activated at different levels of predatory imminence. The pre-encounter mode represents the defensive behavior of an animal before it encounters a predator. The predator-encounter mode represents defensive behavior after the animal has encountered a predator, and the predator-contact mode represents its behavior after the predator has made physical contact.

The predatory imminence continuum.   Animals do one thing when they perceive a low likelihood of injury and other things when the likelihood of injury is higher. The different defensive responses that are elicited by different degrees of perceived danger constitute the **predatory imminence** continuum (Fanselow & Lester, 1988).

The predatory imminence continuum has been investigated most extensively in laboratory rats (Fanselow, 1989, 1994). Rats are subject to predation by various predators, including snakes. Different modes of defensive behavior are activated depending on the rat's perceived likelihood of injury (see Figure 10.7). The pre-encounter response mode is activated if during the course of its foraging, a rat wanders into an area where there is some chance of finding a snake, but the snake has not been encountered yet. In the pre-encounter mode, the rat may move to a safer area. If a safer area is not available, the rat will become more cautious in its foraging. It will go out of its burrow less often and eat larger meals (Fanselow, Lester, & Helmstetter, 1988).

If the pre-encounter defensive responses are not successful and the rat encounters the snake, the predator-encounter response mode is activated. In the predator-encounter mode, freezing is the predominant response. Finally, if this defensive behavior is also unsuccessful and the rat is attacked by the snake, the predator-contact response mode is activated. In the predator contact mode, the rat suddenly leaps into the air, performing what is called a circa strike response (see Figure 10.7).

Preexisting behavioral tendencies are likely to predominate during early avoidance conditioning trials, before much learning has taken place. With continued training, the Pavlovian and instrumental mechanisms presumed by two-factor theory and the safety signal hypothesis will become activated. However, the predatory imminence continuum is also likely to be reflected in the behavioral manifestations of the learning processes that are activated by an avoidance procedure.

As I noted in Chapter 4, conditioning involves incorporating new stimuli into a preexisting behavior system. In an avoidance conditioning situation, the aversive US involves the highest level of predatory imminence and activates the predatory contact response mode. The warning stimulus that occurs before the aversive US is highly predictive of the US and activates the predatory encounter mode. Finally, a conditioned safety signal involves the total absence of predatory imminence. We may expect responses such as freezing that are characteristic of the predatory encounter mode to develop to conditioned stimuli that become associated with an unconditioned aversive event. In contrast, safety signals should elicit recuperative and relaxation responses. These considerations illustrate that even when organisms learn about an aversive situation, their behavior is heavily influenced by the preexisting organization of their defensive behavior system.

Summary

Studies of avoidance learning originated in investigations of Pavlovian conditioning and relied on a discrete-trial method in which a warning signal ended in a brief shock unless the avoidance response was made. Subsequently, free-operant avoidance procedures were developed that did not employ explicit warning signals. Regardless of which method is used, however, avoidance learning is very puzzling because the consequence of an avoidance response is that nothing happens. How can "nothing" motivate learning?

The first major explanation of avoidance learning, two-factor theory, assumed that avoidance behavior is the result of a dynamic reciprocal interaction between Pavlovian and instrumental conditioning. According to the theory, Pavlovian conditioning occurs when the participant fails to make the avoidance response and the warning signal is followed by the aversive US. On the other hand, instrumental conditioning occurs when the avoidance response is made because this terminates the warning signal and reduces conditioned fear. Subsequent research has identified a third factor, safety signal learning, that also contributes to avoidance conditioning. According to the safety signal hypothesis, cues that accompany the omission of the US in an avoidance procedure become conditioned inhibitors of fear and provide instrumental reinforcement for the avoidance response.

Much of the experimental evidence on avoidance learning is compatible with two-factor theory supplemented by safety signal learning, especially when temporal and proprioceptive cues are taken into account. However, these mechanisms require numerous conditioning trials to develop. Therefore, these mechanisms are of little help to an animal that encounters a dangerous predator and has to defend itself successfully the first time or face death or dismemberment. To enable them to cope with such situations, animals have acquired through evolution a rich unconditioned defensive behavioral repertoire. The current view is that unconditioned species-specific defense reactions are organized by predatory imminence, with different defensive response modes activated by different levels of perceived danger from predatory attack.

Suggested Readings

BOLLES, R. C. (1972). The avoidance learning problem. In G. H. Bower (Ed.), *The psychology of learning and motivation* (Vol. 6, pp. 97–145). Orlando, FL: Academic Press.

FANSELOW, M. S. (1997). Species-specific defense reactions: Retrospect and prospect. In M. E. Bouton & M. S. Fanselow (Eds.), *Learning, motivation, and cognition* (pp. 321–341). Washington, DC: American Psychological Association.

FANSELOW, M. S., & LESTER, L. S. (1988). A functional behavioristic approach to aversively motivated behavior: Predatory imminence as a determinant of the topography of defensive behavior. In R. C. Bolles & M. D. Beecher (Eds.), *Evolution and learning* (pp. 185–212). Hillsdale, NJ: Erlbaum.

HERRNSTEIN, R. J. (1969). Method and theory in the study of avoidance. *Psychological Review, 87*, 49–69.

McALLISTER, D. E., & McALLISTER, W. R. (1991). Fear theory and aversively motivated behavior: Some controversial issues. In M. R. Denny (Ed.), *Fear, avoidance, and phobias* (pp. 135–163). Hillsdale, NJ: Erlbaum.

Technical Terms

Aversive stimulus
Discriminated avoidance
Feedback cue
Free-operant avoidance
Nondiscriminated avoidance
One-way avoidance
Predatory imminence
Proprioceptive cue
R-S interval
S-S interval

Safety signal
Shuttle box
Species-specific
    defense reactions (SSDR)
Temporal cues
Two-factor theory
Two-way avoidance
Warning signal
Warning stimulus

CHAPTER ELEVEN

Stimulus Control of Behavior

DID YOU KNOW THAT:

- Differential responding is used to identify control of behavior by a particular stimulus.
- Even simple stimuli have many features or dimensions.
- Control of behavior by one training stimulus often generalizes to other similar stimuli.
- Stimulus generalization and stimulus discrimination are complementary concepts.
- Generalization of behavior from one stimulus to another depends on the individual's training history with the stimuli.
- Discrimination training not only produces differential responding to S^+ and S^- but also increases the steepness of generalization gradients.
- The learning of perceptual concepts involves an interplay between different levels of discrimination and generalization learning.

Throughout the book, we have seen various aspects of behavior that are controlled by environmental events. Elicited behavior and responding that results from Pavlovian conditioning are obvious examples. As we saw in Chapter 6, instrumental behavior also can be regarded as responding that occurs because of the presence of antecedent stimuli. These antecedent stimuli may activate the instrumental response directly or may activate a representation of the response-reinforcer relation.

Clearly, much of learned behavior occurs because of the presence of particular environmental events. Up to this point, however, our discussion of learning has left two critical issues about the stimulus control of behavior unanswered. The first concerns the measurement of stimulus control: How can we determine to what extent a specific stimulus or feature of the environment is responsible for a particular response? Are some types of stimuli more important than others in controlling a particular response? If so, how can we measure such differences in the degree of stimulus control?

Once we know how to measure stimulus control, we can tackle the second issue, which concerns the determinants of stimulus control. What determines which stimulus will gain control over a particular response, and what determines the degree of stimulus control? Why does a response come to be controlled more by one feature of the environment rather than another?

Questions about stimulus control arise in part because of the complexity of environmental events. Even something as simple as a dial tone on the telephone is a complex stimulus with multiple features. The tone can be characterized in terms of its loudness, pitch, how suddenly it begins and ends, tonal complexity, and location in space. How do we determine which of these stimulus features is critical and what makes those features critical?

Measurement of Stimulus Control

Analyzing the stimulus control of behavior in a new situation or in a new species is not unlike trying to figure out what is happening if you are a visitor from a different culture or a different planet. Assume that you are a creature from Mars seeing cars, streets, and traffic lights on earth for the first time. Periodically, the cars go past a traffic light. At other times, they stop and wait. You want to figure out what makes the drivers stop some of the time and continue moving at other times. How might you approach this problem?

The first step would be to formulate a hypothesis or guess about what is going on. The possibilities are limited only by your imagination. Perhaps drivers stop because a sensor in the road near an intersection signals an on-board computer to stop the car. Alternatively, drivers may be sending signals to each other, with a particular gesture indicating "stop" and another indicating "go." Another possibility is that the drivers come to a stop when they need a short break and continue when they have rested a bit. Or there may be an elaborate schedule, known to all drivers, according to which they have to stop at certain times of day and are allowed to continue at other times. Yet another possibility is that stops and starts are controlled by the traffic lights.

IDENTIFYING RELEVANT STIMULI

How could you determine which stimulus causes cars to stop at an intersection? The various possibilities may be tested in different ways. For example, you may test whether drivers are signaling each other by comparing what happens when there is just one car on the road to what happens when several cars are present at the same time. To determine whether the traffic lights have anything to do with it, you could see whether the cars are less likely to stop when the traffic lights are covered up. To determine whether sensors in the road are relevant, you could try to find the sensors and see what happens when they were deactivated.

Notice that each of these tests involves observing the behavior of interest in the presence and absence of the stimulus that we guessed might be responsible for the behavior. To test whether the drivers were signaling each other to stop, we compared their behavior when such signals could not have been transmitted (when there was only one car on the road) to when such signals could have occurred (when there were several cars on the road at the same time). In testing the possibility that the traffic lights were responsible for the stops and starts, we observed what happened when the lights were covered up. These examples illustrate a basic manipulation involved in the measurement of stimulus control:

> The stimulus control of behavior is measured by comparing the behavior of interest in the presence and absence of the test stimulus.

If the presence and absence of the test stimulus does not produce differences in responding, we may conclude that the stimulus does not control the behavior in question. Cars are just as likely to stop at a traffic light whether or not there are other cars on the road. Therefore, we may conclude that stops and starts are not cued by signals between drivers. In contrast, cars are much more likely to stop when the traffic lights are visible than when they are covered up. This provides evidence that the traffic lights control the behavior of interest and illustrates the basic criterion for the stimulus control of behavior:

> A response is said to be under the control of a particular stimulus if the response is altered by changes in that stimulus.

A change in responding related to changes in a stimulus is called **differential responding**. Which possible stimulus is responsible for the target behavior is identified by differential responding related to changes in that

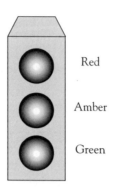

Red

Amber

Green

FIGURE 11.1   Stimulus features of traffic lights.
The lights differ in both color and position.

---

stimulus. If responding is altered by changes in a stimulus, that stimulus is involved in the control of the behavior. If responding is not altered by changes in a stimulus, that stimulus is not relevant to the control of the behavior.

IDENTIFYING RELEVANT STIMULUS FEATURES

Identifying that stops and starts on a road are somehow controlled by traffic lights is progress. However, many details need to be filled in for us to know exactly how drivers respond to traffic lights. For example, traffic lights are often arranged in a vertical array, with the red light on top and the green light on the bottom (see Figure 11.1). Which feature is important, the color of the light or its position? Do drivers stop when they see a red light, or do they stop when the light on top is illuminated?

The strategy for identifying relevant stimulus features is similar to the strategy for identifying relevant stimuli. To determine whether a particular stimulus feature is important, we have to vary that feature without altering other cues and see whether the behavior of interest changes accordingly. To determine whether color rather than position is important in traffic lights, we have to test red and green lights presented in the same position. To determine whether the position rather than color is important, we have to test lights of the same color in different positions.

When we vary one feature of a stimulus while keeping all others constant, we are testing the importance of a particular **stimulus dimension** for the behavior in question. Different stimulus dimensions may be important for different drivers. Drivers who are color blind have to focus on the position of the illuminated light. Others respond primarily to the color of traffic lights. Still other drivers may respond to both the color and the position of the light. Thus, substantial individual differences in stimulus control can occur in response to the same situation.

MEASUREMENT OF THE DEGREE OF STIMULUS CONTROL

Determining whether a response is influenced by the presence versus the absence of a stimulus tells us whether that stimulus is of any relevance to the behavior. However, the presence/absence test does not tell us how precisely the behavior is tuned to a particular stimulus feature. Continuing with the traffic light example, let us assume that a driver stops whenever he sees a red traffic light. What shade of red does the light have to be? To answer this question, we would have to test the driver with a variety of colors, including several different of shades of red.

The wavelength of red light is at the long end of the visual spectrum. Shorter wavelengths of light appear less red and more orange. As the wavelength of light becomes even shorter, the light appears more and more yellow. A detailed test of stimulus control by different colors requires systematically presenting lights of different wavelengths.

Stimulus generalization gradients.   Several different outcomes may occur if a variety of test colors are presented ranging from deep red to deep yellow. If the driver were paying very close attention to color, he would stop only if the light had a perfect red color. Lights that had a tinge of orange would not cause the driver to stop. This possibility is illustrated by curve A in Figure 11.2. At the other extreme, the driver may stop when he sees any color that has a vague resemblance to red. This possibility is illustrated by curve C in Figure 11.2. An intermediate outcome is shown by curve B. In this case, the driver's behavior shows considerable sensitivity to differences in color, but responding is not as closely limited to a particular shade of red as in curve A.

Each of the curves in Figure 11.2 is a **stimulus generalization gradient**. We previously encountered the concept of stimulus generalization in connection with habituation (see Figure 3.3). Generalization gradients can be obtained for any stimulus feature—stimulus position, size, brightness, shape, height, and so on. As Figure 11.2 illustrates, the gradients may be very steep (curve A) or rather shallow (curve C). The steepness or slope of the generalization gradient indicates how closely the behavior is controlled by the stimulus feature in question. A steep generalization gradient indicates strong control by the stimulus feature or dimension. A shallow or flat generalization gradient indicates weak stimulus control.

Stimulus generalization and stimulus discrimination.   Stimulus generalization gradients involve two important phenomena, generalization and

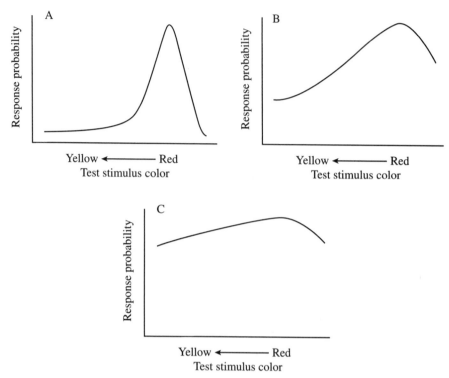

FIGURE 11.2   **Hypothetical stimulus generalization gradients indicating different degrees of control of responding by the color of a stimulus.**
Curve A illustrates strongest stimulus control by color; curve C illustrates weakest stimulus control by color.

discrimination. In **stimulus generalization**, the responding that occurs with one stimulus is also observed when a different stimulus is presented. Points 1 and 2 in Figure 11.3 illustrate the phenomenon of stimulus generalization. In **stimulus discrimination**, changes in a stimulus result in different levels of responding. Points 1 and 3 in Figure 11.3 illustrate the phenomenon of stimulus discrimination. More responding occurred to the stimulus at Point 1 than the stimulus at Point 3. Generalization and discrimination are complementary phenomena. A great deal of generalization among stimuli constitutes lack of discrimination, and a great deal of discrimination among stimuli indicates the lack of generalization.

Theories of generalization. Why do individuals respond similarly to different stimuli? Why do they generalize from one stimulus to another? Early investigators (Pavlov, 1927, for example) proposed a spread-of-effect inter-

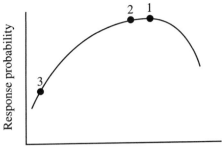

FIGURE 11.3 A hypothetical generalization gradient for responding to different colored stimuli.
Points 1 and 2 illustrate the phenomenon of stimulus generalization. Points 1 and 3 illustrate the phenomenon of stimulus discrimination.

pretation. According to this idea, responses conditioned to one stimulus generalize to other cues because the effects of training spread from the original training stimulus to other similar stimuli. When a child first learns the word for cow, she is likely to use the word "cow" not only when she sees a cow but also when she sees a bull, and perhaps even a horse. According to the spread-of-effect interpretation, such generalization occurs because bulls and horses are similar to cows and the learned response to cows spreads to other similar animals.

The spread-of-effect interpretation was challenged by Lashley and Wade (1946), who proposed that organisms respond similarly to different stimuli because they have not learned to distinguish between them. According to this interpretation, a child will use the word "cow" when she sees cows, bulls, and horses because she has not learned yet to distinguish among those different animals.

The Lashley-Wade hypothesis suggests that stimulus generalization can be limited by appropriate training. I will describe evidence confirming this prediction when I describe learning factors that determine the degree of stimulus control later in the chapter. However, before we get to that, let us consider how stimulus and organismic factors influence stimulus control.

Determinants of Stimulus Control: Stimulus and Organismic Factors

Having identified how to measure the stimulus control of behavior and having identified the complementary phenomena of stimulus generalization and stimulus discrimination, we are ready to tackle the second major question, namely, what factors determine which features of a stimulus will gain control over a particular response? In addressing this question, we will first consider factors related to the type of stimulus and organism involved.

SENSORY CAPACITY

Perhaps the most obvious factor determining whether a particular stimulus feature will influence behavior is the sensory capacity of the organism. An organism cannot respond to a stimulus if it lacks the sense organs needed to detect the stimulus. People are unable to respond to radio waves, ultraviolet light, and sounds above about 20,000 cycles/sec because they lack the sense organs to detect such stimuli. Dogs, in contrast, are able to hear sounds of much higher frequency than human beings and are therefore capable of responding to ultrasounds that are inaudible to people.

Sensory capacity sets a limit on the kinds of stimuli that can come to control an organism's behavior. However, sensory capacity is just a precondition for stimulus control. It does not ensure that behavior will be influenced by a particular stimulus feature. People with a normal sense of smell have the capacity to distinguish the aroma of various red wines. However, to someone with little experience all red wines smell alike. Sensory capacity is just the starting point for bringing behavior under the control of a particular stimulus feature.

SENSORY ORIENTATION

Another prerequisite for stimulus control is the sensory orientation of the organism. For a stimulus to gain control over some aspect of an individual's behavior, the stimulus has to be accessible to the relevant sense organ. If you have a cold and have to breath through your mouth, olfactory stimuli are not likely to reach the nasal epithelium, and you will be unable to make fine distinctions among different odors.

Some stimuli such as sounds and overall levels of illumination spread throughout an environment. Therefore, such stimuli are likely to be encountered whether or not the individual is oriented toward the source of the stimulus. For this reason, tones and overhead lights are popular stimuli in learning experiments. In contrast, a localized visual cue may present a problem because it is encountered only if the individual is facing toward it. For example, if you are watching for traffic signs on the right side of a road, you may miss a sign placed on the left side.

STIMULUS INTENSITY OR SALIENCE

Other things being equal, behavior is more likely to come under the control of intense or salient stimuli than weak ones (e.g., Kamin, 1965). In fact, the presence of an intense stimulus can interfere with the control of behavior

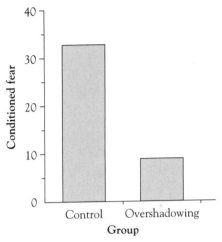

FIGURE 11.4 Levels of conditioned fear elicited by a 50 dB noise CS after pairings with foot shock in which the CS was presented simultaneously with a light CS (overshadowing) or without the light (control).
Based on Kamin (1969).

by a weaker cue. This phenomenon, first identified by Pavlov (1927), is referred to as **overshadowing**.

In one demonstration of overshadowing (Kamin, 1969), two groups of rats were compared in their acquisition of conditioned fear to a fairly soft 50 dB noise using the conditioned suppression procedure. For the overshadowing group, the noise CS was presented simultaneously with a light on each conditioning trial. For the control group the noise was presented without the light. After eight conditioning trials, the fear response of both groups was measured to the noise CS presented alone.

The results of the noise-alone test trials are summarized in Figure 11.4. A substantial level of conditioned fear was observed in the control group. In contrast, much less fear occurred in the overshadowing group. This outcome indicates that the presence of the light during the conditioning trials interfered with, or "overshadowed," the development of conditioned fear to the noise CS.

MOTIVATIONAL FACTORS

The extent to which behavior comes under the control of a particular stimulus is also determined by the motivational state of the organism. Motivational factors in the stimulus control of behavior have not been investigated extensively. However, the available evidence indicates that attention can be shifted away from one type of stimulus to another by a change in motivation. LoLordo and his associates have found, for example, that pigeons conditioned with food as the reinforcer come to respond to visual cues more than to auditory cues. In contrast, pigeons conditioned to avoid pain are more likely to respond to auditory cues than to visual cues (Foree & LoLordo, 1973; Shapiro, Jacobs, & LoLordo, 1980).

The motivational state of the organism appears to activate a stimulus filter that biases the attention of the organism in favor of certain types of cues. When pigeons are hungry and are motivated to find food, they are especially sensitive to visual cues. In contrast, when pigeons are fearful and are motivated to avoid danger, they are especially sensitive to auditory cues. For other species, these motivational influences may take different forms. A species that hunts for live prey at night, for example, may be especially attentive to auditory cues when it is hungry.

Determinants of Stimulus Control: Learning Factors

Given the required sensory capacity and sensory orientation, perhaps the most important factor that determines the extent to which behavior will be controlled by a particular stimulus is the significance or validity of that stimulus. As Pavlov pointed out, biologically significant stimuli (such as food for a hungry animal) can control behavior unconditionally or without prior training. In addition, stimuli that are not significant at the outset can become important through association with stimuli or events that are already significant.

PAVLOVIAN AND INSTRUMENTAL CONDITIONING

An initially ineffective stimulus can come to control behavior through a direct or an indirect association with a US. As I discussed in Chapter 4, simple Pavlovian conditioning procedures make an initially ineffective stimulus (the CS) significant by establishing an association between that event and the US. Stimulus significance also can be established through instrumental conditioning, with either positive or negative reinforcement.

In the case of positive reinforcement, the US or reinforcer (S*) is presented contingent on a response (R) in the presence of an initially neutral stimulus (S). The three-term S-R-S* instrumental contingency increases the significance of stimulus S by establishing an association between S and the reinforcer S* or by having stimulus S signal when the response will be reinforced (see Chapter 6). The situation is similar in the case of negative reinforcement (see Chapter 10). In the discriminated avoidance procedure, for example, the instrumental response results in avoidance of aversive stimulation only if the response occurs in the presence of a warning signal, and this makes the warning signal significant to the organism.

Simple Pavlovian and instrumental conditioning procedures increase the control of behavior by an initially ineffective stimulus, but such procedures do not determine which feature(s) of that stimulus will become most effective. Consider, for example, a compound stimulus that has both auditory and visual features. Whether the visual or the auditory component will gain predominant control over the conditioned response will depend on the stimulus and organismic factors described in the preceding section. If the organism has a keen sense of sight but poor hearing, the visual component will predominate. If both senses are adequate and the organism is motivated by fear, the auditory component may be more important. If the visual component is more intense or salient than the auditory feature, the visual component may overshadow the auditory component.

How about stimulus features that cannot be distinguished on the basis of sensory capacity, sensory orientation, stimulus intensity, or motivation? How can they come to control differential responding? Consider, for example, a car that has been recently filled with gas and one that is about to run out of gas. There is little difference between these two types of cars in terms of the modality and intensity of the stimuli a driver encounters. The only difference is where the fuel gauge indicator points (E or F), and that difference may be just an inch or two. Nevertheless, the difference between having plenty of gas and being nearly empty is highly significant to drivers. People also respond very differently to seeing the word "fire" as compared to the word "hire," even though the visual stimuli features of these two words are nearly identical. How do such highly similar stimuli come to control dramatically different responses? The answer rests with conditioning procedures that provide differential reinforcement in the presence of different stimuli.

STIMULUS DISCRIMINATION TRAINING

Training that provides differential reinforcement in the presence of different stimuli is called **stimulus discrimination training**. Stimulus discrimination training can be conducted with either Pavlovian or instrumental methods. Simple cases of Pavlovian and instrumental conditioning involve only one CS or stimulus condition. In contrast, stimulus discrimination training requires two conditioned stimuli. One of these is called the S^+, and the other is called the S^-. Any two stimuli that are initially ineffective in generating the conditioned or instrumental response may serve as S^+ and S^-. For example, S^+ and S^- may be the letters "f" and "h," a tone and a buzzer, or a light and a noise.

In a Pavlovian discrimination procedure, each presentation of S^+ is paired with the unconditioned stimulus. In contrast, the unconditioned stimulus is omitted on trials when S^- occurs. Thus, S^+ and S^- are associated with different outcomes or differential reinforcement. S^+ and S^- may be two orange cats, for example, one rather friendly and the other aloof. The

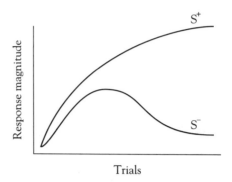

FIGURE 11.5 **Typical results of a Pavlovian discrimination training procedure in which S⁺ is paired with a US and S⁻ is presented equally often alone.** The conditioned responding that develops initially to S⁺ generalizes to S⁻. However, with continued training, a strong discrimination develops between S⁺ and S⁻.

friendly cat (S⁺) is paired with tactile pleasure because it allows people to pet her. The aloof cat (S⁻) does not let people pet her and is therefore not paired with the positive tactile US.

Typical results of a discrimination procedure are illustrated in Figure 11.5. S⁺ and S⁻ trials are randomly alternated during the course of training. Early in training, the conditioned response comes to be elicited by the S⁺, and this responding generalizes to S⁻. The outcome is that the participant responds to some extent to both the S⁺ and the S⁻ during initial stages of training. With continued discrimination training, responding to S⁺ continues to increase, whereas responding to S⁻ gradually declines. The final result is that the participant responds much more to S⁺ than to S⁻. A strong distinction develops between S⁺ and S⁻. At this point, the two stimuli are said to be discriminated.

Let's consider again our example two cats, one friendly and the other aloof. As you start to associate one of the cats with tactile pleasure, any affection that you develop for her may generalize to the other cat. However, as you have additional pleasant encounters with one cat but not with the other, your response to the friendly cat will increase and your response to the aloof cat will decline. You will come to distinguish one cat from the other.

Discrimination training can be conducted in an analogous fashion with instrumental conditioning. In this case, the instrumental response is reinforced on trials when S⁺ is presented (S⁺→R→S*). In contrast, the response is not reinforced when a different stimulus (S⁻) is presented (S⁻→R→ noS*). Thus, S⁺ and S⁻ are again associated with differential reinforcement. As with Pavlovian discrimination procedures, during initial stages of training, responding to S$^+$ may generalize to S$^-$. However, eventually the participant will respond vigorously to S$^+$ and little, if at all, to S$^-$, as in Figure 11.5.

In all stimulus discrimination procedures, different stimuli are associated with different outcomes. In the last examples, differential reinforcement was provided by the delivery versus omission of the US or reinforcer. The presence versus absence of reinforcement represents a common but special case in discrimination training procedures. Any form of differential reinforcement can be used in discrimination training.

Infants, for example, quickly learn to discriminate mom from dad. This does not occur because mom is a source of reinforcement whereas dad is not. Both mom and dad provide pleasure for the infant, but they are likely to provide different types of pleasure. One parent may provide more tactile comfort and nutritional reinforcement, whereas the other may provide primarily sensory reinforcement in the form of tickling or physical play. Each type of reinforcer is associated with a different parent, and that leads the infant to discriminate between the parents.

MULTIPLE SCHEDULES OF REINFORCEMENT

Differential reinforcement also may be programmed in terms of different schedules of reinforcement in the presence of different stimuli. For example, a variable-interval schedule may be in effect in the presence of stimulus A, and a fixed-interval schedule may be in effect in the presence of stimulus B. Such a procedure is called a **multiple schedule of reinforcement**. As a result of training on a multiple VI-FI schedule of reinforcement, participants will come to respond to stimulus A in a manner typical of variable-interval performance and will respond to stimulus B in a manner typical of fixed-interval performance.

Listening to different instructors in different classes, for example, is reinforced on a multiple schedule. The reinforcer is the new information provided in each class. Some professors say lots of new things during their classes, thereby reinforcing listening behavior on a dense variable-interval schedule. Other professors predictably make just four or five important points during a lecture and spend about 10 minutes elaborating each point. This reinforces listening behavior on a fixed-interval schedule. Each schedule of reinforcement is in effect in the presence of the distinct stimuli of each professor and class. Therefore, across both classes listening behavior is reinforced on a multiple schedule that produces differential listening behavior. Students will listen at a steady rate without predictable pauses in the class where listening is reinforced on a dense VI schedule and will show postreinforcement lapses in attention in the class where listening is reinforced on an FI schedule.

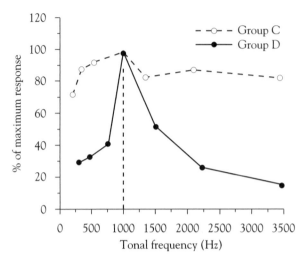

FIGURE 11.6 **Effects of discrimination training on control of the pecking behavior of pigeons by the frequency of different tones.**
Prior to the generalization test, group D received discrimination training in which the S⁺ was a 1000 Hz tone and the S⁻ was the absence of the tone. In contrast, group C received just reinforcement for keypecking in the presence of the 1000 Hz tone. Based on Jenkins & Harrison (1960).

DIFFERENTIAL REINFORCEMENT AND STIMULUS CONTROL

Differential reinforcement in the presence of S⁺ and S⁻ produces differential responding to those stimuli. Interestingly, these effects may extend far beyond the actual stimuli that were used in the discrimination procedure. The far-reaching effects of discrimination training were first identified by Jenkins and Harrison (1960). They compared the stimulus control of pecking behavior in two groups of pigeons. Group D was first conditioned to discriminate between the presence and absence of a tone. These pigeons were reinforced for pecking a response key whenever a tone with a frequency of 1000 Hz was turned on (S⁺) and were not reinforced when the tone was absent (S⁻). The control group (group C) received similar reinforcement for pecking the response key, but for them the tone was on continuously during the training sessions. Thus, group C did not receive differential reinforcement associated with the tone.

Following this contrasting training history, the response of both groups was measured in a test of stimulus generalization. Tones of various frequencies were presented during the test session. The results are summarized in Figure 11.6. The control group, which did not receive discrimination training, responded vigorously to the tone that had been present during training (the 1000 Hz tone). They also responded vigorously to most of the other tones, which they encountered for the first time during the generalization test. Thus, in the absence of discrimination training, a fairly flat generalization gradient was obtained. This indicates that the frequency of the tones did not gain much control over the behavior of these birds.

The results were dramatically different with the pigeons in group D, which were first trained to discriminate between the presence and absence of the 1000 Hz tone. These birds showed a steep generalization gradient. They responded a great deal to the 1000 Hz tone (the S$^+$), but their behavior quickly dropped off when tones of other frequencies were presented. This is a remarkable outcome because the other tones had not been presented during prior discrimination training. None of the other tones had served as the S$^-$ in the discrimination procedure. Even though group D had not encountered nonreinforcement in the presence of tones during training, tones other than S$^+$ did not support much pecking behavior.

The results presented in Figure 11.6 show that the shape of a generalization gradient can be altered by discrimination training. Discrimination training not only produces differential responding to S$^+$ and S$^-$ but also increases the steepness of generalization gradients. Thus, the effects of discrimination training extend beyond the specific stimuli that are used as S$^+$ and S$^-$.

INTERDIMENSIONAL VERSUS INTRADIMENSIONAL DISCRIMINATIONS

So far we have stressed the importance of differential reinforcement in discrimination training procedures. The nature of the S$^+$ and S$^-$ stimuli also determines the outcome of discrimination training. The similarities and differences between S$^+$ and S$^-$ are especially important. If S$^+$ and S$^-$ differ in several respects, the discrimination is called an **interdimensional discrimination**. If S$^+$ and S$^-$ differ in only one respect, the discrimination is called an **intradimensional discrimination**.

Interdimensional discriminations.   Perhaps the most common forms of interdimensional discrimination training are simple Pavlovian or discrete-trial instrumental conditioning procedures, although usually we don't think of these as involving discrimination training. A simple Pavlovian procedure involves just one CS and one US. Presentations of the CS end in delivery of the US. In contrast, the US is not delivered when the CS is absent. Thus, the discrimination is between times when the CS is present and times when the CS is absent (the intertrial interval). All of the features of the CS (its modality, intensity, and location) serve to distinguish the CS from its absence. Therefore, this is an interdimensional discrimination.

In discrete-trial instrumental conditioning, the participant is reinforced for responding in the presence of particular stimuli (the stimuli of a runway, for example), and responding is not reinforced in the absence of those cues. Thus, simple discrete-trial instrumental conditioning similarly involves a discrimination between the stimuli that define a trial versus those that are encountered during the intertrial interval. Because numerous stimulus features distinguish the trial stimuli from the intertrial interval, this is also an interdimensional discrimination.

Interdimensional discriminations also can be set up between discrete stimuli serving as S$^+$ and S$^-$. Discrimination between a red and a green traffic light, for example, is an interdimensional discrimination because red and green traffic lights differ in both color and position. The discrimination learned by an infant between mom and dad is also an interdimensional discrimination. Mom and dad differ in many respects, including visual features, differences in how each holds the infant, differences in voice, differences in the time of day each is likely to interact with the infant, and so on.

Intradimensional discriminations.   Interdimensional discriminations are effective in establishing stimulus control. However, they do not establish a high degree of control over behavior by any particular stimulus feature. For example, since many things distinguish mom from dad, the infant may not respond a great deal to any one distinguishing feature. The most effective way to establish control by a specific stimulus feature is through intradimensional discrimination training (Jenkins & Harrison, 1960, 1962). In intradimensional discrimination training, the stimuli associated with differential reinforcement differ in only one respect.

Many forms of expert performance involve intradimensional discriminations. Reading, for example, requires discriminating between letters that differ in only one respect. The letters "E" and "F" differ only in the horizontal bottom stem, which is present in "E" but not in "F." The physical difference is very small, but the differential consequences in terms of meaning can be substantial. The letters "B" and "P," and "M" and "N" are other pairs that are similar physically but differ greatly in significance. Learning to read involves learning to respond differentially to such similar letters. Thus, reading requires learning many intradimensional discriminations.

One of the interesting things about learning fine intradimensional discriminations is that the participant is not likely to be aware of the physical difference between the stimuli at the outset of training. Initially, the letters "E" and "F" may appear the same to a child. The child may recognize "E" and "F" as being different from "O" but may not be able to tell the difference between "E" and "F." The child may come to recognize the visual difference between the two letters only after being taught to say one thing when shown "E" and something else when shown "F." Differential reinforcement serves to focus attention on physical differences that are otherwise ignored.

Similar effects occur in the acquisition of other forms of expertise. Children learning to sing may not be able to tell at first when they are singing in tune or off key. However, this skill develops through differential reinforcement from a teacher. Likewise, budding ballerinas learn to pay close attention to proprioceptive cues indicating the precise position of their arms and legs, and pool players learn to make precise judgments about angles and trajectories. Intradimensional discrimination training brings behavior under precise control of small variations in a stimulus and thereby serves to increase sensitivity to those small stimulus variations. Thus, sensitivity to variations in environmental stimuli depends not only on sensory capacity but also on one's history of discrimination training.

Shaping of Discriminations and Perceptual Concept Learning

As this discussion indicates, the stimulus control of behavior is not fixed by an organism's sensory capacity but can be shaped by experience. Whether an organism responds in the same manner to certain stimuli or responds differentially depends on its training history. The flexibility and modifiability of stimulus control are critical for the learning of a **perceptual concept**. Perceptual concepts are the means by which organisms categorize the various stimuli they encounter in their world in order to respond similarly to some of them and differently to others.

Consider the perceptual category that consists of various types of dogs. In calling greyhounds, poodles, and dachshunds all "dogs," a child has to ignore differences in the overall size, speed, fur quality, and other features that characterize these breeds. On the other hand, the category "dogs" requires distinguishing greyhounds, poodles, and dachshunds from other mammals such as cats, ferrets, and beavers. Thus, the learning of a perceptual category involves an interplay between generalization and discrimination. The child has to learn to ignore differences among various distinctive dog breeds (**stimulus generalization**) at the same time that she learns to tell the difference between dogs and other mammals (**stimulus discrimination**).

The exact interplay between generalization and discrimination learning depends on the level of the perceptual category. "Dog" is an intermediate-level category. A higher-level category is "mammal" and a lower-level category is a specific type of dog, such as "greyhound." Although various types of dogs differ in numerous respects, dogs are more similar to one another than are animals that belong to the higher level category "mammals." Therefore, learning the category "mammal" requires more generalizations than learning the category "dog." On the other hand, more discrimination learning is required for the lower-level category "greyhound." In responding to an animal as a "greyhound," one has to learn to distinguish greyhounds from other dog breeds.

Successful navigation of the environment requires learning to respond to certain stimuli in the same manner despite their differences (generalization) while responding differentially to other cues (discrimination). Contingencies of reinforcement serve to shape an organism's stimulus generalization and discrimination performance and thereby serve to coordinate the organism's behavior with its ecological niche.

Summary

Organisms have to learn not only what to do but also when and where to do it. When and where a response is made involves the stimulus control of behavior. Stimulus control is identified by differential responding and can be precisely measured by the steepness of generalization gradients. The extent to which a stimulus influences behavior depends on stimulus and organismic variables such as sensory capacity, sensory orientation, stimulus intensity, and the organism's motivational state. Stimuli that cannot be differentiated on the basis of these factors may gain control over behavior as a result differential reinforcement.

Discrimination training may involve either interdimensional stimuli or intradimensional stimuli. Intradimensional discrimination training produces more precise stimulus control than interdimensional training and is the basis for various forms of expert performance. However, learning fine discriminations is not always useful. The formation of perceptual concepts, for example, requires a precise balance between discrimination learning and stimulus generalization. More precise discriminations are required for low-level concepts and more stimulus generalization is required for higher-level concepts.

Suggested Readings

BALSAM, P. D. (1988). Selection, representation, and equivalence of controlling stimuli. In R. C. Atkinson, R. J. Herrnstein, G. Lindzey, & R. D. Luce (Eds.), *Stevens' handbook of experimental psychology* (Vol. 2, pp. 111–166). New York: Wiley.

PEARCE, J. M. (1994). Discrimination and categorization. In N. J. Mackintosh (Ed.), *Animal learning and cognition* (pp. 110–134). San Diego: Academic Press.

WASSERMAN, E. A., & ASTLEY, S. L. (1994). A behavioral analysis of concepts: Its application to pigeons and children. In D. L. Medin (Ed.), *The psychology of learning and motivation* (Vol. 31, pp. 73–132). San Diego: Academic Press.

Technical Terms

Differential responding	S^-
Interdimensional discrimination	Stimulus dimension
Intradimensional discrimination	Stimulus discrimination
Multiple schedule of reinforcement	Stimulus discrimination training
Overshadowing	Stimulus generalization
Perceptual concept	Stimulus generalization gradient
S^+	

CHAPTER TWELVE

Memory Mechanisms

DID YOU KNOW THAT:

- Learning and memory are integrally related.
- Tasks testing memory mechanisms have to be specially designed so that they cannot be solved without the use of memory.
- Memory for even simple stimuli is not a passive or automatic process.
- Memory can improve with learning.
- Memory can be brought under stimulus control.
- Memory can be prospective and involve future rather than past events.
- Failures of memory can be caused by remembering too much or by not remembering enough.
- Seemingly trivial aspects of a learning situation can stimulate retrieval of what was learned.

In Chapter 11, I described mechanisms responsible for the control of behavior by stimuli an organism encounters in its environment. This chapter deals with how behavior can be controlled by events that occurred at an earlier time but are no longer present. Past events influence behavior through memory mechanisms.

Philosophers and scientists have been interested in how people remember things since the time of the ancient Greeks. Studies of memory continue today as a prominent aspect of contemporary research in human cognitive psychology. In contrast, systematic investigations of memory mechanisms in nonhuman animals have a much shorter history. Only in the last 30 years has much experimental research on memory been conducted with various species of animals (Honig & James, 1971; Kendrick, Rilling, & Denny, 1986; Medin, Roberts, & Davis, 1976; Spear & Riccio, 1994).

Why should anyone study memory mechanisms in nonhuman animal species? Why should we care about how rats or pigeons remember things? Animal research on memory mechanisms is important for several reasons. It promises to inform us about the evolution of cognitive processes (Sherry & Schachter, 1987). Such research is also essential for investigations of the physiological bases of memory, for the development and testing of drugs that influence memory, and for the development of systems of artificial intelligence that mimic living organisms. Finally, studies of memory mechanisms promise to help us understand basic mechanisms of conditioning and learning (e.g., Miller, Kasprow, & Schachtman, 1986).

Learning and memory are integrally related. One cannot have one without the other. In fact, research on memory mechanisms in animals makes extensive use of the basic conditioning procedures that I described in earlier chapters. This makes the discussion of memory research appropriate at the end of a book on basic conditioning procedures. However, a fundamental question arises: If all learning involves memory, what distinguishes studies of memory from studies of learning? The answer is that studies of memory focus on a different stage of information processing than studies of learning.

Stages of Information Processing

Memory involves the delayed effects of experience. For experience with stimuli and responses to influence behavior some time later, three things have to happen. First, information about the stimuli and responses must be acquired and encoded in the nervous system in some fashion. This is the **acquisition stage** of information processing. Once encoded, the information has to be stored for later use. This is the **retention stage** of information processing. Finally, when the information is needed at the end of the retention interval, it has to be recovered from storage. This is the **retrieval stage**.

TABLE 12.1   Differences Between Experiments on Learning and Experiments on Memory

Stage	Learning Experiments	Memory Experiments
Acquisition	Varied	Constant
Retention interval	Constant (long)	Varied (short and long)
Retrieval	Constant	Varied

Acquisition, retention, and retrieval are involved in all studies of learning as well as all studies of memory. However, which stage is the focus of interest differs depending on whether one is primarily concerned with learning processes or memory processes (see Table 12.1). Studies of learning focus on the acquisition stage. In studies of learning the circumstances of acquisition are manipulated or varied while the conditions of retention and retrieval are kept constant. In contrast, in studies of memory, the conditions of acquisition are kept constant while the retention interval and the conditions of retrieval are varied.

The Matching-to-Sample Procedure

A variety of different techniques have been used to study memory mechanisms in animals. Memory procedures often require special controls to ensure that the participant's behavior is determined by its past experience rather than by some clue that is inadvertently presented in the test situation. In addition, special procedures have to be designed to isolate particular memory processes. To facilitate illustration of these complexities, I will describe one technique for the study of memory mechanisms in detail—the **matching-to-sample procedure**.

Matching-to-sample is perhaps the most versatile procedure for the study of memory mechanisms. It can be used to investigate memory for a variety of different kinds of stimuli and can be adapted to address a variety of different research questions. Although our discussion will focus on the matching to sample technique, the conceptual issues involved are relevant to all other memory tasks as well.

In the matching-to-sample procedure, the participant is first exposed to a sample stimulus. The sample is then removed for a retention interval. After the retention interval, the participant receives a multiple-choice memory test. Several alternatives are presented, one of which is the same as the sample stimulus that was presented at the start of the trial. If the participant selects the previously presented sample, it is reinforced.

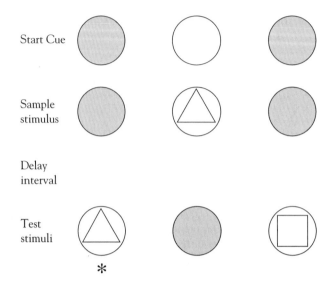

FIGURE 12.1   Illustration of a matching-to-sample trial used with pigeons.
The trial begins with a start cue presented on the center key. The sample stimulus (a triangle) is then presented, also on the center key. The sample is then turned off, and a retention interval begins. At the end of the retention interval, the subject receives two test stimuli on the side keys, one of which matches the sample stimulus. Pecks at the matching test cue are reinforced, as indicated by the asterisk.

The matching procedure has been used with species as diverse as dolphins, rats, and people (Baron & Menich, 1985; Forestell & Herman, 1988; Wallace, Steinert, Scobie, & Spear, 1980), and the procedure has been adapted for various types of sample stimuli, including visual, auditory, and spatial cues. Figure 12.1 illustrates a version of the procedure for use with pigeons.

Pigeons are typically tested in a Skinner box that is provided with three response keys arranged in a row. Each trial begins with a start cue, which might be illumination of the center key with a white light. One peck at the start cue results in presentation of the sample stimulus on the center key. In our example, the sample stimulus is a triangle. After a few seconds, the sample stimulus is turned off and a retention interval begins. At the end of the retention interval, the pigeon receives two test stimuli on the side keys. One of the test stimuli is the same as the previously presented sample (a triangle), whereas the other is different (a square). Pecks at the matching stimulus are reinforced. Pecks at the alternate test stimulus have no consequence.

Simultaneous and Delayed Matching-to-Sample

As you might suspect, the difficulty of a matching-to-sample procedure depends in part on the duration of the retention interval (Grant, 1976). To facilitate learning of a matching task, it is useful to begin training without a retention interval. Such a procedure is called **simultaneous matching-to-sample**. In simultaneous matching-to-sample, each trial begins with a start cue on the center key. This is then followed by presentation of the sample stimulus on the center key. The test stimuli are then presented on the side keys while the sample remains on the center key. Because the sample stimulus is visible at the same time as the test stimuli, the procedure is called simultaneous matching-to-sample.

After the participants have learned to make the accurate choice in a simultaneous matching procedure, a retention interval can be introduced between presentation of the sample and presentation of the test stimuli, as illustrated in Figure 12.1. Because in this case the test stimuli are delayed after presentation of the sample, the procedure is called **delayed matching-to-sample**.

Procedural Controls for Memory

Introducing a retention interval is necessary to make sure that the participant has to remember something about the sample stimulus to respond accurately when the test choices are presented. However, having a retention interval in the procedure is not enough to be sure that the participant is using memory based on the sample stimulus. The sample and test stimuli also have to be varied from one trial to the next.

Consider, for example, a procedure in which every trial was exactly the same as the trial illustrated in Figure 12.1. To respond accurately with repetitions of this trial, the pigeon would just have to learn to peck the left key when the side keys were illuminated. The pigeon would not have to remember anything about the shape of the visual cue that was projected on any of the response keys.

To force pigeons to pay attention to and remember information about the specific stimuli that are presented in a matching procedure, the sample stimulus used and the position of the test stimuli have to be varied across training trials. Figure 12.2 illustrates various types of trials in a matching procedure involving two shape stimuli (triangle and square) and two pattern stimuli (a vertical grid and a horizontal grid). There are eight possible trial types. With each sample stimulus, two types of test trials can be designed, one with the correct stimulus on the left and one with the correct

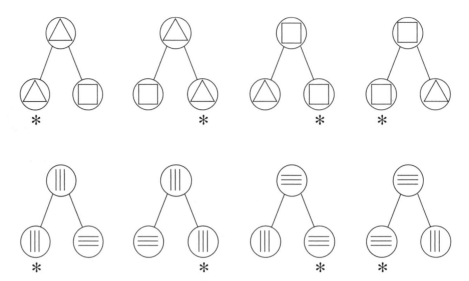

FIGURE 12.2   Eight different types of trials used to make sure that participants in a matching-to-sample procedure are responding on the basis of information obtained from the sample stimulus.
For each trial type the sample is presented on top and the two choice stimuli are presented below. The correct choice is identified by an asterisk.

stimulus on the right. If the eight trial types appear randomly during training, the participant cannot be consistently accurate unless it uses information based on the sample to guide its choice responses.

Types of Memory

Memory is not a homogeneous process. There are different kinds of memory based on what kind of information is remembered, what types of manipulations influence the nature of the memory, and how long the memory lasts. In animal research, distinctions between reference and working memory, active and passive memory, and prospective and retrospective memory have received special attention.

REFERENCE MEMORY AND WORKING MEMORY

What kinds of memory are required to respond successfully in a matching-to-sample procedure? In our discussion of procedural controls for memory, we were concerned with making sure that responses to the test stimuli on a particular trial depended on what the participant remembered from the sample stimulus that was presented on that trial. Such memory is called **working memory**.

Working memory is retention of information that is needed to respond successfully on one trial or task but is not useful in responding on the next trial or task. Because the sample stimulus is varied from one trial to the next in a matching procedure (see Figure 12.2), information from the sample presented on one trial does not help in picking the correct test stimulus on the next trial. Thus, working memory is of limited duration.

The control procedures that we discussed previously (variations in the sample stimulus and in the location of the correct choice stimulus) ensure that matching-to-sample procedures involve working memory. However, to respond successfully participants have to remember more than just information from the sample on a particular trial. They also have to remember general features of the matching procedure that remain constant from one trial to the next. For example, pigeons have to remember to peck the start cue and to peck one of the test stimuli after the retention interval. In addition, they have to remember that correct responses are reinforced and where to obtain the reinforcer once it is delivered. Such memory is called **reference memory**. Because reference memory involves constant features of a task, it is of considerably longer duration than working memory.

The distinction between working and reference memory is applicable to all sorts of situations. Baking a cake, for example, involves both working and reference memory. As you create the batter, you have to remember which ingredients you have already included and which ones to add next. That kind of information is useful only for the cake you are preparing; it will not help you bake the next cake. Therefore, such information involves working memory.

To bake a cake, you also have to have some general information about cooking. You have to know about cake pans, ovens, various ingredients, and how to measure and mix those ingredients. These general skills are useful not just for the cake you happen to be baking but also for any future cakes you might want to make. Therefore, such information involves reference memory.

ACTIVE AND PASSIVE MEMORY

Working and reference memory are distinguished by the type of information that is retained and by how long the information is remembered. Memory mechanisms can also be distinguished by the kinds of procedures that influence them. A fundamental issue is whether memory can be modified or influenced by other psychological processes. This is the basis for the distinction between active and passive memory.

Passive memory processes are assumed to be automatic and not subject to modification by other psychological processes. A prominent passive memory process that has been considered in matching-to-sample experiments is the **trace-decay hypothesis** (Roberts & Grant, 1976). According to this hypothesis, presentation of a sample stimulus activates a neural trace that automatically decays after the end of the stimulus. Information about the sample is available only as long as the trace is sufficiently strong. The gradual fading or decay of the neural trace is assumed to produce progressively less accurate recall.

The initial strength of a neural trace is assumed to depend only on the physical intensity and duration of the sample stimulus. (More intense and longer stimuli presumably activate stronger neural traces.) However, regardless of its initial strength, a neural trace is assumed to gradually fade with time. Consistent with these assumptions, pigeons respond less accurately in delayed matching-to-sample procedures as the retention interval between the sample stimulus and the choice test is increased; in addition, responding is more accurate with longer sample stimuli (Grant, 1976).

According to the trace-decay hypothesis, information about the sample is lost automatically during the retention interval and nothing can be done about that. However, several lines of evidence suggest that memory loss is not an automatic passive process that is immune to modification by other psychological processes. Contrary to the trace-decay hypothesis, memory for a sample stimulus improves with practice (D'Amato, 1973). Memory also can be improved by making the stimulus surprising (Maki, 1979). Finally, evidence suggests that memory mechanisms can be brought under stimulus control (Grant & Soldat, 1995; Roper, Kaiser, & Zentall, 1995). Animals can be conditioned to remember a sample stimulus in one situation but not in another.

The preponderance of evidence suggests that working memory in a matching-to-sample procedure is not the kind of automatic passive process that is assumed by the trace-decay hypothesis. Rather, it is an active process that can be influenced by various psychological processes such as learning, surprisingness, and stimulus control.

RETROSPECTIVE AND PROSPECTIVE MEMORY

So far we have established that the matching to sample task involves both working and reference memory, and working memory is best characterized as an active rather than a passive process. Another important issue concerns the contents of working memory. This refers to what the organism remembers during the retention interval that enables it to make the correct choice at the end of a trial.

Retrospective memory. The most obvious possibility is that information about the sample stimulus is retained during the retention interval, and this enables the participant to select the correct test stimulus. Presumably, the memory of the sample is compared to each of the test stimuli at the end of the trial to determine which alternative best resembles the sample. The participant then selects the test stimulus that best matches the sample.

Remembering attributes of the sample stimulus is a form of **retrospective memory**. Retrospective memory is memory for stimuli (or other types of events) that were encountered previously. It is memory that is retroactive or involves past events.

Retrospective memory is perhaps the most obvious possibility for the contents of working memory in a matching task. However, just because a hypothesis is obvious does not make it correct. What else might a participant keep in mind during the retention interval that would enable it to respond correctly during the choice test?

Prospective memory. Recall that in the typical matching procedure, a limited number of different trial types are repeated over and over again in a random order. Figure 12.2, for example, illustrates a procedure in which there are four possible sample stimuli: a triangle, a square, a vertical grid, and a horizontal grid. For each sample, there is a unique correct test stimulus. Because of this, the matching procedure involves pairs of sample and test stimuli.

Let us represent a sample stimulus as "S" and a test stimulus as "T." Different sample test stimulus pairs can then be represented as S1-T1, S2-T2, S3-T3, and so on. Given these S-T pairings, participants could select the correct choice stimulus in a matching task by thinking of T after presentation of the sample S and storing that information during the retention interval. This involves keeping information about a future stimulus in memory and is called **prospective memory**. Prospective memory involves remembering something that is predicted to occur in the future or prospectively.

Deciding between retrospection and prospection. Retrospective memory involves remembering the sample stimulus S during the retention interval. Prospective memory involves remembering the test stimulus T during the retention interval. How can we distinguish between these possibilities experimentally?

In a matching-to-sample procedure, the sample stimulus S and the correct test stimulus T are physically the same thing. If the sample is a triangle, the correct test stimulus is also a triangle. This makes it virtually impossible to decide whether information stored during the retention interval concerns stimulus S or stimulus T. To distinguish between retrospective and prospective memory, we have to change the matching procedure somewhat so that T is not the same physical stimulus as S. Such a procedure is called symbolic matching to sample.

A symbolic matching procedure is illustrated in the left column of Figure 12.3. Each row represents a different trial type in the procedure. The procedure is based on symbolic relations between sample and test stimuli

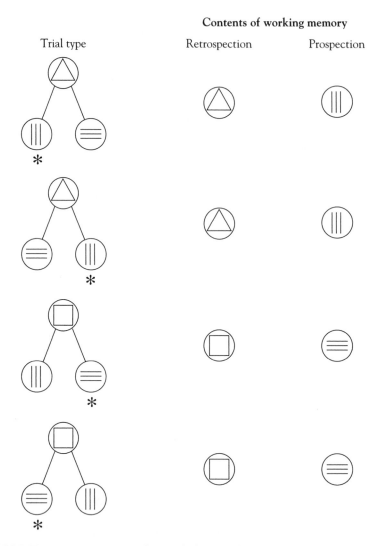

FIGURE 12.3   Diagram of a symbolic matching-to-sample procedure and illustration of the difference between retrospective and prospective working memory.

For each trial type, the test stimuli are shown below the sample stimulus, and the correct test stimulus is indicated by an asterisk.

rather than the identity relation. In Figure 12.3, responding to the vertical grid is reinforced after presentation of a triangle as the sample stimulus, and responding to the horizontal grid is reinforced after presentation of a square as the sample. In a sense, the vertical grid is a symbol for the triangle sample, and the horizontal grid is a symbol for the square sample.

As with the standard matching procedure, in a symbolic matching task the correct test stimulus appears equally often on the left and the right, and there is a delay between the sample and the test stimuli. Therefore, the task involves working memory, just as the standard matching procedure. However, with symbolic matching different things are remembered depending on whether the memory is retrospective or prospective. The differences are shown in the center and right columns of Figure 12.3. On trials with the triangle as the sample, retrospective memory involves retention of information about the triangle. In contrast, prospective memory involves retention of information about the vertical grid test stimulus, which is the correct choice after a triangle sample. On trials with the square as the sample, retrospective memory involves remembering the square, whereas prospective memory involves remembering the horizontal grid.

Using symbolic matching to sample tasks, investigators have found that pigeons use prospective rather than retrospective memory (e.g., Roitblat, 1980; Santi & Roberts, 1985). Research using other kinds of memory tasks also has provided evidence of prospective memory. However, not all instances of working memory involve prospection or memory for events that are predicted to occur in the future. Whether organisms remember a past event (retrospection) or a future event (prospection) appears to depend on which form of memory is more efficient in solving a particular task (Cook, Brown, & Riley, 1985; Zentall, Steirn, & Jackson-Smith, 1990).

Sources of Memory Failure

Instances of the failure of memory can tell us as much about memory mechanisms as instances of successful remembering. Memory may fail for a variety of reasons. You may not remember something because you never encoded or learned the information in the first place. Memory failure may also result from failure to effectively retrieve information that was successfully encoded or stored. Finally, you may perform poorly in a memory task because you remember several different things and are unable to choose correctly among those alternatives. This section provides examples of each of these sources of memory failure in the context of investigations of interference and retrieval failure.

INTERFERENCE

Memory failure caused by interference has been extensively investigated in both human and animal studies. Interference refers to memory failure that results from exposure to stimuli or events that are extraneous to the memory task the individual is tested on. If you were presented with a single visual pattern in an otherwise darkened room, you would show good retention of that stimulus several minutes later. In contrast, if you saw numerous

TABLE 12.2   Distinction Between Proactive and Retroactive Interference

Proactive interference

Extraneous events → Target task → Memory test

Retroactive interference

Target task → Extraneous events → Memory test

---

visual stimuli before and/or after the stimulus that you were tested on, your memory for the test item would be much worse. Exposure to various visual stimuli before and after the test item would interfere with your memory for the test item.

Different kinds of interference effects occur depending on whether the interfering events occur before or after what the participant is to be tested on (see Table 12.2). If the extraneous stimuli that disrupt memory occur before the target event, the phenomenon is called **proactive interference**. In proactive interference, the interfering stimuli act forward, or proactively, to disrupt memory for the target stimulus. In contrast, if the extraneous stimuli occur after the event the participant has to remember, the phenomenon is called **retroactive interference**. In retroactive interference, the extraneous stimuli act backward, or retroactively, to disrupt memory for the target event.

Proactive interference in matching-to-sample.   Both proactive and retroactive interference have been investigated in animal studies using delayed matching-to-sample procedures. In early studies of proactive interference, an explicit extraneous stimulus was presented before the start of a matching trial (and thus before presentation of the sample stimulus for that trial). Subjects performed less accurately on trials preceded by the extraneous stimulus than on control trials conducted in the absence of the extraneous stimulus (Medin, 1980).

Proactive interference is a fairly general phenomenon and can occur even in the absence of the presentation of an explicit extraneous stimulus. The matching-to-sample task involves repeated training trials. If those trials are presented close enough together, what occurs on one trial can disrupt performance on the next trial. Thus, proactive interference may occur because of the close scheduling of successive training trials (Edhouse & White, 1988; Jitsumori, Wright, & Shyan, 1989).

To see how proactive interference may develop between training trials, let us consider again the matching-to-sample task that was summarized in Figure 12.2. In this task one of four sample stimuli could occur on a particular trial (triangle, square, vertical grid, or horizontal grid). Let us assume that the subject receives a trial in which the triangle is the sample stimulus and the correct choice, and this is followed by a trial in which the square is the sample and correct choice. To respond accurately on the trial with the square sample, the subject has to disregard the fact that the triangle was correct on the preceding trial. If the subject fails to disregard what was correct on the preceding trial, it may make an error on the square trial by choosing the triangle (see Figure 12.2).

Proactive interference caused by earlier matching trials is particularly interesting because it is a case in which subjects perform poorly on a memory task not because they remember too little but because they remember too much. The disruption of performance is caused by remembering what happened on an earlier trial and confusing that with the correct response on the current trial. This illustrates the general rule that memory failure can occur for a variety of reasons, not all of which involve the loss of information over time.

Retroactive interference in matching to sample.   Retroactive interference has been investigated by presenting extraneous stimuli during the retention interval after the presentation of the sample stimulus. In some studies with pigeons, for example, the sample and choice stimuli were various visual cues projected on pecking keys. As a test for retroactive interference, on some trials the house lights were turned on during the delay interval after presentation of the sample stimulus; on other trials, the pigeons spent the delay interval in darkness. Illumination of the house lights during the retention interval exposed the pigeon to various visual features of the experimental chamber and produced retroactive interference. The birds were less likely to select the correct test stimulus after illumination of the house lights during the delay interval than if they spent the delay interval in darkness (Roberts & Grant, 1978; see also Grant, 1988).

In contrast to proactive interference, which results from remembering too much, retroactive interference seems to result from failure to retain required information during the delay interval. Presentation of extraneous stimuli during the delay interval disrupts the rehearsal processes that are required to effectively store information based on the sample, and that causes poor performance during the memory test (Wright, Urcuioli, Sands, & Santiago, 1981).

RETRIEVAL FAILURE

Studies of proactive and retroactive interference illustrate two different causes of poor performance in a memory task. Proactive interference can result from remembering too much and confusing the sample stimulus on the current trial with what was correct on the previous trial. In contrast, retroactive interference is usually caused by not remembering enough. The failure to remember enough information may be due to the subject being unable to effectively retrieve information that she previously learned.

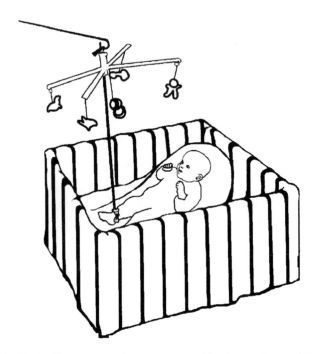

FIGURE 12.4   Experimental situation used by Borovsky and Rovee-Collier (1990) to study the effects of retrieval cues on the memory of human infants for an instrumental conditioning task.
The instrumental response was moving a leg, and the reinforcer was consequent movement of a mobile located in the infant's view.

If poor performance on a memory task is caused by retrieval failure, then procedures that facilitate retrieval should facilitate performance. Retrieval of information is facilitated by exposure to stimuli that were previously associated with the target information. Such stimuli are called **retrieval cues**.

Remarkably insignificant features of the environment may become associated with a learning task and facilitate retrieval of information relevant to that task. In one study (Borovsky & Rovee-Collier, 1990), for example, 6-month-old infant babies received an instrumental conditioning procedure in their playpen at home (see Figure 12.4). Each infant was placed in a baby seat in the playpen with a mobile positioned above in plain view. The mobile was gently attached to one foot of the infant with a satin ribbon. By moving its foot, the infant could make the mobile move. Thus, the instrumental response was a leg movement, and the reinforcer was movement of the mobile.

Infants readily learned the leg-movement task but showed substantial forgetting in as little as 24 hours. Does this rapid forgetting reflect failure to effectively acquire or encode the instrumental contingency or failure to re-trieve what was learned the day earlier? If the instrumental response was not learned effectively in the first place, then there is nothing one can do to counteract the poor performance that is evident 24 hours later. In contrast, if the forgetting was due to retrieval failure, then the presentation of re-trieval or reminder cues should restore the performance.

What might be an effective retrieval cue for the infants in this situation? Borovsky and Rovee-Collier (1990) found that the pattern of the cloth liner that covered the sides of the playpen served as an effective retrieval cue for the instrumental response. Sometimes the liner for the playpen had a striped pattern; on other occasions the liner had a square pattern. Infants for whom the striped pattern was in the playpen during training responded better 24 hours later if they were tested with the striped liner than if they were tested with the square liner. The reverse results were obtained with infants for whom the other liner was used during original training.

The results of this experiment are remarkable because nothing was done to direct the attention of the infants to the cloth liners. The square and striped patterns were both familiar to the infants, and the patterns were not predictive of reinforcement. They served as background cues rather than as discriminative stimuli. Nevertheless, the pattern present during original training became associated with the instrumental task and helped to retrieve information about the task during the memory test 24 hours later.

A variety of different stimuli have been found to be effective as re-trieval cues in various learning situations, including exposure to a condi-tioned stimulus in extinction (Gordon & Mowrer, 1980), internal cues induced by psychoactive drugs (Spear, Smith, Bryan, Gordon, Timmons, & Chiszar, 1980), and exposure to the nonreinforced stimulus in a discrimi-nation procedure (Campbell & Randall, 1976). In addition, retrieval cues have been found to counteract a variety of instances of failed memory in-cluding forgotten early life experiences (Richardson, Riccio, & Jonke, 1983) and amnesia caused by electroconvulsive shock (Gordon & Mowrer, 1980).

Summary

Learning and memory are integrally related, but studies of learning focus on the acquisition stage of information processing, whereas studies of mem-ory focus on the retention and retrieval stages. Working memory is used to retain information that is required just long enough to complete a trial or job. In contrast, reference memory involves aspects of the task or trial that remain constant from one occasion to the next. Early conceptions consid-ered memory to be passive and retrospective. However, more recent evi-dence suggests that in many cases memory involves active processes and the stored information concerns future (prospective) rather than past (retrospective) events.

Studies of what individuals forget can tell us as much about memory mechanisms as studies of successful performance. Memory failure may occur because of prospective or retrospective interference or because of retrieval failure. Prospective interference is often caused by remembering both useful and irrelevant information and not being able to select between them. Retrospective interference is caused by disruptions of rehearsal processes needed for successful memory. But proper rehearsal does not guarantee good memory. Information that is properly retained may not be retrieved during a memory test. Retrieval cues, some of which are seemingly trivial features of the training situation, can facilitate memory performance in cases of retrieval failure.

Suggested Readings

MILLER, R. R., KASPROW, W. J., & SCHACHTMAN, T. R. (1986). Retrieval variability: Sources and consequences. *American Journal of Psychology, 99*, 145–218.

KENDRICK, D. F., RILLING, M. E., & DENNY, M. R. (Eds.). (1986). *Theories of animal memory.* Hillsdale, NJ: Erlbaum.

RICCIO, D. C., & SPEAR, N. E. (1994). *Memory: Phenomena and principles.* Boston: Allyn and Bacon.

Technical Terms

Acquisition stage	Retrieval cues
Delayed matching-to-sample	Retrieval stage
Matching-to-sample procedure	Retroactive interference
Proactive interference	Retrospective memory
Prospective memory	Simultaneous matching-to-sample
Reference memory	Trace-decay hypothesis
Retention stage	Working memory

GLOSSARY

Acquired drive A source of motivation for instrumental behavior caused by the presentation of a stimulus that was previously conditioned with a primary, or unconditioned, reinforcer.

Acquisition stage The first stage of information processing during which information to be remembered is acquired or encoded for later retrieval.

Afferent neuron A neuron that transmits messages from sense organs to the central nervous system.

Appetitive behavior The initial component of a natural behavior sequence. Appetitive behavior is variable, occurs in response to general spatial cues, and serves to bring the organism in contact with releasing stimuli that elicit consummatory responses.

Appetitive conditioning A type of conditioning in which the unconditioned stimulus or reinforcer is a pleasant event, a stimulus the subject tends to approach.

Associative learning Learning in which one event (a stimulus or a response) becomes linked to another, with the result that the first event activates a representation of the second.

Autoshaping Same as *Sign tracking*.

Aversive conditioning A type of conditioning in which the unconditioned stimulus or reinforcer is an unpleasant event, a stimulus that elicits aversion and withdrawal responses.

Aversive stimulus Noxious or unpleasant stimulus that elicits aversion and/or withdrawal responses.

Backward chaining A procedure for training a chain of responses that starts with training the last response or response component. Earlier components are then added in succession, ending with the first component.

Behavior The observable actions of an organism.

Behavior system A system of responses and corresponding behavioral and physiological control mechanisms that are coordinated to achieve particular functions such as feeding or defense against predation.

Behavioral bliss point   The optimal distribution of activities in the absence of constraints or limitations imposed by an instrumental conditioning procedure.

Behavioral regulation   A mechanism that focuses on the allocation or distribution of an animal's responses. It is assumed that animals work to maintain an optimal distribution of activities.

Between-subjects experiment   An experimental design in which two or more independent groups of participants are compared. The focus is on the average performance of the various groups rather than the behavior of the individual participants.

Blocking effect   Interference with the conditioning of a novel stimulus because of the presence of a previously conditioned stimulus.

Chained schedule   A schedule of reinforcement in which the primary reinforcer is delivered only after the subject has performed a sequence of responses, with each response performed in the presence of a different stimulus.

Compound stimulus test   A test procedure that identifies a stimulus as a conditioned inhibitor if that stimulus reduces responding elicited by a conditioned excitatory stimulus.

Concurrent schedule   A reinforcement procedure in which the subject can choose one of two or more simple reinforcement schedules that are available simultaneously. Concurrent schedules allow for the measurement of choice between simple schedule alternatives.

Conditioned drive   A drive state induced by the presentation of a stimulus that was previously conditioned with a primary, or unconditioned, reinforcer.

Conditioned emotional response procedure   Same as **conditioned suppression**.

Conditioned facilitation   Same as *Facilitation*.

Conditioned inhibition   A type of Pavlovian conditioning in which the conditioned stimulus becomes a signal for the absence of the unconditioned stimulus.

Conditioned reinforcer   A stimulus that becomes an effective reinforcer because of its association with a primary, or unconditioned, reinforcer.

Conditioned response   A response that comes to be made to a conditioned stimulus as a result of classical conditioning.

Conditioned stimulus   A stimulus that initially does not elicit a conditioned response or activate a representation of an unconditioned stimulus but comes to do so after pairings with an unconditioned stimulus.

Conditioned suppression   An aversive Pavlovian conditioning procedure in which conditioned responding is measured by the suppression of positively reinforced instrumental behavior.

Constraint on learning   A limitation on learning resulting from the evolutionary history of the organism.

Consummatory behavior   Behavior that brings an elicited behavior sequence to an end; behavior that consummates a sequence of elicited responses.

Contingency   A measure of the extent to which two events are linked or the extent to which the occurrence of one event depends on the other, and vice versa.

Control condition   A condition in which subjects do not receive a training procedure but are treated identically in all other respects to subjects that are trained. Performance in the control condition is compared to performance in the experimental condition in the basic learning experiment.

CS-alone control   A control procedure in which the conditioned stimulus occurs by itself on each trial.

CS-US interval   Same as *Interstimulus interval.*

Cumulative record   A graphical representation of the cumulative number of occurrences of a particular response as a function of the passage of time. The horizontal distance on the record represents the passage of time, the vertical distance represents the total number of responses that have occurred, and the slope represents the rate of responding.

Delayed conditioning   A Pavlovian conditioning procedure in which the conditioned stimulus begins before the unconditioned stimulus on each trial.

Delayed matching-to-sample   A procedure in which subjects are reinforced for responding to a test stimulus that is the same as a previously presented sample stimulus.

Differential probability principle   The principle that assumes that reinforcement depends on how much more likely the individual is to perform the reinforcer response than the instrumental response.

Differential reinforcement of other behavior   An instrumental conditioning procedure in which a positive reinforcer is periodically delivered only if the subject fails to perform a specified response.

Differential responding   Responding in different ways or at different rates in the presence of different stimuli.

Directed forgetting   Stimulus control of memory, achieved by presenting a cue indicating when subjects will, or will not, be required to remember something.

Discrete-trial method   A method of instrumental conditioning in which the subject can perform the instrumental response only during specified periods, usually determined either by placement of the subject in an experimental chamber or by the presentation of a stimulus.

Discriminated avoidance   An avoidance-conditioning procedure in which the occurrence of an aversive unconditioned stimulus is signaled by a conditioned stimulus or warning signal. Responding during the conditioned stimulus terminates that stimulus and prevents the delivery of the aversive unconditioned stimulus.

Discrimination control   A control procedure for Pavlovian conditioning in which one conditioned stimulus (the CS$^+$) is paired with the unconditioned stimulus whereas another conditioned stimulus (the CS$^-$) is presented without the unconditioned stimulus. The development of responding during the CS⁺ but not during the CS⁻ is considered evidence of Pavlovian conditioning.

Discrimination hypothesis   An explanation of the partial reinforcement extinction effect according to which extinction is slower after partial reinforcement than after continuous reinforcement because the onset of extinction is more difficult to detect following partial reinforcement.

Discriminative punishment   A type of punishment procedure in which responses are punished in the presence of a discriminative stimulus but not when the discriminative stimulus is absent.

Dishabituation   Recovery of a habituated response as a result of presentation of a strong extraneous stimulus.

Disinhibition   Recovery of a partly extinguished conditioned response as a result of presentation of a novel stimulus.

Drive reduction theory   A theory of reinforcement according to which reinforcers are effective because they reduce the subject's drive state and return the subject to the homeostatic level.

Drive state   A motivational state that exists when a system is not at its homeostatic level. Return of the system to its homeostatic level reduces the drive state.

Dual-process theory   A theory that describes how habituation and sensitization processes jointly determine the vigor of elicited behavior.

Efferent neuron   A neuron that transmits impulses from the central nervous system to muscles.

Elicited behavior   A specific behavior or action pattern that occurs reliably upon presentation of a particular stimulus (its eliciting stimulus).

Equipotentiality assumption   The idea that the rate of learning is independent of the combination of conditioned and unconditioned stimuli or responses and reinforcers that are used.

Ethology   A specialization in biology concerned with the evolution and development of behavior.

Evolution   Change in a physical or behavioral trait that occurs across successive generations because of differential reproductive success.

Experimental condition   A condition in which subjects receive a training procedure. Performance in the experimental condition is compared to performance in the control condition in the basic learning experiment.

Experimental observation   Observation of behavior under conditions specifically designed by an investigator to test particular factors or variables that might influence the learning or performance of the behavior.

External inhibition   Same as *Disinhibition*.

Extinction   See *Extinction effect*; *Extinction procedure*.

Extinction effect   Reduction of a learned response that occurs because the conditioned stimulus is no longer paired with the unconditioned stimulus (in classical conditioning) or because the response is no longer reinforced (in instrumental conditioning).

Extinction procedure   The procedure of repeatedly presenting a conditioned stimulus without the unconditioned stimulus or no longer providing reinforcement for an instrumental response.

Facilitation   A Pavlovian conditioning procedure in which a conditioned stimulus is presented on trials when a second stimulus is paired with a US but not on trials when the second stimulus is presented alone. In such a procedure, one cue designates when another cue will be reinforced.

Fatigue   A temporary decrease in behavior caused by repeated or excessive use of the muscles involved in the behavior.

Feedback cue   A stimulus that results from the performance of a response.

Feedback function   The relation between rates of responding and rates of reinforcement allowed by a particular reinforcement schedule.

Fixed-action pattern   A response pattern that occurs in much the same way most of the time and in most members of a species. Fixed-action patterns are often used as basic units of behavior in ethological investigations of behavior.

Fixed-interval schedule   A reinforcement schedule in which reinforcement is delivered for the first response that occurs after a fixed amount of time following the last reinforcer.

Fixed-ratio schedule   A reinforcement schedule in which a fixed number of responses must occur in order for the next response to be reinforced.

Flavor neophobia   An aversion based on the unfamiliarity of the flavor of a new food.

Focal search mode   A response mode in the feeding system that is activated once a potential source of food has been identified.

Free-operant avoidance   Same as *Nondiscriminated avoidance*.

Free-operant method   A method of instrumental conditioning that permits uninterrupted repetition of the instrumental response, in contrast to the discrete trial method.

Frustration   An aversive emotional reaction that results from the unexpected absence of reinforcement.

Frustration theory   A theory of the partial reinforcement extinction effect, according to which extinction is retarded after partial reinforcement because the instrumental response becomes conditioned to the anticipation of frustrative nonreward.

Fundamental learning experiment   The basic experiment required to demonstrate a learning effect. The experiment requires an experimental condition in which subjects receive a training procedure and a control condition in which subjects are treated the same way, but without the training procedure. Contrasting performance under the two conditions is used to infer that learning has taken place.

General search mode   The initial response mode of the feeding system. In this mode, the organism reacts to general features of the environment with responses that enable it to come in contact with a variety of potential sources of food.

Habituation effect   A progressive decrease in the vigor of an elicited response that may occur with repeated presentations of the eliciting stimulus.

Heterogeneous chain   A sequence of response components, each involving a different response. Each component is characterized by a distinctive stimulus and its own schedule requirement.

Higher-order stimulus relation   A relation in which a stimulus signals a relationship between two other stimuli rather than signaling just the presence or absence of another stimulus. In a higher-order Pavlovian relation, one CS signals whether or not another CS is paired with a US.

Homeostatic level   The target or desired range within which a physiological or behavioral system is maintained by regulatory processes.

Homeostasis   The process of maintaining a homeostatic level.

Homogeneous chain   A sequence of response components, all involving the same response. Each component is characterized by a distinctive stimulus and its own schedule requirement.

Hydraulic model   A model proposed by ethologists according to which certain factors lead to the buildup of a particular type of motivation or drive that increases the likelihood of corresponding fixed-action patterns. Performance of the fixed-action patterns reduces or discharges the motivational state.

Instrumental behavior   An activity that is effective in producing a particular consequence or reinforcer.

Instrumental conditioning   A type of conditioning procedure in which the presentation of a reinforcer depends on the prior occurrence of a designated instrumental response.

Interdimensional discrimination   A discrimination between two stimuli that differ in several different respects.

Interneuron   A neuron in the spinal cord that transmits impulses from afferent (of sensory) to efferent (or motor) neurons.

Interstimulus interval   The interval in a Pavlovian conditioning procedure between the start of the conditioned stimulus and the start of the unconditioned stimulus.

Interval schedule   A reinforcement schedule in which a response is reinforced only if it occurs more than a set amount of time after the last delivery of the reinforcer.

Intradimensional discrimination   A discrimination between stimuli that differ in only one stimulus characteristic, such as color, brightness, or pitch.

Law of Effect   A rule for instrumental behavior proposed by Thorndike according to which reinforcement of an instrumental response strengthens the association between the response and the stimulus in the presence of which the response occurred.

Learning   An enduring change in the mechanisms of behavior involving specific stimuli and/or responses that results from prior experience with those stimuli and responses.

Limited hold   A restriction on how much time a subject has to obtain an available reinforcer. A limited hold can be added to interval and other schedules or reinforcement.

Long-delay learning   A classical conditioning procedure in which the conditioned stimulus is presented long before the unconditioned stimulus on each conditioning trial.

Long-term habituation   A type of habituation that results in a response decrement that lasts for a week or more.

Long-term sensitization   A form of sensitization that is persistent or slow to decay.

Marking stimulus   A brief visual or auditory cue presented after an instrumental response that makes the instrumental response more memorable and helps overcome the deleterious effect of delayed reinforcement.

Matching Law   A rule for instrumental behavior proposed by Herrnstein according to which the relative rate of response on a particular response alternative equals the relative rate of reinforcement for that response alternative.

Matching-to-sample procedure   A procedure in which subjects are reinforced for selecting a stimulus that corresponds to the sample presented on that trial.

Maturation   A change in behavior caused by physical or physiological development.

Memory   A theoretical term used to characterize instances in which behavior at one point in time is determined by some aspect of experience at an earlier point in time.

Memory retrieval   The recovery of information from a memory store.

Motivation   A hypothetical state that increases the probability of a coordinated set of activities or activates a system of behaviors that functions to satisfy a goal such as feeding, predatory defense, infant care, or copulation.

Motor neuron   Same as *Efferent neuron.*

Multiple schedule of reinforcement   A procedure in which different reinforcement schedules are in effect in the presence of different stimuli presented in succession. Generally, each stimulus comes to evoke a pattern of responding that corresponds to whatever reinforcement schedule is in effect in the presence of that stimulus.

Naturalistic observations   Observations of behavior as it occurs under natural conditions, in the absence of interventions or manipulations introduced by the investigator.

Negative CS-US contingency   A situation in which the probability of encountering the US is lower in the presence of the CS than in the absence of the CS.

Negative reinforcement   An instrumental conditioning procedure in which there is a negative contingency between the instrumental response and an aversive stimulus. If the instrumental response is performed, the aversive stimulus is terminated or prevented from occurring; if the instrumental response is not performed, the aversive stimulus is presented.

Negative reinforcer   Same as *Aversive stimulus*.

Nondiscriminated avoidance   An avoidance-conditioning procedure in which the aversive stimulus is not signaled by an external warning signal. In the absence of avoidance behavior, the aversive stimulus occurs periodically, as determined by the S-S interval. Each occurrence of the avoidance response restarts a certain amount of time without aversive stimulation, as determined by the R-S interval.

One-way avoidance   An avoidance-conditioning procedure in which the required instrumental response is always to cross from one compartment of a shuttle box to the other in the same direction.

Operant behavior   A response that is defined by the effect it produces in the environment. Examples include pressing a lever and opening a door. Any sequence of movements that depresses the lever or opens the door constitutes an instance of that particular operant.

Operant conditioning   A type of conditioning procedure in which the presentation of a reinforcer depends on the prior occurrence of a designated operant response.

Opponent process   A compensatory mechanism that ensures that deviations of a system from a set or homeostatic level are counteracted so as to return the system to that homeostatic level.

Orienting response   A reaction to novel stimuli that usually involves turning towards the source of the stimulus.

Outcome   Same as *Reinforcer*.

Overshadowing   Interference with the conditioning of a stimulus because of the simultaneous presence of another stimulus that is easier to condition.

Partial reinforcement extinction effect   More persistence performance of an instrumental response in extinction after partial (intermittent) reinforcement training than after continuous reinforcement training.

Perceptual concept   Learning to respond in a certain way to various objects (or views of an object) that belong to a set or category and in a different way to objects that do not belong to that category.

Performance   An organism's activities at a particular time.

Persistence   The continued performance of an instrumental response after an extinction procedure has been introduced.

Positive occasion setting   Same as *Facilitation*.

Postreinforcement pause   A pause in responding that typically occurs after the delivery of the reinforcer on fixed-ratio and fixed-interval schedules of reinforcement.

Practice   Repetition of a response or behavior, usually with the intent of improving performance.

Predatory imminence   The perceived likelihood of being attacked by a predator. Different species' typical defense responses are assumed to be performed in the face of different degrees of predatory imminence.

Premack principle   Given two responses with different baseline probabilities of occurrence, the opportunity to perform the higher probability response will reinforce or increase performance of the lower probability behavior.

Primary reinforcer   A reinforcer that is effective without prior conditioning.

Proactive interference   Disruption of memory by exposure to stimuli before the event to be remembered.

Proprioceptive cue   An internal response feedback stimulus that arises from the movement of muscles and/or joints.

Prospective memory   Memory of a plan for future action. Also called *Prospection.*

Punishment   A type of instrumental conditioning procedure in which occurrence of the instrumental response results in delivery of an aversive stimulus.

Puzzle box   A type of experimental chamber used by Thorndike to study instrumental conditioning. The subject was put in the chamber and had to perform a specified behavior to be released from it.

R-S interval   The interval between the occurrence of an avoidance response and the next scheduled presentation of the aversive stimulus in a nondiscriminated avoidance procedure.

R-S* association   An association between the instrumental response (R) and the reinforcer (S*).

Random control   A control procedure for Pavlovian conditioning in which the conditioned and unconditioned stimuli are presented at random times relative to each other.

Rate of responding   A measure of how often a response is repeated in a unit of time; for example, the number of responses that occur per hour.

Ratio run   The high and invariant rate of responding observed after the postreinforcement pause on fixed-ratio reinforcement schedules. The ratio run ends when the necessary number of responses has been performed and the subject is reinforced.

Ratio schedule   A reinforcement schedule in which reinforcement depends only on the number of responses the subject performs, irrespective of when these responses occur.

Reference memory   The retention of background information a subject has to have to respond successfully in a situation. (Compare with working memory.)

Reflex   A unit of elicited behavior involving a specific environmental event and its corresponding specific elicited response.

Reflex arc   Neural structures, consisting of the afferent (sensory) neuron, interneuron, and efferent (motor) neuron, that enable a stimulus to elicit a reflex response.

Reinforcer   A stimulus whose delivery shortly following a response increases the future probability of that response. (Also called *Outcome*).

Releasing stimulus   Same as *Sign stimulus.*

Reminder treatment   The presentation of a retrieval cue that reactivates a memory or facilitates memory retrieval.

Renewal effect   Recovery of responding when subjects are returned to the training context after receiving an extinction procedure in a distinctively different environment.

Response deprivation hypothesis   An explanation of reinforcement according to which reduced access to a particular response is sufficient to make the opportunity to perform that response an effective positive reinforcer.

Retardation-of-acquisition test   A test procedure that identifies a stimulus as a conditioned inhibitor if that stimulus is slower to acquire conditioned excitatory properties than a comparison stimulus.

Retention stage   The second stage of information processing when acquired information is stored in memory for later use or retrieval.

Retrieval cue   A stimulus related to an experience that facilitates the recall of other information related to that experience.

Retrieval failure   A deficit in recovering information from a memory store.

Retrieval stage   The third stage of information processing during which previously stored information is reactivated or recovered for use.

Retroactive interference   Disruption of memory by exposure to stimuli following the event to be remembered.

Retrospection   Same as *Retrospective memory*.

Retrospective memory   Memory for a previously experienced event.

S^+   A discriminative stimulus that signals the availability of reinforcement for an instrumental response.

S^-   A discriminative stimulus that signals the absence of reinforcement for an instrumental response.

S-R association   An association between a stimulus and a response, with the result that the stimulus comes to elicit the response.

S-R learning   The learning of an association between a stimulus and a response, with the result that the stimulus comes to elicit a response.

S-R system   The shortest neural pathway that connects the sense organs stimulated by an eliciting stimulus and the muscles involved in making the elicited response.

S(R-S*) association   A higher-order relation in instrumental conditioning situations, according to which a discriminative or contextual stimulus (S) activates an association between the instrumental response and the reinforcer (R-S*).

S-S interval   The interval between successive presentations of the aversive stimulus in a nondiscriminated avoidance procedure when the avoidance response is not performed.

S-S learning   Same as *Stimulus-stimulus learning*.

S-S* association   An association between a stimulus (S) in the presence of which an instrumental response is reinforced and the reinforcer (S*).

Safety signal   A stimulus that signals the absence of an aversive event.

Schedule line   A line on a graph of different rates of instrumental and reinforcer behavior indicating how much access to the reinforcer activity is provided for various rates of instrumental responding on a particular schedule of reinforcement.

Schedule of reinforcement A program, or rule, that determines how and when the occurrence of a response will be followed by the delivery of the reinforcer.

Secondary reinforcer Same as *Conditioned reinforcer*.

Selective association Association formed more readily between one combination of conditioned and unconditioned stimuli than between other combinations.

Sensitization effect An increase in the vigor of elicited behavior that may result from repeated presentations of the eliciting stimulus.

Sensory neuron Same as *Afferent neuron*.

Sensory reinforcement Reinforcement provided by presentation of a stimulus unrelated to a biological need or drive.

Sequential theory A theory of the partial reinforcement extinction effect according to which extinction is retarded after partial reinforcement because the instrumental response becomes conditioned to the memory of nonreward.

Shaping Reinforcement of successive approximations to a target instrumental response, typically used to condition responses that are not in the subject's existing repertoire of behavior.

Short-term habituation A habituation effect that lasts a relatively short period of time, sometimes less than a minute.

Short-term sensitization A sensitization effect that lasts a relatively short period of time, sometimes less than a minute.

Shuttle box An apparatus for the study of avoidance behavior consisting of two compartments connected end-to-end. The avoidance response involves moving from one compartment to the other (shuttling between the compartments).

Sign stimulus A specific feature of an object or animal that elicits a fixed-action pattern.

Sign tracking A form of appetitive Pavlovian conditioning in which a localized stimulus serves as the conditioned stimulus. As a result, the subject comes to approach (track) and sometimes manipulate the conditioned stimulus.

Simultaneous conditioning A Pavlovian conditioning procedure in which the conditioned stimulus and the unconditioned stimulus are presented simultaneously on each conditioning trial.

Simultaneous matching-to-sample A procedure in which subjects are reinforced for responding to a test stimulus that is the same as a sample stimulus. The sample and the test stimuli are presented at the same time.

Single-subject experiment An experiment in which learning is investigated through extensive observations of the behavior of a single individual. The individual's behavior has to be sufficiently well known to permit accurate assumptions about how the subject would have behaved if he had not received the training procedure.

Skinner box   A small experimental chamber provided with something the subject can manipulate repeatedly, such as a response lever. This allows a subject to perform a particular response repeatedly without being removed from the experimental situation. The chamber usually also has a mechanism that can deliver a reinforcer, such as a pellet of food.

Species-typical behavior   Behavior that is characteristic of most members of a species.

Species-specific defense reactions   Species-typical responses animals perform in aversive situations. The responses may involve freezing, fleeing, or fighting.

Spontaneous recovery   Recovery of a response produced by a period of rest after habituation or extinction.

SSDR   Abbreviation for *Species-specific defense reaction.*

Startle response   A sudden jump or tensing of the muscles that may occur when an unexpected stimulus is presented.

State system   Neural structures that determine the organism's general level of responsiveness or readiness to respond.

Stimulus   An event external or internal to the organism that activates sensory neurons and may elicit or cue behavior.

Stimulus dimension   The feature (color, for example) that distinguishes a series of stimuli in a test of stimulus generalization.

Stimulus discrimination   Differential responding in the presence of two or more stimuli.

Stimulus discrimination training (in classical conditioning)   One conditioned stimulus (the CS^+) is paired with an unconditioned stimulus whereas another conditioned stimulus (the CS^-) is presented without the unconditioned stimulus.

Stimulus discrimination training (in instrumental conditioning)   A procedure in which reinforcement for responding is available whenever one stimulus (the S^+) is present and is not available whenever another stimulus (the S^-) is present.

Stimulus generalization   The occurrence of behavior learned through habituation or conditioning in the presence of stimuli that are different from the stimulus used during training.

Stimulus generalization gradient   A gradient of responding that may be observed if subjects are tested with stimuli that increasingly differ from the stimulus that was present during training.

Stimulus generalization of habituation   See *Stimulus generalization.*

Stimulus-stimulus learning   The learning of an association between two stimuli, such that presentation of one of the stimuli activates a neural representation of the other.

Straight-alley runway   A straight alley with a start box at one end and a goal box at the other. Animals are placed in the start box at the start of a trial and allowed to run to the goal box.

Summation test   Same as *Compound stimulus test.*

Taste aversion learning   A type of Pavlovian conditioning in which the taste of a novel food serves as the conditioned stimulus and gastrointestinal illness serves as the unconditioned stimulus. Taste aversions can be learned even if the illness is delayed several hours after exposure to the taste.

Temporal contiguity   The simultaneous occurrence of two or more events.

Temporal cues   Stimuli related to the passage of time.

Temporal encoding   The learning of a temporal code for when the US occurs in relation to the CS. This enables the organism to predict the precise point in time when the US will occur.

Time-out   A period during which the opportunity to obtain reinforcement is removed. This may involve removal of the individual from a situation where reinforcers may be obtained.

Token economy   A system in which individuals are reinforced with tokens or points for performing low probability responses targeted by a training program. The points or tokens can then be exchanged for the chance to engage in other activities that the individuals are much more likely to do.

Trace conditioning   A classical conditioning procedure in which the unconditioned stimulus is presented on each trial after the conditioned stimulus has been terminated for a short period.

Trace-decay hypothesis   The theoretical idea that exposure to a stimulus produces changes in the nervous system that gradually decrease after the stimulus has been terminated.

Trace interval   The interval between the end of the conditioned stimulus and the start of the unconditioned stimulus in trace-conditioning trials.

Two-factor theory   A theory of avoidance learning involving two forms of conditioning: (1) Pavlovian conditioning of fear to a stimulus that signals aversive stimulation, and (2) instrumental conditioning of the avoidance response by fear reduction.

Two-way avoidance   A shuttle avoidance procedure in which trials can start in either compartment of a shuttle box, and the avoidance response consists of going from the occupied compartment to the unoccupied compartment.

Unconditioned response   The response that occurs to an unconditioned stimulus without the necessity of learning.

Unconditioned stimulus   A stimulus that elicits vigorous responding in the absence of prior training.

US-alone control   A control procedure for classical conditioning that involves presentations of just the unconditioned stimulus. Such a control is typically not considered to be sufficient in studies of classical conditioning.

US devaluation   A procedure that reduces the effectiveness of an unconditioned stimulus to elicit unconditioned behavior.

US inflation   A procedure that increases the effectiveness of an unconditioned stimulus to elicit unconditioned behavior.

Variable-interval schedule   A reinforcement schedule in which reinforcement is provided for the first response that occurs after a variable amount of time from the last reinforcement.

Variable-ratio schedule   A reinforcement schedule in which the number of responses necessary to obtain reinforcement varies from trial to trial. The value of the schedule refers to the average number of responses needed for reinforcement.

Warning stimulus or warning signal   The stimulus in a discriminated avoidance procedure that reliably precedes scheduled presentations of the aversive unconditioned stimulus.

Working memory   The retention of information that is needed only to respond successfully on the task at hand, as contrasted with reference memory that involves background information that is also needed for future similar tasks.

REFERENCES

ALCOCK, J. (1993). *Animal behavior* (5th Ed.). Sunderland, MA: Sinauer.

ALLISON, J. (1983). *Behavioral economics*. New York: Praeger.

ALLISON, J. (1989). The nature of reinforcement. In S. B. Klein & R. R. Mowrer (Eds.), *Contemporary learning theories: Instrumental conditioning theory and the impact of biological constraints on learning* (pp. 13–39). Hillsdale, NJ: Erlbaum.

ALLISON, J., & TIMBERLAKE, W. (1974). Instrumental and contingent saccharin-licking in rats: Response deprivation and reinforcement. *Learning and Motivation, 5,* 231–247.

AMSEL, A. (1958). The role of frustrative nonreward in noncontinuous reward situations. *Psychological Bulletin, 55,* 102–119.

AMSEL, A. (1967). Partial reinforcement effects on vigor and persistence. In K. W. Spence & J. T. Spence (Eds.), *The psychology of learning and motivation* (Vol. 1, pp. 1–65). Orlando, FL: Academic Press.

AMSEL, A. (1992). *Frustration theory: An analysis of dispositional learning and memory.* Cambridge, England: Cambridge University Press.

AMSEL, A., & RASHOTTE, M.E. (1984). *Mechanisms of adaptive behavior: Clark L. Hull's theoretical papers, with commentary.* New York: Columbia University Press.

ANGER, D. (1963). The role of temporal discrimination in the reinforcement of Sidman avoidance behavior. *Journal of the Experimental Analysis of Behavior, 6,* 477–506.

AZRIN, N. H. (1959). Punishment and recovery during fixed-ratio performance. *Journal of the Experimental Analysis of Behavior, 2,* 301–305.

AZRIN, N. H. (1960). Effects of punishment intensity during variable-interval reinforcement. *Journal of the Experimental Analysis of Behavior, 3,* 123–142.

AZRIN, N. H., & HOLZ, W. C. (1961). Punishment during fixed-interval reinforcement. *Journal of the Experimental Analysis of Behavior, 4,* 343–347.

AZRIN, N. H., & HOLZ, W. C. (1966). Punishment. In W. K. Honig (Ed.), *Operant behavior: Areas of research and application* (pp. 380–447). New York: Appleton-Century-Crofts.

AZRIN, N. H., HOLZ, W. C., & HAKE, D. F. (1963). Fixed-ratio punishment. *Journal of the Experimental Analysis of Behavior, 6,* 141–148.

BABKIN, B. P. (1949). *Pavlov: A biography.* Chicago: University of Chicago Press.

BAERENDS, G. P. (1988). Ethology. In R. C. Atkinson, R. J. Herrnstein, G. Lindzey, & R. D. Luce (Eds.), *Stevens' handbook of experimental psychology* (Vol. 1, pp. 765–830). New York: Wiley.

BALSAM, P. D. (1988). Selection, representation, and equivalence of controlling stimuli. In R. C. Atkinson, R. J. Herrnstein, G. Lindzey, & R. D. Luce (Eds.), *Stevens' handbook of experimental psychology* (Vol. 2, pp. 111–166). New York: Wiley.

BALSAM, P. D., & TOMIE, A. (Eds.) (1985). *Context and conditioning.* Hillsdale, NJ: Erlbaum.

BARNET, R. C., GRAHAME, N. J., & MILLER, R. R. (1993). Temporal encoding as a determinant of blocking. *Journal of Experimental Psychology: Animal Behavior Processes, 19,* 327–341.

BARON, A., & MENICH, S. R. (1985). Reaction times of younger and older men: Effects of compound samples and a prechoice signal on delayed matching-to-sample performances. *Journal of the Experimental Analysis of Behavior, 44,* 1–14.

BASHINSKI, H., WERNER, J., & RUDY, J. (1985). Determinants of infant visual attention: Evidence for a two-process theory. *Journal of Experimental Child Psychology, 39,* 580–598.

BECHTEREV, V. M. (1913). *La psychologie objective.* Paris: Alcan.

BENEDICT, J. O., & AYRES, J. J. B. (1972). Factors affecting conditioning in the truly random control procedure in the rat. *Journal of Comparative and Physiological Psychology, 78,* 323–330.

BERLYNE, D. E. (1969). The reward value of indifferent stimulation. In J. Tapp (Ed.), *Reinforcement and behavior* (pp. 178–214). New York: Academic Press.

BEST, M. R., BATSON, J. D., MEACHUM, C. L., BROWN, E. R., & RINGER, M. (1985). Characteristics of taste-mediated environmental potentiation in rats. *Learning and Motivation, 16,* 190–209.

BITTERMAN, M. E. (1964). Classical conditioning in the gold fish as a function of the CS-US interval. *Journal of Comparative and Physiological Psychology, 58,* 359–366.

BITTERMAN, M. E. (1975). The comparative analysis of learning. *Science, 188,* 699–709.

BOAKES, R. (1984). *From Darwin to behaviorism: Psychology and the minds of animals.* Cambridge, England: Cambridge University Press.

BOAKES, R. A. (1979). Interactions between type I and type II processes involving positive reinforcement. In A. Dickinson & R. A. Boakes (Eds.), *Mechanisms of learning and motivation* (pp. 233–268). Hillsdale, NJ: Erlbaum.

BOAKES, R. A., POLI, M., LOCKWOOD, M. J., & GOODALL, G. (1978). A study of misbehavior: Token reinforcement in the rat. *Journal of the Experimental Analysis of Behavior, 29,* 115–134.

BOLLES, R. C. (1970). Species-specific defense reactions and avoidance learning. *Psychological Review, 71,* 32–48.

BOLLES, R. C. (1972a). Reinforcement, expectancy, and learning. *Psychological Review, 79,* 394–409.

BOLLES, R. C. (1972b). The avoidance learning problem. In G. H. Bower (Ed.), *The psychology of learning and motivation* (Vol. 6, pp. 97–145). Orlando, FL: Academic Press.

BOLLES, R. C., & RILEY, A. L. (1973). Freezing as an avoidance response: Another look at the operant-respondent distinction. *Learning and Motivation, 4,* 268–275.

BOROVSKY, D., & ROVEE-COLLIER, C. (1990). Contextual constraints on memory retrieval at six months. *Child Development, 61,* 1569–1583.

BOUTON, M. E. (1986). Slow reacquisition following the extinction of conditioned suppression. *Learning and Motivation, 17,* 1–15.

BOUTON, M. E. (1993). Context, time, and memory retrieval in the interference paradigms of Pavlovian learning. *Psychological Bulletin, 114,* 80–99.

BOUTON, M. E., & BOLLES, R. C. (1980). Conditioned fear assessed by freezing and by the suppression of three different baselines. *Animal Learning & Behavior, 8,* 429–434.

BOUTON, M. E., & SWARTZENTRUBER, D. (1989). Slow reacquisition following extinction: Context, encoding, and retrieval mechanisms. *Journal of Experimental Psychology: Animal Behavior Processes, 15,* 43–53.

BOUTON, M. E., & SWARTZENTRUBER, D. (1991). Sources of relapse after extinction in Pavlovian and instrumental learning. *Clinical Psychology Review, 11,* 123–140.

BOWER, G. H., & HILGARD, E. R. (1981). *Theories of learning* (5th Ed.). Englewood Cliffs, NJ: Prentice Hall.

BRAVEMAN, N. S., & BRONSTEIN, P. (Eds.). (1985). *Experimental assessments and clinical applications of conditioned food aversions.* Annals of the New York Academy of Sciences: Vol. 443. New York: New York Academy of Sciences.

BRELAND, K., & BRELAND, M. (1961). The misbehavior of organisms. *American Psychologist, 16,* 681–684.

BROGDEN, W. J., LIPMAN, E. A., & CULLER, E. (1938). The role of incentive in conditioning and extinction. *American Journal of Psychology, 51,* 109–117.

BROOKS, D. C., & BOUTON, M.E. (1993). A retrieval cue for extinction attenuates spontaneous recovery. *Journal of Experimental Psychology: Animal Behavior Processes, 19,* 77–89.

CAMP, D. S., RAYMOND, G. A., & CHURCH, R. M. (1967). Temporal relationship between response and punishment. *Journal of Experimental Psychology, 74,* 114–123.

CAMPBELL, B. A., & RANDALL, P. K. (1976). The effect of reinstatement stimulus conditions on the maintenance of long-term memory. *Developmental Psychobiology, 9,* 325–333.

CAPALDI, E. J. (1967). A sequential hypothesis of instrumental learning. In K. W. Spence & J. T. Spence (Eds.), *The psychology of learning and motivation* (Vol. 1, pp. 67–156). Orlando, FL: Academic Press.

CAPALDI, E. J. (1971). Memory and learning: A sequential viewpoint. In W. K. Honig & P. H. R. James (Eds.), *Animal memory* (pp. 115–154). Orlando, FL: Academic Press.

CHARLOP, M. H., KURTZ, P. F., & CASEY, F. G. (1990). Using aberrant behaviors as reinforcers for autistic children. *Journal of Applied Behavior Analysis, 23,* 163–181.

CHURCH, R. M. (1964). Systematic effect of the random error in the yoked control design. *Psychological Bulletin, 62,* 122–131.

CHURCH, R. M. (1969). Response suppression. In B. A. Campbell & R. M. Church (Eds.), *Punishment and aversive behavior* (pp. 111–156). New York: Appleton-Century-Crofts.

CHURCH, R. M., & RAYMOND, G. A. (1967). Influence of the schedule of positive reinforcement on punished behavior. *Journal of Comparative and Physiological Psychology, 63,* 329–332.

COHEN, L. B. (1988). An information processing view of infant cognitive development. In L. Weiskrantz (Ed.), *Thought without language* (pp. 211–228). Oxford: Oxford University Press.

COLE, R. P., BARNET, R. C., & MILLER, R. R. (1995). Temporal encoding in trace conditioning. *Animal Learning & Behavior, 23,* 144–153.

COLWILL, R. M., & RESCORLA, R. A. (1986). Associative structures in instrumental learning. In G. H. Bower (Ed.) *The psychology of learning and motivation* (Vol. 20, pp. 55–104). San Diego: Academic Press.

COLWILL, R. M., & RESCORLA, R. A. (1990). Evidence for the hierarchical structure of instrumental learning. *Animal Learning & Behavior, 18,* 71–82.

COOK, R. G., BROWN, M. F., & RILEY, D. A. (1985). Flexible memory processing by rats: Use of prospective and retrospective information in the radial maze. *Journal of Experimental Psychology: Animal Behavior Processes, 11,* 453–469.

CUNNINGHAM, C. L. (1997). Drug conditioning and drug-seeking behavior. In W. T. O'Donohue (Ed.) *Learning and behavior therapy* (pp. 518–544). Boston: Allyn & Bacon.

D'AMATO, M. R. (1973). Delayed matching and short-term memory in monkeys. In G. H. Bower (Ed.), *The psychology of learning and motivation* (Vol. 7, pp. 227–269). New York: Academic Press.

D'AMATO, M. R., FAZZARO, J., & ETKIN, M. (1968). Anticipatory responding and avoidance discrimination as factors in avoidance conditioning. *Journal of Comparative and Physiological Psychology, 77,* 41–47.

DARDANO, J. F., & SAUERBRUNN, D. (1964). An aversive stimulus as a correlated block counter in FR performance. *Journal of the Experimental Analysis of Behavior, 7,* 37–43.

DAVIS, M. (1970). Effects of interstimulus interval length and variability on startle-response habituation in the rat. *Journal of Comparative and Physiological Psychology, 72,* 177–192.

DAVIS, M. (1974). Sensitization of the rat startle response by noise. *Journal of Comparative and Physiological Psychology, 87,* 571–581.

DAVIS, M., HITCHCOCK, J. M., & ROSEN, J. B. (1987). Anxiety and the amygdala: Pharmacological and anatomical analysis of the fear-potentiated startle paradigm. In G. H. Bower (Ed.), *The psychology of learning and motivation* (Vol. 21, pp. 263–304). Orlando, FL: Academic Press.

DAVISON, M., & McCARTHY, D. (1988). *The matching law: A research review.* Hillsdale, NJ: Erlbaum.

DEAN, S. J., & PITTMAN, C. M. (1991). Self-punitive behavior: A revised analysis. In M. R. Denny (Ed.), *Fear, avoidance, and phobias* (pp. 259–284). Hillsdale, NJ: Erlbaum.

DEICH, J. D., ALLAN, R. W., & ZEIGLER, H. P. (1988). Conjunctive differentiation of gape during food reinforced keypecking in the pigeon. *Animal Learning & Behavior, 16,* 268–276.

DINSMOOR, J. A. (1952). A discrimination based on punishment. *Quarterly Journal of Experimental Psychology, 4,* 27–45.

DINSMOOR, J. A. (1977). Escape, avoidance, punishment: Where do we stand? *Journal of the Experimental Analysis of Behavior, 28,* 83–95.

DOMJAN, M. (1976). Determinants of the enhancement of flavored-water intake by prior exposure. *Journal of Experimental Psychology: Animal Behavior Processes, 2,* 17–27.

DOMJAN, M. (1977). Attenuation and enhancement of neophobia for edible substances. In L. M. Barker, M. R. Best, & M. Domjan (Eds.), *Learning mechanisms in food selection* (pp. 151–179). Waco, TX: Baylor University Press.

DOMJAN, M. (1994). Formulation of a behavior system for sexual conditioning. *Psychonomic Bulletin & Review, 1,* 421–428.

DOMJAN, M. (1997). Behavior systems and the demise of equipotentiality: Historical antecedents and evidence from sexual conditioning. In M. E. Bouton & M. S. Fanselow (Eds.), *Learning, motivation, and cognition* (pp. 31–51). Washington, DC: American Psychological Association.

DOMJAN, M., & GILLAN, D. (1976). Role of novelty in the aversion for increasingly concentrated saccharin solutions. *Physiology & Behavior, 16,* 537–542.

DOMJAN, M., & NASH, S. (1988). Stimulus control of social behaviour in male Japanese quail, *Coturnix coturnix japonica. Animal Behaviour, 36,* 1006–1015.

DOMJAN, M., & WILSON, N. E. (1972). Specificity of cue to consequence in aversion learning in the rat. *Psychonomic Science, 26,* 143–145.

EDHOUSE, W. V., & WHITE, K. G. (1988). Sources of proactive interference in animal memory. *Journal of Experimental Psychology: Animal Behavior Processes, 14,* 56–70.

EISENBERGER, R., KARPMAN, M., & TRATTNER, J. (1967). What is the necessary and sufficient condition for reinforcement in the contingency situation? *Journal of Experimental Psychology, 74,* 342–350.

ESTES, W. K., & SKINNER, B. F. (1941). Some quantitative properties of anxiety. *Journal of Experimental Psychology, 29,* 390–400.

FANSELOW, M. S. (1989). The adaptive function of conditioned defensive behavior: An ecological approach to Pavlovian stimulus-substitution theory. In R. J. Blanchard, P. F. Brain, D.C. Blanchard, & S. Parmigiani (Eds.), *Ethoexperimental approaches to the study of behavior* (NATO ASI Series D., Vol. 48, pp. 151–166). Boston: Kluwer Academic Publishers.

FANSELOW, M. S. (1994). Neural organization of the defensive behavior system responsible for fear. *Psychonomic Bulletin & Review, 1*, 429–438.

FANSELOW, M. S. (1997). Species-specific defense reactions: Retrospect and prospect. In M. E. Bouton & M. S. Fanselow (Eds.), *Learning, motivation, and cognition* (pp. 321–341). Washington, DC: American Psychological Association.

FANSELOW, M. S., & LESTER, L. S. (1988). A functional behavioristic approach to aversively motivated behavior: Predatory imminence as a determinant of the topography of defensive behavior. In R. C. Bolles & M. D. Beecher (Eds.), *Evolution and learning* (pp. 185–212). Hillsdale, NJ: Erlbaum.

FANSELOW, M. S., LESTER, L. S., & HELMSTETTER, F. J. (1988). Changes in feeding and foraging patterns as an antipredator defensive strategy: A laboratory simulation using aversive stimulation in a closed economy. *Journal of the Experimental Analysis of Behavior, 50*, 361–374.

FELTON, M., & LYON, D. O. (1966). The post-reinforcement pause. *Journal of the Experimental Analysis of Behavior, 9*, 131–134.

FERSTER, C. B., & PERROTT, M. C. (1968). *Behavior principles.* New York: Appleton-Century-Crofts.

FERSTER, C. B., & SKINNER, B. F. (1957). *Schedules of reinforcement.* New York: Appleton-Century-Crofts.

FOREE, D. D., & LOLORDO, V. M. (1973). Attention in the pigeon: The differential effects of food-getting vs. shock avoidance procedures. *Journal of Comparative and Physiological Psychology, 85*, 551–558.

FORESTELL, P. H., & HERMAN, L. M. (1988). Delayed matching of visual materials by a bottlenosed dolphin aided by auditory symbols. *Animal Learning & Behavior, 16*, 137–146.

FUDIM, O. K. (1978). Sensory preconditioning of flavors with a formalin-produced sodium need. *Journal of Experimental Psychology: Animal Behavior Processes, 4*, 276–285.

GALBICKA, G. (1988). Differentiating the behavior of organisms. *Journal of the Experimental Analysis of Behavior, 50*, 343–354.

GARCIA, J., ERVIN, F. R., & KOELLING, R. A. (1966). Learning with prolonged delay of reinforcement. *Psychonomic Science, 5*, 121–122.

GARCIA, J., & KOELLING, R. A. (1966). Relation of cue to consequence in avoidance learning. *Psychonomic Science, 4*, 123–124.

GOODALL, G. (1984). Learning due to the response-shock contingency in signalled punishment. *Quarterly Journal of Experimental Psychology, 36B*, 259–279.

GORDON, W. C., & MOWRER, R. R. (1980). An extinction trial as a reminder treatment following electroconvulsive shock. *Animal Learning & Behavior, 8*, 363–367.

GORMEZANO, I., KEHOE, E. J., & MARSHALL, B. S. (1983). Twenty years of classical conditioning research with the rabbit. In J. M. Sprague & A. N. Epstein (Eds.), *Progress in psychobiology and physiological psychology* (Vol. 10, pp. 197–275). Orlando, FL: Academic Press.

GRANT, D. S. (1976). Effect of sample presentation time on long-delay matching in the pigeon. *Learning and Motivation, 7,* 580–590.

GRANT, D. S. (1988). Sources of visual interference in delayed matching-to-sample with pigeons. *Journal of Experimental Psychology: Animal Behavior Processes, 14,* 368–375.

GRANT, D. S., & SOLDAT, A. S. (1995). A postsample cue to forget does initiate an active forgetting process in pigeons. *Journal of Experimental Psychology: Animal Behavior Processes, 21,* 218–228.

GREEN, L., & FREED, D. E. (1993). The substitutability of reinforcers. *Journal of the Experimental Analysis of Behavior, 60,* 141–158.

GREEN, L., & RACHLIN, H. (1991). Economic substitutability of electrical brain stimulation, food, and water. *Journal of the Experimental Analysis of Behavior, 55,* 133–143.

GROVES, P. M., LEE, D., & THOMPSON, R. F. (1969). Effects of stimulus frequency and intensity on habituation and sensitization in acute spinal cat. *Physiology & Behavior, 4,* 383–388.

GROVES, P. M., & THOMPSON, R. F. (1970). Habituation: A dual-process theory. *Psychological Review, 77,* 419–450.

HEARST, E., BESLEY, S., & FARTHING, G. W. (1970). Inhibition and the stimulus control of operant behavior. *Journal of the Experimental Analysis of Behavior, 14,* 373–409.

HEARST, E., FRANKLIN, S., & MUELLER, C. G. (1974). The "disinhibition" of extinguished operant behavior in pigeons: Trial-tempo shifts and novel-stimulus effects. *Animal Learning & Behavior, 2,* 229–237.

HEARST, E., & JENKINS, H. M. (1974). *Sign tracking: The stimulus-reinforcer relation and directed action.* Austin, TX: Psychonomic Society.

HEILIGENBERG, W. (1974). Processes governing behavioral states of readiness. In D. S. Lehrman, J. S. Rosenblatt, R. Hinde, & E. Shaw (Eds.), *Advances in the study of behavior* (Vol. 5, pp. 173–200). New York: Academic Press.

HERRNSTEIN, R. J. (1969). Method and theory in the study of avoidance. *Psychological Review, 87,* 49–69.

HERRNSTEIN, R. J. (1970). On the law of effect. *Journal of the Experimental Analysis of Behavior, 13,* 243–266.

HOGAN, J. A. (1994). Structure and development of behavior systems. *Psychonomic Bulletin & Review, 1,* 439–450.

HOLLAND, P. C. (1977). Conditioned stimulus as a determinant of the form of the Pavlovian conditioned response. *Journal of Experimental Psychology: Animal Behavior Processes, 3,* 77–104.

HOLLAND, P.C. (1984). Origins of behavior in Pavlovian conditioning. In G. H. Bower (Ed.), *The psychology of learning and motivation* (Vol. 18, pp. 129–174). Orlando, FL: Academic Press.

HOLLAND, P. C. (1986). Temporal determinants of occasion setting in feature-positive discriminations. *Animal Learning & Behavior, 14*, 111–120.

HOLLAND, P. C. (1989). Feature extinction enhances transfer of occasion setting. *Animal Learning & Behavior, 17*, 269–279.

HOLLAND, P. C. (1992). Occasion setting in Pavlovian conditioning. In G. Bower (Ed.), *The psychology of learning and motivation* (Vol. 28, pp. 69–125). Orlando, FL: Academic Press.

HOLLIS, K. L. (1984). The biological function of Pavlovian conditioning: The best defense is a good offense. *Journal of Experimental Psychology: Animal Behavior Processes, 10*, 413–425.

HOLLIS, K. L. (1990). The role of Pavlovian conditioning in territorial aggression and reproduction. In D. A. Dewsbury (Ed.), *Contemporary issues in comparative psychology* (pp. 197–219). Sunderland, MA: Sinauer.

HOLLIS, K. L. (1997). Contemporary research on Pavlovian conditioning: A "new" functional analysis. *American Psychologist, 52*, 956–965.

HOLLIS, K. L., PHARR, V. L., DUMAS, M. J., BRITTON, G. B., & FIELD, J. (1997). Classical conditioning provides paternity advantage for territorial male blue gouramis (*Trichogaster trichopterus*). *Journal of Comparative Psychology, 111*, 219–225.

HOLLOWAY, K. S., & DOMJAN, M. (1993b). Sexual approach conditioning: Tests of unconditioned stimulus devaluation using hormone manipulations. *Journal of Experimental Psychology: Animal Behavior Processes, 19*, 47–55.

HOLZ, W. C., & AZRIN, N. H. (1961). Discriminative properties of punishment. *Journal of the Experimental Analysis of Behavior, 4*, 225–232.

HOMME, L. E., DEBACA, P. C., DEVINE, J. V., STEINHORST, R., & RICKERT, E. J. (1963). Use of the Premack Principle in controlling the behavior of nursery school children. *Journal of the Experimental Analysis of Behavior, 6*, 544–548.

HONIG, W. K., & JAMES, P. H. R. (Eds.). (1971). *Animal memory.* New York: Academic Press.

HULL, C. L. (1930). Knowledge and purpose as habit mechanisms. *Psychological Review, 30*, 511–525.

HULL, C. L. (1931). Goal attraction and directing ideas conceived as habit phenomena. *Psychological Review, 38*, 487–506.

HUMPHREYS, L. G. (1939). The effect of random alternation of reinforcement on the acquisition and extinction of conditioned eyelid reactions. *Journal of Experimental Psychology, 25*, 141–158.

JENKINS, H. M. (1962). Resistance to extinction when partial reinforcement is followed by regular reinforcement. *Journal of Experimental Psychology, 64*, 441–450.

JENKINS, H. M., & HARRISON, R. H. (1960). Effects of discrimination training on auditory generalization. *Journal of Experimental Psychology, 59*, 246–253.

JENKINS, H. M., & HARRISON, R. H. (1962). Generalization gradients of inhibition following auditory discrimination. *Journal of the Experimental Analysis of Behavior, 5*, 435–441.

JITSUMORI, M., WRIGHT, A. A., & SHYAN, M. R. (1989). Buildup and release from proactive interference in a rhesus monkey. *Journal of Experimental Psychology: Animal Behavior Processes, 15,* 329–337.

KAMIL, A. C., & CLEMENTS, K. C. (1990). Learning, memory, and foraging behavior. In D. A. Dewsbury (Ed.), *Contemporary issues in comparative psychology* (pp. 7–30). Sunderland, MA: Sinauer.

KAMIN, L. J. (1965). Temporal and intensity characteristics of the conditioned stimulus. In W. F. Prokasy (Ed.), *Classical conditioning* (pp. 118–147). New York: Appleton-Century-Crofts.

KAMIN, L. J. (1969). Predictability, surprise, attention, and conditioning. In B. A. Campbell & R. M. Church (Eds.), *Punishment and aversive behavior* (pp. 279–296). New York: Appleton-Century-Crofts.

KAPLAN, P. S., WERNER, J. S., & RUDY, J. W. (1990). Habituation, sensitization, and infant visual attention. In C. Rovee-Collier & L. P. Lipsitt (Eds.), *Advances in infancy research* (Vol. 6, pp. 61–109). Norwood, NJ: Ablex.

KAZDIN, A. E. (1985). The token economy. In R. M. Turner & L. M. Ascher (Eds.), *Evaluating behavior therapy outcome* (pp. 225–253). New York: Springer.

KENDRICK, D. F., RILLING, M. E., & DENNY, M. R. (Eds.) (1986). *Theories of animal memory.* Hillsdale, NJ: Erlbaum.

KIMBLE, G. A. (1961). *Hilgard and Marquis' conditioning and learning.* New York: Appleton-Century-Crofts.

KREMER, E. F. (1974). The truly random control procedure: Conditioning to the static cues. *Journal of Comparative and Physiological Psychology, 86,* 700–707.

LASHLEY, K. S., & WADE, M. (1946). The Pavlovian theory of generalization. *Psychological Review, 53,* 72–87.

LEATON, R. N. (1976). Long-term retention of the habituation of lick suppression and startle response produced by a single auditory stimulus. *Journal of Experimental Psychology: Animal Behavior Processes, 2,* 248–259.

LIEBERMAN, D. A., McINTOSH, D. C., & THOMAS, G. V. (1979). Learning when reward is delayed: A marking hypothesis. *Journal of Experimental Psychology: Animal Behavior Processes, 5,* 224–242.

LOGUE, A. W., OPHIR, I., & STRAUSS, K. E. (1981). The acquisition of taste aversions in humans. *Behaviour Research and Therapy, 19,* 319–333.

LOLORDO, V. M., & DROUNGAS, A. (1989). Selective associations and adaptive specializations: Taste aversions and phobias. In S. B. Klein & R. R. Mowrer (Eds.), *Contemporary learning theories: Instrumental conditioning theory and the impact of biological constraints on learning* (pp. 145–179). Hillsdale, NJ: Erlbaum.

LOLORDO, V. M., & FAIRLESS, J. L. (1985). Pavlovian conditioned inhibition: The literature since 1969. In R. R. Miller & N. E. Spear (Eds.), *Information processing in animals: Conditioned inhibition* (pp. 1–49). Hillsdale, NJ: Erlbaum.

LORENZ, K. Z. (1981). *The foundations of ethology.* New York: Springer-Verlag.

MACKINTOSH, N. J. (1974). *The psychology of animal learning.* Orlando, FL: Academic Press.

MACKINTOSH, N. J. (1977). Stimulus control: Attentional factors. In W. K. Honig & J. E. R. Staddon (Eds.), *Handbook of operant behavior* (pp. 481–513). Englewood Cliffs, NJ: Prentice-Hall.

MAKI, W. S. (1979). Pigeon's short-term memories for surprising vs. expected reinforcement and nonreinforcement. *Animal Learning & Behavior, 7,* 31–37.

MAKI, W. S., BEATTY, W. W., HOFFMAN, N., BIERLEY, R. A., & CLOUSE, B. A. (1984). Spatial memory over long retention intervals: Nonmemorial factors are not necessary for accurate performance on the radial arm maze by rats. *Behavioral and Neural Biology, 41,* 1–6.

MARLIN, N. A., & MILLER, R. R. (1981). Associations to contextual stimuli as a determinant of long-term habituation. *Journal of Experimental Psychology: Animal Behavior Processes, 7,* 313–333.

McALLISTER, D. E., & McALLISTER, W. R. (1991). Fear theory and aversively motivated behavior: Some controversial issues. In M. R. Denny (Ed.), *Fear, avoidance, and phobias* (pp. 135–163). Hillsdale, NJ: Erlbaum.

McDOWELL, J. J., & WIXTED, J. T. (1988). The linear system theory's account of behavior maintained by variable ratio schedules. *Journal of the Experimental Analysis of Behavior, 49,* 143–169.

MEDIN, D. L. (1980). Proactive interference in monkeys: Delay and intersample interval effects are noncomparable. *Animal Learning & Behavior, 8,* 553–560.

MEDIN, D. L., ROBERTS, W. A., & DAVIS, R. T. (1976). *Processes of animal memory.* Hillsdale, NJ: Erlbaum.

MILLER, D. B. (1985). Methodological issues in the ecological study of learning. In T.D. Johnston & A. T. Pietrewicz (Eds.), *Issues in the ecological study of learning* (pp. 73–95). Erlbaum.

MILLER, N. E. (1951). Learnable drives and rewards. In S. S. Stevens (Ed.), *Handbook of experimental psychology* (pp. 435–472). New York: Wiley.

MILLER, N. E. (1960). Learning resistance to pain and fear: Effects of overlearning, exposure, and rewarded exposure in context. *Journal of Experimental Psychology, 60,* 137–145.

MILLER, R. R., KASPROW, W. J., & SCHACHTMAN, T. R. (1986). Retrieval variability: Sources and consequences. *American Journal of Psychology, 99,* 145–218.

MILLER, R. R., & MATZEL, L. D. (1989). Contingency and relative associative strength. In S. B. Klein & R. R. Mowrer (Eds.), *Contemporary learning theories: Pavlovian conditioning and the status of learning theory* (pp. 61–84). Hillsdale, NJ: Erlbaum.

MINEKA, S., & GINO, A. (1980). Dissociation between conditioned emotional response and extended avoidance performance. *Learning and Motivation, 11,* 476–502.

MORRIS, R. G. M. (1974). Pavlovian conditioned inhibition of fear during shuttlebox avoidance behavior. *Learning and Motivation, 5,* 424–447.

MORRIS, R. G. M. (1975). Preconditioning of reinforcing properties to an extero-ceptive feedback stimulus. *Learning and Motivation, 6,* 289–298.

MOWRER, O. H. (1947). On the dual nature of learning: A reinterpretation of "conditioning" and "problem-solving." *Harvard Education Review, 17,* 102–150.

MOWRER, O. H., & LAMOREAUX, R. R. (1942). Avoidance conditioning and signal duration: A study of secondary motivation and reward. *Psychological Monographs, 54* (Whole No. 247).

OLTON, D. S., & SAMUELSON, R. J. (1976). Remembrance of places passed: Spatial memory in rats. *Journal of Experimental Psychology: Animal Behavior Processes, 2,* 97–116.

PAPINI, M. R., & BITTERMAN, M. E. (1990). The role of contingency in classi-cal conditioning. *Psychological Review, 97,* 396–403.

PAVLOV, I. (1927). *Conditioned reflexes.* G. V. Anrep, trans. London: Oxford Uni-versity Press.

PEAR, J. J., & LEGRIS, J. A. (1987). Shaping by automated tracking of an arbi-trary operant response. *Journal of the Experimental Analysis of Behavior, 47,* 241–247.

PEELE, D. B., CASEY, J., & SILBERBERG, A. (1984). Primacy of interresponse-time reinforcement in accounting for rate differences under variable-ratio and variable-interval schedules. *Journal of Experimental Psychology: Animal Behavior Processes, 10,* 149–167.

PELCHAT, M. L., & ROZIN, P. (1982). The special role of nausea in the acquisi-tion of food dislikes by humans. *Appetite, 3,* 341–351.

PERRY, D. G., & PARKE, R. D. (1975). Punishment and alternative response training as determinants of response inhibition in children. *Genetic Psychology Monographs, 91,* 257–279.

PREMACK, D. (1965). Reinforcement theory. In D. Levine (Ed.), *Nebraska sympo-sium on motivation* (Vol. 13, pp. 123–180). Lincoln: University of Nebraska Press.

RACHLIN, H. (1976). *Behavior and learning.* San Francisco: W. H. Freeman. See especially Chapter 3, pp. 102–154.

RACHLIN, H. C. (1978). A molar theory of reinforcement schedules. *Journal of the Experimental Analysis of Behavior, 30,* 345–360.

REBERG, D. (1972). Compound tests for excitation in early acquisition and after prolonged extinction of conditioned suppression. *Learning and Motivation, 3,* 246–258.

REBERG, D., & BLACK, A. H. (1969). Compound testing of individually condi-tioned stimuli as an index of excitatory and inhibitory properties. *Psychonomic Science, 17,* 30–31.

REPP, A. C., & SINGH, N. N. (Eds.). (1990). *Perspectives on the use of nonaversive and aversive interventions for persons with developmental disabilities.* Sycamore, IL: Sycamore.

RESCORLA, R. A. (1967). Pavlovian conditioning and its proper control proce-dures. *Psychological Review, 74,* 71–80.

RESCORLA, R. A. (1969). Pavlovian conditioned inhibition. *Psychological Bulletin, 72*, 77–94.

RESCORLA, R. A. (1972). Informational variables in Pavlovian conditioning. In G. H. Bower (Ed.), *The psychology of learning and motivation* (Vol. 6, pp. 1–46). Orlando, FL: Academic Press.

RESCORLA, R. A. (1973). Effect of US habituation following conditioning. *Journal of Comparative and Physiological Psychology, 82*, 137–143.

RESCORLA, R. A. (1985). Conditioned inhibition and facilitation. In R. R. Miller & N. E. Spear (Eds.), *Information processing in animals: Conditioned inhibition* (pp. 299–326). Hillsdale, NJ: Erlbaum.

RESCORLA, R. A. (1988). Pavlovian conditioning: It's not what you think it is. *American Psychologist, 43*, 151–160.

RESCORLA, R. A., & DURLACH, P. J., & GRAU, J. (1985). Contextual learning in Pavlovian conditioning. In P. Balsam & A. Tomie (Eds.), *Context and learning* (pp. 23–56). Hillsdale, NJ: Erlbaum.

RESCORLA, R. A. & FREBERG, L. (1978). The extinction of within-compound flavor associations. *Learning and Motivation, 9*, 411–427.

RESCORLA, R. A., & GILLAN, D. J. (1980). An analysis of the facilitative effect of similarity on second-order conditioning. *Journal of Experimental Psychology: Animal Behavior Processes, 6*, 339–351.

RESCORLA, R. A., & SOLOMON, R. L. (1967). Two-process learning theory: Relationships between Pavlovian conditioning and instrumental learning. *Psychological Review, 74*, 151–182.

REYNOLDS, G. S. (1975). *A primer of operant conditioning*. Glenview, IL: Scott, Foresman.

RICHARDSON, R., RICCIO, D. C., & JONKE, T. (1983). Alleviation of infantile amnesia in rats by means of a pharmacological contextual state. *Developmental Psychobiology, 16*, 511–518.

RILLING, M. (1977). Stimulus control and inhibitory processes. In W. K. Honig & J. E. R. Staddon (Eds.), *Handbook of operant behavior* (pp. 432–480). Englewood Cliffs, NJ: Prentice-Hall.

ROBBINS, S. J. (1990). Mechanisms underlying spontaneous recovery in autoshaping. *Journal of Experimental Psychology: Animal Behavior Processes, 16*, 235–249.

ROBERTS, W. A., & GRANT, D. S. (1976). Studies of short-term memory in the pigeon using the delayed matching to sample procedure. In D. L. Medin, W. A. Roberts, & R. T. Davis (Eds.), *Processes of animal memory* (pp. 79–112). Hillsdale, NJ: Erlbaum.

ROBERTS, W. A., & GRANT, D. S. (1978). An analysis of light-induced retroactive inhibition in pigeon short term memory. *Journal of Experimental Psychology: Animal Behavior Processes, 4*, 219–236.

ROITBLAT, H. L. (1980). Codes and coding processes in pigeon short-term memory. *Animal Learning & Behavior, 8*, 341–351.

ROPER, K. L., KAISER, D. H., & ZENTALL, T. R. (1995). True directed forgetting in pigeons may occur only when alternative working memory is required on forget-cue trials. *Animal Learning & Behavior, 23*, 280–285.

ROSS, R. T. (1983). Relationships between the determinants of performance in serial feature-positive discriminations. *Journal of Experimental Psychology: Animal Behavior Processes, 9*, 349–373.

SANTI, A., & ROBERTS, W. A. (1985). Prospective representation: The effects of varied mapping of sample stimuli to comparison stimuli and differential trial outcomes on pigeons' working memory. *Animal Learning & Behavior, 13*, 103–108.

SCHEIN, M. W., & HALE, E. B. (1965). Stimuli eliciting sexual behavior. In F. A. Beach (Ed.), *Sex and behavior* (pp. 440–482). New York: Wiley.

SCHMAJUK, N. A., & HOLLAND, P. C. (Eds.) (1998). *Occasion setting.* Washington, DC: American Psychological Association.

SCHNEIDERMAN, N., & GORMEZANO, I. (1964). Conditioning of the nictitating membrane of the rabbit as a function of the CS-US interval. *Journal of Comparative and Physiological Psychology, 57*, 188–195.

SCHWARTZ, B. (1981). Reinforcement creates behavioral units. *Behavioural Analysis Letters, 1*, 33–41.

SHAPIRO, K. L., JACOBS, W. J., & LOLORDO, V. M. (1980). Stimulus-reinforcer interactions in Pavlovian conditioning of pigeons: Implications for selective associations. *Animal Learning & Behavior, 8*, 586–594.

SHERRY, D. F., & SCHACHTER, D. L. (1987). The evolution of multiple memory systems. *Psychological Review, 94*, 439–454.

SHETTLEWORTH, S. J. (1975). Reinforcement and the organization of behavior in golden hamsters: Hunger, environment, and food reinforcement. *Journal of Experimental Psychology: Animal Behavior Processes, 1*, 56–87.

SHIMP, C. P. (1969). Optimum behavior in free-operant experiments. *Psychological Review, 76*, 97–112.

SIDMAN, M. (1953). Avoidance conditioning with brief shock and no exteroceptive warning signal. *Science, 118*, 157–158.

SIDMAN, M. (1960). *Tactics of scientific research.* New York: Basic Books.

SIEGEL, S. (1974). Flavor preexposure and "learned safety." *Journal of Comparative and Physiological Psychology, 87*, 1073–1082.

SIEGEL, S. (1975). Conditioning insulin effects. *Journal of Comparative and Physiological Psychology, 89*, 189–199.

SIMONS, R. C. (1996). *Boo! Culture, experience, and the startle reflex.* New York: Oxford University Press.

SKINNER, B. F. (1938). *The behavior of organisms.* New York: Appleton-Century.

SKINNER, B. F. (1953). *Science and human behavior.* New York: Macmillan.

SKINNER, B. F. (1956). A case study in scientific method. *American Psychologist, 11*, 221–233.

SMALL, W. S. (1899). An experimental study of the mental processes of the rat: I. *American Journal of Psychology, 11*, 133–164.

SMALL, W. S. (1900). An experimental study of the mental processes of the rat: II. *American Journal of Psychology, 12*, 206–239.

SMITH, J. C., & ROLL, D. L. (1967). Trace conditioning with X-rays as an aversive stimulus. *Psychonomic Science, 9*, 11–12.

SMITH, M. C., COLEMAN, S. R., & GORMEZANO, I. (1969). Classical conditioning of the rabbit's nictitating membrane response at backward, simultaneous, and forward CS-US intervals. *Journal of Comparative and Physiological Psychology, 69,* 226–231.

SOLOMON, R. L., KAMIN, L. J., & WYNNE, L. C. (1953). Traumatic avoidance learning: The outcomes of several extinction procedures with dogs. *Journal of Abnormal and Social Psychology, 48,* 291–302.

SPEAR, N. E., & RICCIO, D. C. (1994). *Memory: Phenomena and principles.* Boston: Allyn & Bacon.

SPEAR, N. E., SMITH, G. J., BRYAN, R. G., GORDON, W. C., TIMMONS, R., & CHISZAR, D. A. (1980). Contextual influences on the interaction between conflicting memories in the rat. *Animal Learning & Behavior, 8,* 273–281.

SPENCE, K. W. (1956). *Behavior theory and conditioning.* New Haven, CT: Yale University Press.

STADDON, J. E. R. (1979). Operant behavior as adaptation to constraint. *Journal of Experimental Psychology: General, 108,* 48–67.

STEWART, J., & EIKELBOOM, R. (1987). Conditioned drug effects. In L. L. Iversen, S. D. Iversen, & S. H. Snyder (Eds.), *Handbook of psychopharmacology* (Vol. 19, pp. 1–57). New York: Plenum.

SULZER-AZAROFF, B., & MAYER, G. R. (1991). *Behavior analysis for lasting change.* Fort Worth: Holt, Rinehart, and Winston.

TESTA, T. J. (1974). Causal relationships and the acquisition of avoidance responses. *Psychological Review, 81,* 491–505.

THEIOS, J. (1962). The partial reinforcement effect sustained through blocks of continuous reinforcement. *Journal of Experimental Psychology, 64,* 1–6.

THEIOS, J., LYNCH, A. D., & LOWE, W. F., JR. (1966). Differential effects of shock intensity on one-way and shuttle avoidance conditioning. *Journal of Experimental Psychology, 72,* 294–299.

THOMAS, G. V., & LIEBEMAN, D. A. (1990). Commentary: Determinants of success and failure in experiments on marking. *Learning and Motivation, 21,* 110–124.

THOMPSON, R. F., & SPENCER, W. A. (1966). Habituation: A model phenomenon for the study of neuronal substrates of behavior. *Psychological Review, 73,* 16–43.

THORNDIKE, E. L. (1898). Animal intelligence: An experimental study of the association processes in animals. *Psychological Review Monograph, 2* (Whole No. 8).

THORNDIKE, E. L. (1911). *Animal intelligence: Experimental studies.* New York: Macmillan.

THORNDIKE, E. L. (1932). *The fundamentals of learning.* New York: Teachers College, Columbia University.

TIERNEY, K. J. (1995). Molar regulatory theory and behavior therapy. In W. O'Donohue and L. Krasner (Eds.), *Theories of behavior therapy* (pp. 97–128). Washington, DC: American Psychological Association.

TIMBERLAKE, W. (1980). A molar equilibrium theory of learned performance. In G. H. Bower (Ed.), *The psychology of learning and motivation* (Vol. 14, pp. 1–58). Orlando, FL: Academic Press.

TIMBERLAKE, W. (1984). Behavior regulation and learned performance: Some misapprehensions and disagreements. *Journal of the Experimental Analysis of Behavior, 41*, 355–375.

TIMBERLAKE, W. (1994). Behavior systems, associationism, and Pavlovian conditioning. *Psychonomic Bulletin & Review, 1*, 405–420.

TIMBERLAKE, W., & ALLISON, J. (1974). Response deprivation: An empirical approach to instrumental reinforcement. *Psychological Review, 81*, 146–164.

TIMBERLAKE, W., & FARMER-DOUGAN, V. A. (1991). Reinforcement in applied settings: Figuring out ahead of time what will work. *Psychological Bulletin, 110*, 379–391.

TIMBERLAKE, W., & LUCAS, G. A. (1989). Behavior systems and learning: From misbehavior to general principles. In S. B. Klein & R. R. Mowrer (Eds.), *Contemporary learning theories: Instrumental conditioning theory and the impact of biological constraints on learning* (pp. 237–275). Hillsdale, NJ: Erlbaum.

TIMBERLAKE, W., WAHL, G., & KING, D. (1982). Stimulus and response contingencies in the misbehavior of rats. *Journal of Experimental Psychology: Animal Behavior Processes, 8*, 62–85.

TINBERGEN, N. (1951). *The study of instinct.* Oxford: Clarendon Press.

TINBERGEN, N. (1952). The behavior of the stickleback. *Scientific American, 187*, 22–26.

TINBERGEN, N., & PERDECK, A.C. (1950). On the stimulus situation releasing the begging response in the newly hatched herring gull chick (*Larus argentatus argentatus* Pont.). *Behaviour, 3*, 1–39.

TOMIE, A., BROOKS, W., & ZITO, B. (1989). Sign-tracking: The search for reward. In S. B. Klein & R. R. Mowrer (Eds.), *Contemporary learning theories: Pavlovian conditioning and the status of learning theory* (pp. 191–223). Hillsdale, NJ: Erlbaum.

TOMIE, A., MURPHY, A. L., FATH, S., & JACKSON, R. L. (1980). Retardation of autoshaping following pretraining with unpredictable food: Effects of changing the context between pretraining and testing. *Learning and Motivation, 11*, 117–134.

TURKKAN, J. S. (1989). Classical conditioning: The new hegemony. *The Behavioral and Brain Sciences, 12*, 121–179.

WALLACE, J., STEINERT, P. A., SCOBIE, S. R., & SPEAR, N. E. (1980). Stimulus modality and short-term memory in rats. *Animal Learning & Behavior, 8*, 10–16.

WASSERMAN, E. A., FRANKLIN, S. R., & HEARST, E. (1974). Pavlovian appetitive contingencies and approach vs. withdrawal to conditioned stimuli in pigeons. *Journal of Comparative and Physiological Psychology, 86*, 616–627.

WEISMAN, R. G., & LITNER, J. S. (1972). The role of Pavlovian events in avoidance training. In R. A. Boakes & M. S. Halliday (Eds.), *Inhibition and learning.* London: Academic Press.

WHITLOW, J. W., JR., & WAGNER, A. R. (1984). Memory and habituation. In H. V. S. Peeke & L. Petrinovich (Eds.), *Habituation, sensitization, and behavior* (pp. 103–153). New York: Academic Press.

WILLIAMS, B. A. (1994). Reinforcement and choice. In N. J. Mackintosh (Ed.), *Animal learning and cognition* (pp. 81–108). San Diego: Academic Press.

WINTER, J., & PERKINS, C. C. (1982). Immediate reinforcement in delayed reward learning in pigeons. *Journal of the Experimental Analysis of Behavior, 38,* 169–179.

WRIGHT, A. A., URCUIOLI, P. J., SANDS, S. F., & SANTIAGO, H. C. (1981). Interference of delayed matching to sample in pigeons: Effects of interpolation at different periods within a trial and stimulus similarity. *Animal Learning & Behavior, 9,* 595–603.

ZENTALL, T. R., STEIRN, J. N., & JACKSON-SMITH, P. (1990). Memory strategies in pigeons' performance of a radial-arm-maze analog task. *Journal of Experimental Psychology: Animal Behavior Processes, 16,* 358–371.

Name Index

Alcock, J., 17
Allan, R. W., 89
Allison, J., 128, 129, 130, 134
Amsel, A., 94, 117, 118, 122
Anger, D., 159
Astley, S. L., 184
Atkinson, R. C., 24, 184
Ayres, J. J. B., 55
Azrin, N. H., 138, 140, 142, 143, 148

Babkin, B. P., 43
Baerends, G. P., 17, 24
Balsam, P. D., 55, 184
Barnet, R. C., 67
Baron, A., 188
Bashinski, H., 28, 30
Batson, J. D., 53
Baum, W. M., 118
Bechterev, V. M., 151, 152, 157
Beecher, M. D., 166
Benedict, J. O., 55
Berlyne, D. E., 125
Best, M. R., 53
Bitterman, M. E., 55, 61, 64, 80, 115
Boakes, R. A., 42, 44, 48
Bolles, R. C., 45, 162, 163, 166
Borovsky, D., 198, 199
Bouton, M. E., 45, 57, 59, 60, 61, 76, 166
Bower, G. H., 61, 97, 121
Braveman, N. S., 66
Breland, K., 14, 96
Breland, M., 14, 96
Britton, G. B., 4
Brogden, W. J., 156, 157
Bronstein, P., 66
Brooks, D. C., 57
Brooks, W., 44
Brown, E. R., 53
Brown, M. F., 195
Bryan, R. G., 199

Camp, D. S., 139, 140
Campbell, B. A., 80, 148, 199
Capaldi, E. J., 117, 118
Casey, F. G., 127
Casey, J., 108
Charlop, M. H., 127
Chiszar, D. A., 199
Church, R. M., 10, 80, 138, 139, 140, 142, 148
Clements, K. C., 14
Cohen, L. B., 31
Cole, R. P., 67
Coleman, S. R., 64, 66
Colwill, R. M., 94, 97
Cook, R. G., 195
Culler, E., 156
Cunningham, C. L., 48

D'Amato, M. R., 162, 192
Dardano, J. F., 143
Davis, M., 29, 34, 35, 36
Davis, R. T., 186
Davison, M., 113
Dean, S. J., 144
deBaca, P. C., 126
Deich, J. D., 89
Denny, M. R., 166, 186, 200
Déscartes, R. 15, 16, 26, 37
Devine, J. V., 126
Dinsmoor, J., 142, 160
Domjan, M., 14, 19, 33, 34, 36, 49, 50, 51, 52
Droungas, A., 44, 61
Dumas, M. J., 4
Durlach, P. J., 78

Edhouse, W. V., 196
Eikelboom, R., 48
Eisenberger, R., 129
Epstein, A. N., 80
Ervin, F. R., 67
Estes, W. K., 45
Etkin, M., 162

Fanselow, M. S., 49, 164, 166
Farmer-Dougan, V. A., 134
Fath, S., 55, 70
Fazzaro, J., 162
Felton, M., 102
Ferster, C. B., 103, 105, 110, 119
Field, J., 4
Foree, D. D., 176
Forestell, P. H., 188
Franklin, S. R., 48
Freberg, L., 51
Freed, D. E., 132
Fudim, O. K., 51

Galbicka, G., 89
Garcia, J., 52, 53, 67
Gillan, D. J., 34, 54
Gino, A., 159
Goodall, G., 48, 139
Gordon, W. C., 199
Gormezano, I., 46, 64, 65, 66, 80
Grahame, N. J., 67
Grant, D. S., 189, 192, 197
Grau, J., 78
Green, L., 132
Groves, P. M., 34, 35, 36, 39, 40

Hake, D. F., 140
Hale, E. B., 20
Harrison, R. H., 180, 182
Hearst, E., 14, 44, 48
Heiligenberg, W., 35

Helmstetter, F. J., 164
Herman, L. M., 188
Herrnstein, R. J., 24, 113, 166, 184
Hilgard, E. R., 121
Hitchcock, J. M., 29
Holland, P. C., 43, 44, 45, 61, 77, 78, 79, 80
Hollis, K. L., 4, 14, 43, 61
Holloway, K. S., 49, 50, 51
Holz, W. C., 138, 140, 142, 143, 148
Homme, L. E., 126
Honig, W. K., 118, 148, 186
Hull, C. L., 94, 122, 123, 124, 125, 126
Humphreys, L. G., 114

Jackson, R. L., 55, 70
Jackson-Smith, P., 195
Jacobs, W. J., 53, 176
James, P. H. R., 118, 186
Jenkins, H. M., 14, 44, 116, 180, 182
Jitsumori, M., 196
Jonke, T., 199

Kaiser, D. H., 192
Kamil, A. C., 14
Kamin, L. J., 65, 66, 68, 80, 159, 174, 175
Kaplan, P. S., 31, 34, 35, 40
Karpman, M., 129
Kasprow, W. J., 186, 200
Kazdin, A. E., 127
Kehoe, E. J., 46, 80
Kendrick, D. F., 186, 200
Kimble, G. A., 46
King, D., 14, 96
Klein, S. B., 61, 97
Koelling, R. A., 52, 53, 67
Krasner, L., 134
Kremer, E. F., 55
Kurtz, P. F., 127

Lamoreaux, R. R., 150
Lashley, K. S., 173
Leaton, R. N., 34
Lee, D., 34
Legris, J. A., 89
Lester, L. S., 164, 166
Lieberman, D. A., 92
Lindzey, G., 24, 184
Lipman, E. A., 156
Litner, J. S., 161
Lockwood, M. J., 48
Logue, A. W., 53
LoLordo, V. M., 44, 53, 61, 176
Lorenz, K. Z., 21
Lowe, W. F., Jr., 154
Lucas, G. A., 48, 97
Luce, R. D., 24, 184

Lynch, A. D., 154
Lyon, D. O., 102

Mackintosh, N. J., 47, 119
Maki, W. S., 192
Marlin, N. A., 34
Marshall, B. S., 46, 80
Matzel, L. D., 70
Mayer, G. R., 111
McAllister, D. E., 116
McAllister, W. R., 116
McCarthy, D., 113
McDowell, J. J., 108
McIntosh, D. C., 92
Meachum, C. L., 53
Medin, D. L., 97, 184, 186, 196
Menich, S. R., 188
Miller, D. B., 8
Miller, N. E., 140, 157
Miller, R. R., 34, 67, 70, 186, 200
Mineka, S., 159
Morris, R. G. M., 161
Mowrer, O. H., 150, 157
Mowrer, R. R., 61, 97, 199
Murphy, A. L., 55, 70

Nash, S., 19

O'Donohue, W., 134
Ophir, I., 53

Papini, M. R., 55, 61, 80
Parke, R. D., 143
Pavlov, I., 41, 42, 43, 52, 57, 71, 83, 172,
    175, 176
Pear, J. J., 89
Pearce, J. M., 184
Peeke, H. V. S., 40
Peele, D. B., 108
Pelchat, M. L., 53
Perdeck, A. C., 20
Perkins, C. C., 91
Perrott, M. C., 110
Perry, D. G., 143
Petrinovich, L., 40
Pharr, V. L., 4
Pittman, C. M., 144
Poli, M., 48
Premack, D., 125, 126, 127, 128, 129,
    133, 134

Rachlin, H. C., 14, 24
Randall, P. K., 199

Rashotte, M. E., 122
Raymond, G. A., 139, 142
Reberg, D., 76
Repp, A. C., 148
Rescorla, R. A., 10, 43, 49, 51, 54, 55,
    69, 78, 79, 94, 97
Reynolds, G. S., 108
Riccio, D. C., 186, 199, 200
Richardson, R., 199
Rickert, E. J., 126
Riley, A. L., 163
Riley, D. A., 195
Rilling, M. E., 186, 200
Ringer, M., 53
Robbins, S. J., 57
Roberts, W. A., 186, 192, 195, 197
Roitblat, H. L., 195
Roll, D. L., 66
Roper, K. L., 192
Rosen, J. B., 29
Ross, R. T., 79
Rovee-Collier, C., 198, 199
Rozin, P., 53
Rudy, J. W., 28, 31, 40

Sands, S. F., 197
Santi, A., 195
Santiago, H. C., 197
Sauerbrunn, D., 143
Schachter, D. L., 186
Schachtman, T. R., 186, 200
Schein, M. W., 20
Schmajuk, N. A., 78, 80
Schneiderman, N., 65, 66
Schwartz, B., 88
Scobie, S. R., 188
Shapiro, K. L., 53, 176
Sherry, D. F., 186
Shettleworth, S. J., 96
Shyan, M. R., 196
Sidman, M., 154
Siegel, S., 33, 43
Silberberg, A., 108
Simons, R. C., 29
Singh, N. N., 148
Skinner, B. F., 10, 14, 43, 45, 47, 83, 85,
    86, 87, 94, 96, 97, 103, 105, 119,
    125, 128, 136, 138, 139, 144, 154
Small, W. S., 85
Smith, G. J., 199
Smith, J. C., 66
Smith, M. C., 64, 66
Soldat, A. S., 192

Solomon, R. L., 94, 97, 159
Spear, N. E., 186, 188, 199, 200
Spence, K. W., 94
Spencer, W. A., 31, 32, 34, 35
Sprague, J. M., 80
Steinert, P. A., 188
Steinhorst, R., 126
Steirn, J. N., 195
Stewart, J., 48
Strauss, K. E., 53
Sulzer-Azaroff, B., 111
Swartzentruber, D., 60, 76

Testa, T. J., 54
Theios, J., 116, 154
Thomas, G. V., 92
Thompson, R. F., 31, 32, 34, 35, 35, 39,
    40
Thorndike, E. L., 81, 83, 84, 85, 93, 95,
    96, 97, 121, 122, 128, 136, 139,
    144
Tierney, K. J., 134
Timberlake, W., 14, 22, 24, 48, 96, 97,
    128, 129, 130, 134
Timmons, R., 199
Tinbergen, N., 17, 18, 20, 24
Tomie, A., 44, 55, 70
Trattner, J., 129
Turkkan, J. S., 43

Urcuioli, P. J., 197

Wade, M., 173
Wagner, A. R., 34
Wahl, G., 14, 96
Wallace, J., 188
Wasserman, E. A., 48, 184
Weisman, R. G., 161
Werner, J. S., 28, 31, 40
White, K. G., 196
Whitlow, J. W., Jr., 34
Williams, B. A., 113
Wilson, N. E., 52
Winter, J., 91
Wixted, J. T., 108
Wright, A. A., 196, 197
Wynne, L. C., 159

Zeigler, H. P., 89
Zentall, T. R., 192, 195
Zito, B., 44